Witnessing Unbound

Witnessing Unbound

Holocaust Representation and the Origins of Memory

EDITED BY
Henri Lustiger Thaler
and Habbo Knoch

WAYNE STATE UNIVERSITY PRESS
DETROIT

© 2017 by Wayne State University Press, Detroit, Michigan 48201. All rights reserved. No part of this book may be reproduced without formal permission. Manufactured in the United States of America.

ISBN 978-0-8143-4301-2 (paperback); ISBN 978-0-8143-4302-9 (ebook)
Library of Congress Cataloging Number: 2017941002

Wayne State University Press
Leonard N. Simons Building
4809 Woodward Avenue
Detroit, Michigan 48201-1309

Visit us online at wsupress.wayne.edu

Dedicated to the memory of Geoffrey Hartman

Contents

Acknowledgments   ix

Introduction   1
Henri Lustiger Thaler with the collaboration
of Habbo Knoch

1. The Afterdeath of the Holocaust   15
   Lawrence L. Langer

2. Witnesses and Witnessing: Some *Reflections*   31
   Annette Wieviorka

3. Halakhic Witnessing: The Auschwitz Memoir
   of Berish Erlich   54
   Henri Lustiger Thaler

4. Memoirs Not Forgotten: Rabbis Who Survived
   the Holocaust   81
   Esther Farbstein

5. "Solidarity and Suffering": Lager Vapniarka
   among the Camps of Transnistria   105
   Leo Spitzer

6. Interview with Father Patrick Desbois   131
   Henri Lustiger Thaler

7. The Flight and Evacuation of Civilian Populations
   in the USSR: New Sources, New Publications,
   New Questions   144
   Paul A. Shapiro

Contents

8. Ravensbrück Women's Concentration Camp:
   Memories in Situ 168
   Insa Eschebach

9. The Belzec Memorial and Museum:
   Personal Reflections 192
   Michael Berenbaum

10. Locating Loss: The Physical Contexts
    of Genocide Memorials 218
    Paul Williams

    Contributors 235
    Index 239

Acknowledgments

The editors gratefully acknowledge the Stiftung niedersächsische Gedenkstätten Bergen-Belsen in Germany and The School of Social Sciences and Human Services of Ramapo College of New Jersey for their support during the early and later stages of production of this volume. We also take this opportunity to thank all those who have been directly or indirectly related to the production of this volume, with special mention of the readers commissioned by Wayne State University Press and of Ms. Allison Gutworth, whose organizational skills and acumen were everpresent.

The title of this volume was inspired by artist Barbara Rose Haum's video memory installation titled "Book Unbound."

Introduction

HENRI LUSTIGER THALER
with the collaboration of Habbo Knoch

> All sorrows can be borne if you put them into a story or tell a story about them.
>
> Isak Dinesen
> (quoted in Hannah Arendt,
> *The Human Condition*)

This volume brings together a collection of diverse reflections on witnessing and memory. Primary witnessing, in its various forms and genres—from survivor and bystander testimonies to memoirs and diaries—informs our cultural understanding of the multiple subjective experiences of the Holocaust. These personal accounts, however, forecast an external movement, much like a clock's weighted pendulum, swinging back and forth between the rawness of survivors' experiences and the stylization of their voices, or what Berel Lang has called their "representation-as."[1] The multiple expressions of primary witnessing are particularly germane today with the hastening decline of the survivor population and the cultural void it leaves in its wake, in addition to the inevitable search for generational relevancy. At the very least, the multiple logics of representation, its uses and abuses, caution us that the voices and artifacts left to us by primary witnesses, counterposed against what Geoffrey Hartman has referred to as "adoptive and intellectual witnessing,"[2] may be engaged in the first act of an undeclared if empathetic tension. The trauma of original experience and its reimagination within contemporary frameworks of meaning-making indicate a widening interpretive and risk-filled landscape from which to make sense of an event that continues to adapt and change metaphorically and globally.

This book is largely about primary witnesses, the voices of the subject, before the temporal and cumulative effects of years of listening, repetition, reification, and even "technical issues of communicability."[3] The essays in this volume are by some of the leading figures on the subject of witnessing as well as by scholars exploring new primary sources of knowledge about the Holocaust and genocide and the multi-layered subjectivities they continue to express through a variety of approaches. These include a focus on the victims, the perished as well as the survivors, and their experiential worlds captured in testimonies, diaries, and memoirs; on peasant bystanders to the terror; on the value of religious historical/meta-historical writing during and after the war, which act as proto-memoirs for destroyed communities; and on the recently opened Soviet archives that now function as an extended actualization of historical memory, or the archive as witness to its own historicity.

Lawrence Langer has been one of the most poignant interpreters of the complexities of survivors' fragmented selves. In his chapter "The Afterdeath of the Holocaust," he describes his experience as an eyewitness in 1964 at the trial of SS General Karl Wolff, and later at the Auschwitz Prozess (trials)[4] in Frankfurt of SS guards and camp personnel. All the perpetrators in these proceedings denied complicity. Langer contrasts the "evasive memory" of the murderers with the "deep memory" of survivors. For Langer, it is only by confronting the dark and cruel revelations of "deep memory" at the very core of the Holocaust that it can enter human consciousness. He explains:

> When dealing with the Holocaust, the difficult challenge before us is to identify with the target of deep memory, that intellectual and emotional terrain where the clear borders between living and dying merge and we are faced with the condition of being what I call "deathlife" (the Afterdeath of the Holocaust), a territory we instinctively flee because it is uninhabitable by reasonable creatures like ourselves.

Langer raises important points in our continued understanding of, and grappling with, the transmitted *lebensvelt* of the primary witness, the survivor: what residue of memories of the perished and survivors do we want readers, students, museum visitors, now and in the future, to absorb about the Holocaust? What is the level of discursive sanitization that occurs as the modern history of the Holocaust is fragmented into multiple themes and subjects in scholarly research, in arts and letters? How can the brutality of the core details of the Holocaust compete with other phases of its historical trajectories and contingencies that are much more palatably absorbed? What form does "evasive memory" take today when the horror of how mass slaughter was meted out exists alongside the very limits of human understanding in history and literature, "offering us," as Langer argues, "no exit from the trap of this darkest secret of the Holocaust."

Annette Wieviorka, in her chapter "Witnesses and Witnessing: Some Reflections," examines the multiplicity of experiences captured in survivor testimonies. She exposes the everpresent tension between a historian's quest for historical truth and overly authored survivor testimonies. Yet regardless of this phenomena of "self-representation," which may indeed indicate a variety of subjective truths that compose the meaning of a given event, she clearly acknowledges the importance of drawing the witness experience methodologically closer to problems of historical writing.[5] The testimonies of survivors, she argues, contain the concealed and untold story. Wieviorka notes that during an evacuation march from the camps at Auschwitz, Simone Veil and other prisoners found themselves in a vast camp. Veil is unwilling to fully recount the historical event. She explains: "Those who, for one reason or another, had had some responsibilities at the camp or still had some strength would start to launch into a bit of blackmail: 'I have not seen a woman in years. . . .' Meanwhile in another part of the camp a selection was taking place and the SS were continuing their deadly task. . . . Few of us lived through the experience but it did take place and it is very difficult to talk about it."

In the immediate postwar period, the collective consciousness of Europe was replete with conflicting symbols of victory. In Israel, the ascent of the "new Jew" and decline of the "diasporic Jew" were dominant and powerful tropes for modern Jewish renewal in the post-bellum period. In Eastern Europe, Soviet collectivist ideologies and their resonance in the German Democratic Republic (GDR) supported the heroic nature of the victorious battle against fascism. These political/cultural contexts left little space for Jewish memory within the immediate postwar period. In spite of this, survivors of the Holocaust, immediately after 1945, created historical commissions in Germany, France, Poland, Austria, and Italy. They focused on exposing the crimes of National Socialism, demanding legal and moral redress as well as creating a basis for future historical research on the Holocaust. They consciously related this investigative work within the Jewish tradition of *khurbn-forshung* (destruction research) utilized by Eastern European Jews to document antisemitic atrocities in the early twentieth century. As Laura Jockusch has argued, "On a more abstract level, the commission workers viewed their accumulated documents and chronicles of the past as 'memorials' or 'gravestones' for their dead."[6] Survivors and their families—certainly after 1950, with the closing of the displaced persons camps and the new State of Israel—were virtually alone in commemorating the genocide of European Jewry. In the postwar Orthodox world, rabbis and talmudic scholars offered a variety of ontological reasons and theological responsa in face of the sheer scale of the mass killings. Memory in its various expressive, liturgical, and literary forms and genres—both religious and secular—circulated largely amongst survivors. The postwar silence of survivors had been overstated in Holocaust literature.[7] Survivors were not quiescent. Rather, the cultural contexts of listeners in Europe and America were not yet developed and hence largely absent. Early attempts to elicit testimony from survivors, such as David Boder's interviews in 1946, did not lead to additional oral histories.[8] The work of the historical commissions and eyewitness accounts written shortly after 1945 disappeared from the public sphere a few short years after the liberation: world attention looked elsewhere, but not for survivors. The displaced person camps of Europe became unique sites of rebirth and reflection for the still raw experiences of the war years.

Henri Lustiger Thaler, in "Halakhic Witnessing: The Auschwitz Memoir of Berish Erlich," examines an Orthodox survivor's memoir, written in early 1946 in the Landsberg displaced person camp in the American Military Zone of Occupied Germany. The memoir illuminates a radically different form and subjective context for cultural memory and witnessing. Lustiger Thaler examines "the relationality of being" between faith-based Jews and rabbis during the Holocaust, through what he refers to as "halakhic witnessing," as a counterpoint to Primo Levi's dictum of "speaking in another's stead." Erlich's memoir has two sections: life in the Warsaw ghetto and his internment in Auschwitz. The Auschwitz portion of the memoir is published in its entirety for the first time in this book. It was written in three languages, Yiddish, German, and English, triptych-like, in a small US Army–issued notebook, as part of an English lesson in the Landsberg displaced person camp. In examining the memoir, Lustiger Thaler provides intersecting and fragmented biographical information on Erlich, culled from the files of the International Tracing Service of the International Red Cross. He explains how a reading of the memoir, through symbolic codes associated with Orthodox Jewish perspectives, provides new methodological instruments to decipher the cultural meanings of witnessing at the intersection of religious beliefs, its embodied comportment, and everyday life in the ghettos and camps.

Esther Farbstein is a key contributor to the relatively new area of Orthodox Jewish historiography. She examines scholarly rabbinic writings of wartime experiences in her chapter "Memoirs Not Forgotten: Rabbis Who Survived the Holocaust." These writings took the form of prefaces to rabbinic texts. Farbstein demonstrates how such introductions to scholarly rabbinic works were the chosen genre for discourses on suffering and Jewish tragedy from the Orthodox perspective. Hence, in this form of Jewish historiography, dilemmas encountered amongst the faithful are viewed through the lens of the rabbi, the communal spokesperson. Farbstein argues that the "forgotten memoirs" embedded in rabbinic prefaces underscore their search for the meaning of events in liturgical texts and offer new knowledge about faith-based survivor perspectives, largely ignored until now, or given token reference under the rubric of "spiritual resistance."

Varied cultural understandings of witnessing, its presence in the archive and scholarship, have emerged as objects of theoretical reflection, as well as an alternate source for methodological inquiry and source for historical writing.[9] The specificities of different forms of witnessing are today matters of intensive research, based on a deepening understanding of the cultural and political backgrounds of the perished and survivors. Leo Spitzer's chapter, "'Solidarity and Suffering': Lager Vapniarka among the Camps of Transnistria," is based on witness testimony and memoirs. They juxtapose the historical evidence of the Romanian Holocaust against solidaristic networks that developed in Lager Vapniarka in Transnistria. In the midst of mass poisonings, starvation, forced labor, disease, and deprivation, clandestine networks of association developed amongst the inmates. An underground political committee took control of everyday life in the camp. Spitzer reconstructs the surreptitious life of prisoners exchanging stories, precious food, information from the front, and the bribing of guards. In so doing, Spitzer draws upon resistance— the *Vita Activa* of the inmates—and their agency as witnesses to the terror of their internment.

Father Patrick Desbois, a Catholic priest, is on a singular and unique mission: to find the mass graves of Jews murdered in the former Soviet Union. In so doing he examines the peasant bystander as witness. Henri Lustiger Thaler interviewed Father Desbois for this book. Desbois and his team have gathered the testimonies of peasants in the remote villages of Eastern Europe. As he explains, "My point of view is from the farm. So of course it's not perfect. A farmer sees a killing in his role as a neighbor." He defines the village bystander as a witness of a particular sort. Individuals become witnesses, he argues, because we listen to them. Before Father Desbois arrived, the last inquiry about the massacres in these remote villages was associated with the Soviet Commission of 1946. Using data from these interviews, Father Desbois is able to contrast bystander witness testimonies that he gathers today with witness testimonies that appeared in early skeletal form in the Soviet Commission reports.

The Soviet archive as a knowledge-based repository of a neglected history provides a yet different mode of witnessing. Paul Shapiro's chapter on the Jewish refugee and evacuation experience in the Occupied Soviet territories reveals new parameters for contemporary inquiry. These once inaccessible archives expose what was long considered hidden or lost: histories of the Jewish experience in the Soviet Union which reappear in the form of memoirs, diaries, letters, and testimonies that reveal the dramatic hardships of war evacuations and refugee experiences, opening up new research vistas about the "Holocaust in the East." Shapiro brings to our attention the saliency of evacuee and refugee experiences as critical to the broader context of Holocaust historiography. His mining of the Soviet evacuee and refugee experience revisits the empirical and now largely political question of the actual number of Jewish victims murdered during the Holocaust, once Soviet history is fully examined.

Insa Eschebach's chapter, "Ravensbrück Women's Concentration Camp: Memories in Situ," looks at the postwar history of an internment camp in the GDR, where the recognition of Jewish survivors was virtually negligible in postwar memorial commemorations. Witness testimony did not play an important role in the constructed memory of the camp. As Eschebach states: "The genocide of the Jewish people is not mentioned once; Jewish prisoners, in general, figure only marginally into this narrative, and if they do, they serve as a dark background against which the actions of the political prisoners—which figured large in the camp—appear all the more heroic." Ravensbrück was the largest women's concentration camp in Nazi Germany, incarcerating 139,000 women and children and 20,000 men from roughly thirty countries. Jewish women constituted about one-fifth of the camp's total inmates. Eschebach's chapter informs us of the complex postwar memorialization of a camp in the GDR. In this Soviet commemorative framework, personal and collective memories of the deaths and sufferings were sublimated and neglected in favor of a GDR narrative honoring dead heroes through a motif more appropriate to German soldiers who fell in the act of their "patriotic" duties than to concentration camp prisoners. To a large extent, the commingling of historical sites with political symbolism was also true for Poland: major sites like Auschwitz-Birkenau and Majdanek were transformed into open-air martyrological spaces, mainly representing the suffering of Poles.[10]

In the period of postwar German denial, activists argued that the Holocaust as a German crime must be publicly acknowledged within the physicality of the landscape itself. In West Germany and particularly in the State of Lower Saxony, a small group of German memorial activists fought for the political and public recognition of former concentration camp sites as memorial and learning sites.[11] On the one hand, they saw this as the best guarantee for the sustenance of postwar democratic political culture in Germany. On the other hand, these sites underscored the necessity of bringing the life stories of survivors into the public realm: survivors of the Nazi crimes came to be seen as authentic voices on desecrated ground, and were slowly adopted as symbolic citizens.[12] This reflected a new generational stance that protested the absence of empathy for the victims of the Holocaust in their parents' generation. In turn, they adopted the responsibility for memorial sites as a gesture to the rebuilding of a national and collective German identity. In the borrowed lexicon of truth and reconciliation committees in post-conflict societies, memorials at sites of destruction within Germany became spatial markers of a partial reconciliation.

Today, sites of destruction—particularly in Germany—have incorporated museums or monuments within the former landscape of terror. These mediate between the historical site and visitors while offering multi-layered interpretations of the past. The sites are today venues that are interpreted by docents with the aid of apps, testimony stations, leaflets, and electronic technologies. Memorial landscapes have become objects of immediate explanation, accompanied by a Permanent Exhibit, and forensic explorations of its archaeological character. These locations are ultimately filled with spatial and post-spatial tensions: what Walter Benjamin understood as the effect of aura upon original objects and experiences, on the one hand, and on the other, containment, rationality, and systems of information.

These sites and their associated exhibits encompass old and yet new forms of hauntings of the perished, as well as the specter of the increasingly absent Holocaust survivor. The sites themselves as locations for witnessing strive to delineate a balance between the forensic traces of the past and the dolorous subjectivity and desubjectivization of its former inmates. Michael Berenbaum recounts his experience as a conceptual developer of the Belzec death camp in Poland in "The Belzec Memorial and Museum: Personal Reflections." Belzec offers a special case of witnessing. Somewhere in the vicinity of 500,000 Jews were murdered there, with only two survivor witnesses. Berenbaum's chapter delves into the vacuum of absent voices that haunt the memorial site. He draws our attention to a voice that is at the very center of the Belzec exhibition in Poland, the testimony of one of the two Belzec survivors, Rudolf Reder, a Sonderkommando:

> I was chosen to be one of the workers. I would stand on the side of the courtyard with my group of gravediggers and looked at my brothers, sister, friends and acquaintances herded toward death. While the women were rounded up naked and shaved, whipped like cattle into a slaughterhouse, the men were already dying in the gas chambers. It took two hours to shave the women and two hours to murder them. Many SS men using whips and sharp bayonets pushed the women

toward the building with the chambers. Then the *askars* counted out 750 persons per chamber.

As the survivor population declines, the memorial significance to these sites becomes infused with novel frameworks for witnessing. Paul Williams, in the closing chapter of this volume, "Locating Loss: The Physical Contexts of Genocide Memorials," examines the global relationship of memorial sites to history and memory. Williams directs his attention to the function of landscape in the service of multiple political, cultural, national, and local interests. Sites of destruction emerge as privileged sites for secondary witnessing, in that they project powerful situated experiences for the memorial visitor. Williams quotes Pierre Nora's dictum that "memory attaches itself to sites, whereas history attaches itself to events." In this sense, Williams recalls the Oklahoma City Memorial that features an empty chair for each person killed there in April 1995, capturing the subjective themes associated with unfulfilled lives. His chapter demonstrates that memorial sites, however aesthetically imagined or conceived, allow for the promulgation of multiple experiences about "the past in the present" that emit an increasingly global significance.

Post-Holocaust Culture: The Peril of Lost Origins

The demographic decline of the survivor population is a watershed moment in Holocaust memory and historical consciousness. Survivors as witnesses have master-framed the very idea of origins within the Holocaust, and in so doing have represented the voices closest to millions of the perished. Primary witnesses have thus come to occupy a cultural location well beyond historical reportage. Indeed, the experiences and perspectives of the primary witnesses (collective, national, faith-based) are having an increasingly evident effect on historical writing, thereby shifting subjective experiences to the fore. The extremity of survivor stories—and how to convey them—opens more widely than ever the gates of representation. A recent effort in this direction deserves some mention in the context of this volume, because of its proximity to generational practices, technological advances, and digital manipulations. The Shoah History Foundation and the New Dimensions in Technology division of the University of Southern California have created what has been referred to as "The World's First 3-D Interactive Holocaust Survivor"[13] through a hologram image of a survivor of Buchenwald, Pinchas Gutter. Siri-based technology interacts with the viewer through an algorithm that improves with usage as it responds to newly formed questions. Gutter's digital file has been engineered to gesture and respond to questions. The hologram not only answers questions, but also produces the expected aesthetic response from the viewer, through an expectation of empathetic association. The photo-realistic speaker not only anticipates questions but also re-creates the expected aesthetic response through the aural effect of the archetypal survivor: generating yet further layers of distanciation from the original moment of speech (see Trezise, *Witnessing Witnessing*, on this critical point). This informationalized practice at the problematic intersection of pedagogical technique and memory shifts a historic sequence, begun in a dimly lit world of tragedy: from the speaker to the listener, from the listener to a digitally prepared algorithm mimicking the plausibility of an answer.

Much is assumed here. The potential for the greater accessibility of the survivor's story—the promise of the hologram—is negatively balanced by the experiential loss of listening and viewing an authentic encounter between the interviewer and the survivor, which defines this unique relational genre. Marshall McLuhan's poignant insight that "the medium is the message"[14] continues to provide a useful cautionary tale for an ethics of Holocaust representation. The medium is everpresent in any message it conveys, in that it influences how the message is perceived. Is our empathetic association with the primary witness entering a cold watershed moment, where the medium of reception fully becomes the message? What will rescue these stories, however mediated they already are, from programmed ennui in an unfettered world of informationalization? These questions make the present volume all the more germane. Not far beneath the surface of these essays rests a fundamental premise, about individual and collective trauma, experienced at the intersection of everyday life and the cruelty of mass murder.[15]

In a moment of subjective self-exploration about his imprisonment in Auschwitz, Primo Levi unwittingly exposes the contemporary problem of reception of the memory of the Holocaust, as a form of preparation for witnessing itself. It is a daunting reminder of the labyrinthine lessons of origins and the still unsolved challenge of securely transmitting them to the next generations of listeners.

> I still have a visual and acoustic memory of experiences there that I cannot explain ... sentences in languages I do not know have remained etched in my memory, like on a magnetic tape. I have repeated them to Poles and Hungarians and have been told that the sentences are meaningful. For some reason that I cannot explain, something anomalous happened to me, I would say almost an unconscious preparation for bearing witness.[16]

Notes

1. Berel Lang, *Holocaust Representation: Art within the Limits of History and Ethics* (Baltimore: Johns Hopkins University Press, 2000), 87.

2. Geoffrey Hartman, "The Humanities of Testimony: An Introduction," *Poetics Today* 27, no. 2 (2006): 260.

3. Ibid., 257.

4. Auschwitz Prozess refers to a series of trials from December 20, 1963, to August 19, 1965. Twenty-two defendants were charged under German criminal law. The defendants were mid- to low-level officials in Auschwitz-Birkenau and its surrounding camp system.

5. On this precise methodological question, see Saul Friedländer, *Nazi Germany and the Jews: The Years of Extermination 1939–1945* (New York: HarperCollins, 2007), and *Probing the Limits of Representation: Nazism and the Final Solution* (Cambridge, MA: Harvard University Press, 2007).

6. See Laura Jockusch, *Collect and Record! Jewish Holocaust Documentation in Early Postwar Europe* (Oxford: Oxford University Press, 2012), 165.

7. Henri Lustiger Thaler, "History and Memory: The Orthodox Experience in the Bergen-Belsen Displaced Persons Camp," *Holocaust and Genocide Studies* 27, no. 1 (2013): 30–56.

8. David P. Boder, *I Did Not Interview the Dead* (Urbana: University of Illinois Press, 1949).

9. Saul Friedlander, ed., *Probing the Limits of Representation: Nazism and the Final Solution* (Cambridge, MA: Harvard University Press, 1992); Dan

Stone, ed., *The Holocaust and Historical Methodology* (New York: Berghahn Books, 2015).

10. James E. Young, *The Texture of Memory: Holocaust Memorials and Meaning* (New Haven, CT: Yale University Press, 1993).

11. On memorial activism in Lower Saxony, see Henri Lustiger Thaler and Wilfried Wiedemann, "Hauntings of Anne Frank: Sitings in Germany," in *Anne Frank Unbound: Media, Imagination, Memory*, ed. Barbara Kirshenblatt-Gimblett and Jeffrey Shandler (Bloomington: Indiana University Press, 2012), 137–59. See also Habbo Knoch, "Die Rückkehr der Zeugen. Gedenkstätten als Gedächtnisorte der Bundesrepublik," in *Öffentliche Erinnerung und Medialisierung des Nationalsozialismus. Eine Bilanz der letzten dreißig Jahre*, ed. Gerhard Paul and Bernhard Schossig, 116–37 (Göttingen: Wallstein Verlag, 2010).

12. Robert G. Moeller, *War Stories: The Search for a Usable Past in the Federal Republic of Germany* (Berkeley: University of California Press, 2001); Christina Morina, *Legacies of Stalingrad: Remembering the Eastern Front in Germany since 1945* (New York: Cambridge University Press, 2011).

13. Britta Lokting, "Meet the World's First Interactive Holocaust Survivor," *Forward*, November 24, 2015.

14. Marshall McLuhan, *Understanding Media: The Extention of Man* (New York: Mentor, 1964).

15. See Michael Rothberg on this point in *Traumatic Realism: The Demands of Holocaust Representation* (Minneapolis: University of Minnesota Press, 2000).

16. Primo Levi quoted in Giorgio Agamben, *Remnants of Auschwitz: The Witness and the Archive* (New York: Zone Books, 2002), 16.

Bibliography

Arendt, Hannah. *The Human Condition*. Chicago: University of Chicago Press, 1998.

Auger, Marc. *Non Places: Introduction to an Anthropology of Supermodernity*. London: Verso, 2009.

Boder, David P. *I Did Not Interview the Dead*. Urbana: University of Illinois Press, 1949.

Confino, Alon. "Narrative Form and Historical Sensation: On Saul Friedlander's 'The Year of Extermination.'" *History and Theory* 48, no. 3 (2009): 199–219.

Friedländer, Saul. *Nazi Germany and the Jews: The Years of Extermination 1939–1945*. New York: HarperCollins, 2007.
———. *Probing the Limits of Representation: Nazism and the Final Solution*. Cambridge, MA: Harvard University Press, 1992.
Hartman, Geoffrey. "The Humanities of Testimony: An Introduction." *Poetics Today* 27, no. 2 (2006): 249–.60.
Jockusch, Laura. *Collect and Record! Jewish Holocaust Documentation in Early Postwar Europe*. Oxford: Oxford University Press, 2012.
Klei, Alexandra. *Der erinnerte Ort. Geschichte durch Architektur. Zur baulichen und gestalterischen Repräsentation der nationalsozialistischen Konzentrationslager, Bielefeld*. Transcript, 2011.
Knoch, Habbo. "Die Rückkehr der Zeugen. Gedenkstätten als Gedächtnisorte der Bundesrepublik." In *Öffentliche Erinnerung und Medialisierung des Nationalsozialismus. Eine Bilanz der letzten dreißig Jahre*, ed. Gerhard Paul and Bernhard Schossig, 116–37. Göttingen: Wallstein Verlag, 2010.
Lang, Berel. *Holocaust Representation: Art within the Limits of History and Ethics*. Baltimore: Johns Hopkins University Press, 2000.
Lokting, Britta. "Meet the World's First Interactive Holocaust Survivor." *Forward*, November 24, 2015.
Lustiger Thaler, Henri. "History and Memory: The Orthodox Experience in the Bergen-Belsen Displaced Persons Camp." *Holocaust and Genocide Studies* 27, no. 1 (2013): 30–56.
Lustiger Thaler, Henri, and Wilfried Wiedemann. "Hauntings of Anne Frank: Sitings in Germany." In *Anne Frank Unbound: Media, Imagination, Memory*, ed. Barbara Kirshenblatt-Gimblett and Jeffrey Shandler, 137–59. Bloomington: Indiana University Press, 2012.
McLuhan, Marshall. *Understanding Media: The Extention of Man*. New York: Mentor, 1964.
Moeller, Robert G. *War Stories: The Search for a Usable Past in the Federal Republic of Germany*. Berkeley: University of California Press, 2001.
Morina, Christina. *Legacies of Stalingrad: Remembering the Eastern Front in Germany since 1945*. New York: Cambridge University Press, 2011.
Moyn, Samuel. "Bearing Witness: Theological Roots of a New Secular Morality." In *The Holocaust and Historical Methodology*, ed. Dan Stone, 127–42. New York: Berghahn Books, 2015.
Rothberg, Michael. *Traumatic Realism: The Demands of Holocaust Representation*. Minneapolis: University of Minnesota Press, 2000.
Sabrow, Martin, and Norbert Frei, eds. *Die Geburt des Zeitzeugen nach 1945*. Göttingen: Wallstein Verlag, 2012.

Stone, Dan, ed. *The Holocaust and Historical Methodology*. New York: Berghahn Books, 2015.

Trezise, Thomas. *Witnessing Witnessing: On the Reception of Holocaust Survivor Testimony*. Bronx, NY: Fordham University Press, 2013.

Young, James E. *The Texture of Memory: Holocaust Memorials and Meaning*. New Haven, CT: Yale University Press, 1993.

1

The Afterdeath of the Holocaust

LAWRENCE L. LANGER

> When the exiled and the dead outnumber the living, it is the dead who start talking instead of the living. There are simply not enough of the living left to be able to maintain a whole reality.
> Steve Sem-Sandberg, *The Emperor of Lies*

In the summer of 1964, I found myself in a Munich courtroom at the trial of SS General Karl Wolff, adjutant to Heinrich Himmler and liaison to Hitler. Nearly twenty years after the war, he was charged with responsibility for the deportation of more than 300,000 Jews from the Warsaw Ghetto to Treblinka, where most were murdered upon arrival. Neatly dressed in a modest pinstripe suit with white shirt and tie, thinning gray hair, and a pleasant expression on his face, he showed nothing in his appearance that connected our memory to such a monstrous crime. Nor did his testimony help. When the presiding judge asked him if he had ever been in the Warsaw Ghetto, he replied, "Mein Gott, nein!" When a young prosecuting attorney who looked half the sixty-four-year-old Wolff's age offered unassailable evidence that Wolff was lying, the judge asked the accused, "Herr Zeugnis [witness], was sagen Sie dazu?" Wolff calmly replied, "Herr Vorsitzende [Chairman], ich bin ein alter Mann. Ich kann mich nicht alles gut erinnern." To this the judge, leaning forward, responded, "If I had been in the Warsaw Ghetto, I would never have forgotten it!"

It should come as no surprise that people like Wolff were afflicted with convenient amnesia in regard to their crimes. A short time later, I attended the so-called Auschwitz Prozess (trial) in Frankfurt of twenty-one SS guards and camp personnel, and heard notorious killers like Oswald Kaduk and Josef Klehr deny that they had anything to do with murdering Jews. Accused of "Abspritzen," or fatally injecting phenol into the heart muscle of hundreds of prisoners, Klehr insisted that he must have been home on leave when such crimes were taking place. This was not a case of "Ich kann nicht" but of "Ich *will* nicht mich gut erinnern," and this formula, "I don't want to remember very well," extends beyond the claims of those guilty of war crimes to those who feel uncomfortable tracing the journey of "deep memory" into an abyss of horror where they would prefer not to plunge.[1]

Any monument to the Holocaust worthy of its name must include many roads, one of which would invite memory to pursue its winding path toward a destination called "atrocity." Kaduk and Klehr, together with several of the other accused, listened to the testimony of survivors and built around it a wall of what we might call "evasive memory," and the proprietors of this stance, whether guilty or not—an important distinction, to be sure—continue to use it to insulate themselves from the crimes of Auschwitz and its fellow killing sites. But if the Holocaust is to enter human consciousness, as it must, as an integral part of the narrative of modernity, that consciousness must voluntarily explore the contents of "deep memory" wherever it leads, however dark and cruel its revelations, whatever inroads it makes on the so-called moral and spiritual value of the quest for truth and the meaning of being human.

The expression "deep memory" (*memoire profonde*) was introduced into Holocaust discourse by Charlotte Delbo,[2] a French survivor of Auschwitz who in the three volumes evoking her camp experience, *Auschwitz and After*, and in the slim work she finished shortly before her death, *Days and Memory*, struggled to find a link between her Auschwitz self and the self who enjoyed what she considered the luxury of survival. Neither logic nor intuition can explain what one of her fellow survivors meant when she announced to Delbo, "I died in Auschwitz, but no one sees it."[3] But Primo Levi understood well the paradox of a life consumed by the aura of death even as it continued to exist, to breathe, to think, and, perhaps surprisingly, to hope. Forced to witness the hanging of a prisoner, but unable to raise a word or gesture of protest, Levi cannot escape the burden of that moment of remembered shame. Deep memory is at work as he writes, "It has not been easy, nor quick, but you Germans have succeeded.... Because we also are broken, conquered: even if we know how to adapt ourselves, even if we have finally learnt how to find out food and to resist the fatigue and cold, even if we return home."[4] Unlike Levi, Delbo speaks of shedding her Auschwitz ordeal as a snake sheds its old skin, but in so doing, she ironically reminds us of what cannot so easily be left behind: "the leaden stare out of sunken eyes, the tottering gait, the frightened gestures." After all, she finally admits, "Rid of its old skin, it's still the same snake. I'm the same too, apparently." Inside Auschwitz, she is unable to find consolation in thinking about more amiable prewar or postwar conditions: "In the camp, one could never pretend, never take refuge in the imagination.... It's impossible. One can't imagine either being somebody else or being somewhere else." It is easy to extract fragments from her narrative and flaunt them as victorious moments—for example, "To think, to remember was a great victory over the horror"—and to use them as examples of the triumph of the human spirit, but this is to ignore her immediately following insistence that thinking "never lessened" the horror: "Reality was right there, killing. There was no possible getting away from it."[5]

Monuments and museums that do not focus on the killing reality of the Holocaust are risking failure in their missions, if their missions are to capture for present and future generations the depth and the scope of the atrocity. The paradox that Delbo and so many survivors in their testimonies convey is that life stopped at Auschwitz and other camps and ghettos and life went on afterward, giving birth to two selves whose contradictory natures must somehow be transmitted to us, the observers. The Auschwitz self Delbo captures with vivid candor: "Hardly able to stand on my feet, my throat tight, my heart beating wildly, frozen to the marrow, filthy, skin and bones; the suffering I feel is so unbearable, so identical to the pain endured there, that I feel it physically, I feel it throughout my whole body which becomes a mass of suffering; and I feel death fasten on me, I feel that I am dying." The other self, as she says, is "the person you know, who can talk to you about Auschwitz without exhibiting or registering any anxiety or emotion."⁶ "Memoire profonde," deep memory, gives us access to the first; what she calls "memoire ordinaire," common or ordinary memory, reflects the second.

We sympathize cheerfully with the objects of ordinary memory because they do not threaten our well-being, our consciousness, or the integrity of our personalities or worldviews. When dealing with the Holocaust, the difficult challenge before us is to identify with the target of deep memory, that intellectual and emotional terrain where the clear borders between living and dying merge and we are faced with the condition of being what I call "deathlife" (the Afterdeath of the Holocaust), a territory we instinctively flee because it is uninhabitable by reasonable creatures like ourselves. Talking about Auschwitz, Delbo argues, comes from "intellectual memory, the memory connected with thinking processes." And this has its value, but also its limitations: it does not evoke the "killing reality" of the place. That is reserved for deep memory, which "preserves sensations, physical imprints. It is the memory of the senses." Delbo uses the example of thirst, which nearly proved fatal for her in Auschwitz, to clarify her idea. Ordinary memory sees thirst as a condition that is abated by taking a drink; deep memory instantly evokes her camp self, "haggard, halfway crazed, near to collapse; I physically feel that real thirst and it is an atrocious nightmare."⁷

And try as we might to find a context of meaning for the murder of European Jewry, it remains an "atrocious nightmare," a black hole in the cosmos of consciousness, so that efforts to locate traces of a bright galaxy in its orbit only risk allowing the temptations of evasive memory to infiltrate our response. Evasive memory elevates the horrors of the Holocaust to a manageable level by shifting the emphasis from the cruelty of the ordeal to a frame of mind that translates mass murder into a narrative of suffering and redemption. Viktor Frankl is a good example, and his testimony about Auschwitz—where he spent no more than three days—in *Man's Search for Meaning* continues to mislead readers about the nature of the Holocaust experience. Frankl seems constitutionally incapable of acknowledging the physical and moral devastation wrought by that event, though the impact of his work remains undiminished, especially in America, where his book has sold more than nine million copies and the Library of Congress, after a national survey, declared it *one of the ten most influential works ever published in the United States*. If deep memory were allowed to play its proper role in Holocaust discourse, excavating and displaying the monumental cruelty of the catastrophe, sentimentalized versions of its impact like Frankl's could never prevail. Nor could the literal examples of false witnessing like Benjamin Wilkomirski's *Fragments* (*Bruchstücke*) or Misha Defonseca's *Misha: A Memoire of the Holocaust Years* have gained the following they did, especially the latter, which became a best-seller in France and Italy and was made into a successful film. In February 2008, the author finally admitted that the memoir was fake and that she was not even Jewish. Only widely disseminated testimonies based on authentic witnessing, including large doses of deep memory, can discredit such counterfeit narratives before they are distributed.

But the most dangerous examples of evasive memory come from the murderers themselves, authentic witnesses who exploit false witnessing to deflect attention from the horror of their crimes. One illustration from among many will have to suffice. Earlier, I mentioned the SS man Josef Klehr, a defendant in the Auschwitz trial who was accused of murdering no fewer than 465 inmates by injecting phenol into the heart muscle, a tactic that proved instantly fatal. Klehr received a life sentence plus fifteen years in 1965, was released in 1988 at the age of eighty-four, and died a few months later. In 1978, a German television journalist was allowed to interview him in prison. Klehr spoke with a crude bluntness, since he no longer had anything to lose, but his "testimony" demonstrates that if evasive memory can elevate the Holocaust to a spiritual level it has not earned, it can also deflate the ordeal to a plane of moral insensitivity that gives us a rare but valuable glimpse into the mental terrain of the killer. In spite of the biographies of figures like Heinrich Himmler and Ernst Kaltenbrunner, and Robert Jay Lifton's detailed portraits of Nazi doctors, such mental terrain remains a speculative realm that eludes total comprehension.

The interviewer asks Klehr to describe the process of "Abspritzen," or injection, to which he vaguely replies: "Yes, I reported the incident to my superior, that prisoners were being injected without the approval of the camp doctor." No, the interrogator protests, that is not what he meant, since he had asked Klehr to describe the course of events during "injections" after he himself has been ordered to carry them out. "Yes," Klehr responds at length, and we note how he excludes himself as an agent and adopts the role of witness during the deadly drama he describes:

I made my own observations at that time. I was amazed that the prisoners didn't even weep or defend themselves. They sat down on a stool and waited, until it was all over [*bis es soweit war*]. I had my own thoughts about that then, and I still have them today: no prisoner resisted and no prisoner cried. Because they knew, it was an open secret: they had been "selected," they knew where they were headed. That was clear, it was an open secret. And nevertheless when the time for "injection" arrived no prisoner resisted. And should a prisoner have resisted, I would have . . .[8]

And Klehr's thought, such as it is, trails off into silence. It reminded me of the moment at the Auschwitz trial in Frankfurt when one of Klehr's prisoner assistants during the Abspritzen was on the witness stand, testifying that one morning Klehr asked him why he had been weeping the afternoon before and he had replied, "The man you injected then was my father," to which Klehr had responded, "Why didn't you tell me? I would have let him go!" As we all know, myths are born of false witnessing like Klehr's, myths that shift the blame from the murderer to the victims, reproaching them for not doing enough to protect themselves or fighting back. Like so many others, Klehr mistakes the paralysis that seizes doomed individuals in the final moments of existence for passivity or cowardice, although we can never be certain how many of his candidates for death were conscious of what was about to occur.

In his comments in prison, Klehr consistently deflects attention from the "killing reality" for which he was responsible. Evasive memory suffers from a delinquent or reluctant imagination and may be viewed as a variation on the mental approach to the Holocaust that steers us away from the revelations of deep memory. With a cool detachment that insulates him from the nightmare of atrocity as it must have been experienced by his victims, Klehr explains that the phenol injection was preferable to gassing because it was instantly fatal, whereas asphyxiation from gas could take as long as ten minutes. He admits that gassing was "*grausamer*," more terrible than a phenol injection, but this is merely a comparative comment rather than an absolute condemnation. Such testimony is valuable for what it does not express even more than for what it does, since it exposes us to the possibility of a Holocaust discourse that treats deep memory as a response to be avoided.

Testimonies that pay tribute to survival, rescue, or resistance are examples of this discourse, and the temptation to follow this route is strong among all witnesses. We may call it celebratory memory, and it is designed to compensate for the irreducible pain that deep memory explores. Among the documents in the Oyneg Shabbos archives of Emanuel Ringelblum is one composed by a journalist named Leyb Goldin, who was assigned to provide a written account of what a soup kitchen in the Warsaw Ghetto would have looked like to a hungry "customer" in October 1941. In order to objectify his piece and give it a literary flair, Goldin creates a character named "Arke" and presents him as a creature trying to assess the value of the mutual aid groups in the ghetto that supply daily bowls of soup to those too poor to feed themselves. Knowing that future generations will rely on such reports in determining how to remember existence in the ghetto, Goldin divides his persona into two voices, much as Charlotte Delbo had done when she split herself into the Auschwitz inmate who responds to deep memory and the Auschwitz survivor who tries (unsuccessfully) to live afterward through "memoire ordinaire." In Goldin's piece, we witness the birth of both selves, as his character seeks to preserve his dignity despite the starvation that dampens his spirit and threatens his very integrity.

Goldin calls his account "Chronicle of a Single Day," and in it he records the dual responses that Delbo identified as deep and ordinary memory. "At one time," we learn, "he had been an intellectual who had greatly appreciated modern Jewish and European literature: Peretz, Mann, and Goethe. In the good old days, he could think of time as a literary trope, just as Thomas Mann had done in *Magic Mountain*, where Hans Castorp went to the mountain to pay a short visit and stayed for seven years." So much for ordinary memory. "But now," we are informed, "he is in the ghetto; it is 5:00 a.m. and time has assumed a totally different meaning. His mind can only focus on the eight hours that separate himself from his daily bowl of soup at the public kitchen."[9] What we are really witnessing is testimony from the dead, since most of these candidates for daily bowls of soup perished from starvation or were deported to death camps. Such testimony gives us an incisive clue to how we should imagine the "killing reality" of the Holocaust. In one of his essays, Elie Wiesel defined a man in Auschwitz as a starved stomach, and in conjuring up his soup-kitchen client, Leyb Goldin makes a similar discovery: "Now his stomach is doing all his thinking." He also discovers what Jean Améry meant when he wrote, "Es führte keine Brücke vom Tod in Auschwitz zum *Tod in Venedig*" (No bridge led from death in Auschwitz to *Death in Venice*).[10] But he is less prone than Améry to let culture concede defeat to hunger (though Améry would have substituted torture for hunger). He knows that written testimony is a literary event as well as a documentary account, and with a surprising postmodernist fervor he incorporates this insight into his monologue as dialogue: "That kind of split was all right at one time when one was full. Then [with a covert allusion to Goethe's *Faust*] one could say, 'Two people are battling within me,' and one could make a dramatic martyred face. Yes, this kind of thing can be found quite often in literature. But today? Don't talk nonsense—it's you and your stomach. It's your stomach and you. It's 90 percent your stomach and a little bit you, an insignificant remnant of the Arke who once was."[11] Oral Holocaust testimonies are full of the struggle between what we might call civilized memory and the memory of atrocity, though a trained writer like Goldin can translate it into a self-conscious dispute and articulate the need for a resolution.

Walking back from his bowl of soup, "the Arke who once was" passes the small ghetto hospital where surgeons are operating to save a child's life, and he is filled with a sudden surge of dignity: "Each day the profiles of our children, or our wives, acquire the mournful look of foxes, dingoes, kangaroos. Our howls are like the cry of jackals. . . . But we are not animals. We operate on our infants. It may be pointless or even criminal. But animals do not operate on their young!" But he knows this is a voice of desperation, not of triumph, as he concludes: "The world's turning upside down. A planet melts in tears. And I—I am hungry, hungry. I am hungry."[12] Leyb Goldin, I should add, died of starvation in 1942. Deep memory of the Holocaust assaults our idea of normalcy with an irrepressible sense of how, in the midst of life, we are in death in a way not intended by the makers of the original phrase. Finally, Ringelblum himself had to admit that remembering the Holocaust would become an excursion into the archeology of death, though subsequent investigators of the terrain would substitute for "death" the more accurate designation of "mass murder."

When we speak of commemorating the Holocaust, we have to ask ourselves what kind of memory work we want the student, the spectator, and the visitor to museums and monuments to undertake. It is easy enough to transform an archeology of death into an excavation of rebirth and to focus on the future, as Steven Spielberg does at the end of *Schindler's List* when he reminds us of how many descendants resulted from Schindler's saved remnant. But he neglects to speculate about how many offspring might have been born of the millions of Jews who were not rescued and did not survive. Ringelblum established his archives with the hope of documenting for future generations a multidisciplinary record of the conduct of the Jewish community in Warsaw under duress, with no inkling of the coming catastrophe when he began. His shift from hope to despair parallels our passage from ordinary to deep memory, a journey that ends with a confrontation with the heartlessness that lies at the center of the Holocaust experience. We do not need to imagine how the initially sanguine Ringelblum faced this discovery, since he tells us himself. Reflecting in May 1942 on the self-help organization in the ghetto that he was instrumental in founding, he is forced to admit that it "does not solve the problem [of hunger], it only saves people for a short time, and then they will die anyway. The [soup kitchens] prolong the suffering but cannot bring salvation.... It is an absolute fact that the clients of the soup kitchens will all die if all they have to eat is the soup they get there and the bread they get on their ration cards." Ringelblum could not know that in less than two months the Germans would find a swifter end for the ghetto's starving population at a place called Treblinka. The value of Ringelblum's surviving archive cannot be overestimated; it is not, however, the story of the life of a community but of its "deathlife," of its valiant but vain struggle, as its recent historian Samuel Kassow concludes, "to hold onto some morality, some humanity, in the middle of hell."[13]

But at an unhindered level of inquiry into the Holocaust, such an ambition proves fruitless, and this is the chaotic realm where deep memory presides. As the recent work of Father Patrick Desbois confirms, it is a territory where a certain kind of dying ceases to be a trope and becomes a truth. The testimony he extracts from witnesses, a burden for decades, reveals a landscape where "deep" has a physical as well as a metaphorical—to say nothing of metaphysical—meaning. Father Desbois tells us that his investigation of mass graves in Ukraine was inspired by the experience of his grandfather, who during the war was an inmate of a labor camp in the area established by the Germans for French prisoners of war who had attempted multiple escapes from their POW barracks in Germany. Through an odd coincidence, the labor camp in Rawa-Ruska was the same one where French author Pierre Gascar was held and which he used as the basis for his neglected Holocaust masterpiece, the semi-autobiographical novella *The Season of the Dead* (*Les Temps des Mort*), which won the Prix Goncourt in 1953. Both works offer testimony to what I have called the archaeology of death, and reading Gascar's *The Season of the Dead* in tandem with Father Desbois's *The Holocaust by Bullets* gives us sharp comparative glimpses into how deep memory operates in literature, as well as in history.

The resemblance between certain portions of the two works is nothing less than uncanny. Gascar's narrator is in charge of caring for the small cemetery that the Germans have established for the French prisoners of war who die in captivity, from disease or malnutrition. As their number grows, the narrator extends the cemetery's border closer and closer to the nearby forest, until one day, his shovel uncovers a strange twisted corpse, and in an instant he begins to comprehend the difference between a burial ground and a mass grave, a distinction that is already clear to Father Desbois in his grim investigations. The narrator has unwittingly unearthed the site of the murder of members of the local Jewish community, whose tangled decaying remains leave him stunned with revulsion. We hear the testimony of deep memory at work as Gascar's narrator struggles to find an imagery that will do justice to his discovery: "I was overwhelmed by the somber horror of it and the truth it revealed. This was death—these liquefying muscles, this half-eaten eye, those teeth like a dead sheep's; death, no longer decked with grasses, no longer ensconced in the coolness of a vault, no longer lying sepulchered in stone, but sprawling in a bog full of bones, wrapped in a drowned man's clothes, with its hair caught in the earth."[14] There are few clearer examples of how a literature of the Holocaust can find a voice for the archaeology of death that usually only history reports, vital as those reports may be.

Still clearer, however, as evidenced by Father Desbois's work, is how history can occasionally trump even literature through the detailed candor of its so-called bystanders. Most Holocaust testimonies gathered in archives around the world come from survivors. Father Desbois faced the more difficult—many would have thought it impossible—task of collecting accounts from observers, who for decades had chosen evasive memory as the salve to soothe the scars of the atrocities they had seen, or were complicit in. He was determined to follow what he calls the "trail of memory" to the "killing reality" at its end—literally its dead end—stirring deep memory through a strategy that threatened both speaker and interviewer. He offers a lucid description of the problem:

> I had to successfully skirt around the guilt they may have felt about receiving a Jewish garment, about the role they played in the assassination, or even about the simple fact of having been there when it occurred. During the interviews, we were often confronted with horror. I had to accept to hear the unspeakable. I had to get over the disgust provoked by the accounts of infinite sadism.[15]

Such intimacy with the minutiae of atrocity that temporarily suspends both judgment of the speaker and loathing for what is spoken is an essential attitude for anyone who listens to Holocaust testimony in hopes of arriving at the heartlessness at its center. It is asking too much to expect a permanent state of emotional detachment as these stories of the murderers' savagery emerge from the alcoves of deep memory, but it is a helpful and perhaps a necessary point of departure. Each monument to the Holocaust must find its own way of negotiating such treacherous terrain; to avoid it is to join the ranks of evasive memory. But how to commemorate savagery remains an elusive goal, as Father Desbois was to discover. He brings clarity of vision to our journey into atrocity, but little comprehension: *tout comprendre, c'est tout pardonner* (to understand everything is to forgive everything) is a maxim that does not apply to the Holocaust. Unfortunately, such journeys do not offer a guide to the perplexed, only more confusion about the reasons for the total collapse of ethical systems and moral restraints. Primo Levi wrote that he could never understand why the Germans did not simply execute on site two residents in their mid-nineties from a Jewish home for the elderly in northern Italy instead of forcing them to endure the travail of a boxcar transfer to Auschwitz. The testimony elicited by Father Desbois from his witnesses assaults the imagination with hammer blows of unthinkable cruelty that demolish all barricades insulating us from such scenarios, leaving us defenseless and spiritually forlorn.

There is no need to describe too many of the excavations of deep memory that Father Desbois uncovered—a few will suffice. They represent the searing core of the Holocaust experience, to which evasive memory over the decades has turned a deaf ear and a blind eye. In a sense, they restore speech to an awful empire of silence whose reign after the war the killers would obviously refuse to examine and the doomed would be unable to portray. One of the former prisoners of Rawa-Ruska who accompanied Father Desbois on his journey recalls that because the Germans had requisitioned all the animals from the farms, they summoned Jewish women from the nearby village to do the harvesting. "They came in the morning with their children," he says. "The German who was guarding them could not stand their crying and whenever it irritated him too much, he would get hold of a little child and bludgeon it to death against a cart. In the evening all that remained were the women, carts, and hay."[16] After so many years, the teller is given a chance to speak, and we call this testimony. But more important is that we are given a chance to listen, and what we hear plunges us into the darkest corners of deep memory, where the most hideous dramas of the Holocaust were enacted.

Such witnesses are rare, because they give us direct access to the vantage point of those who were, at least temporarily, immune from the killing process. The episode raises the difficult and perhaps insoluble issue of whether witnessing, under certain circumstances, can itself be a form of complicity. A bent and ancient Ukrainian, a young bride at the time of the mass murders, tells of working in the fields when she saw two German trucks filled with standing Jewish women approaching: "She suddenly recognized a friend of her mother's who began shouting 'Olena, Olena, save me!'... The more she shouted, the more I hid myself in the wheat. I was afraid that the Germans would kill us like they were killing the Jews. The woman shouted until they took her to the pit. Right until the last moment I heard her shouting: 'Olena, Olena, save me!'"[17] She revives for us the voice of sheer naked terror from a doomed woman who does not want to die. Witnesses like these resemble modern Virgils leading us through the German inferno, though their narrative twists Dante's scenario since here it is the guilty who survive while the innocent perish. And there is no trace of divine guidance to be seen.

These accounts strip from the story of the Holocaust the burden of bravado or the consolations of the heroic gesture. One last piece of evidence uncovered by Father Desbois is presented with such brutal honesty that even the most courageous imagination intuitively seeks to censor its message of historical truth. It helps us to understand what Charlotte Delbo meant when she tried to distinguish in her account of Auschwitz between the "worst," which many of us are familiar with, and the unthinkable. Many years ago, I interviewed a survivor who was in one of the smaller labor camps that grew up around the larger killing centers. The barracks were not far from a nearby forest, and he tells of a plan that some barrack leaders drew up for a mass escape. At the last moment, something went awry and the plan was canceled, but a few members of the group defied their leaders' decision and made the attempt anyway. They were caught, brought back to camp, a large pit was dug, and they were executed and buried in the mass grave. The interviewee says that from his barrack, he had a clear view of the site, and for the next few days he could see the earth there moving, as he reported, up and down, up and down, up and down. At the time, I assumed that the source of the motion was gas escaping from the decaying corpses, but Father Desbois's investigations offer convincing evidence for an alternative explanation.

He presents us with a shuddering revelation, and here the long journey of deep memory toward the "killing reality" of the Holocaust reaches its most desolate destination:

> These peasants also spoke to me of the pits as if they were alive. How was I to understand what they meant? How was I to accept the witnesses' repeated assertion that the pits "breathed" for three days afterward? I attributed it, without yet having explained it, to the deterioration process of the bodies. And then, on a different day in another village, someone who had been requisitioned as a child to dig that pit told us that a hand coming out of the ground had grabbed hold of his spade. I understood then that all the witnesses who had told us about the pits moving, accompanying their words by an up-and-down movement of the hand, had signified in fact that a pit took three days to quiet down because many of the victims had been buried alive.[18]

Here, the imagination pauses, lowers its lids, and struggles to resist the tempting lure of evasive memory. Here, too, history reaches its limit, offering us no exit from the trap of this darkest secret of the Holocaust. We must return to the fiction of Pierre Gascar in *The Season of the Dead*, which traces a parallel theme, but offers a glimmer of light through a question that at least challenges the mind to further thought: "When death has come, has one finished dying?"[19]

This is the afterdeath of the Holocaust. Gascar's narrator, like those of us devoted to Holocaust memory, is a caretaker of the dead, but just as he learns that after the war he will have to contend with the difference between decent burial and anonymous mass murder, so too are we now faced with the thankless task of following deep memory to a place we do not wish to visit and finding a monument to express and commemorate the end of more than a million Jews in places they did not wish to be, dying in ways that no creatures on Earth should ever be made to die.

Notes

1. For extensive excerpts from trial testimony, see Bernd Naumann, *Auschwitz: A Report on the Proceedings against Robert Karl Ludwig Mulka and Others before the Court at Frankfurt* (New York: Frederick A. Praeger, 1966). For a more comprehensive history of the trial, see Devin O. Pendas, *The Frankfurt Auschwitz Trial, 1963–1965: Genocide, History, and the Limits of the Law* (Cambridge: Cambridge University Press, 2006).

2. Charlotte Delbo, *Days and Memory*, trans. Rosette C. Lamont (Marlboro, VT: Marlboro Press, 1990), 3.

3. Charlotte Delbo, *Auschwitz and After*, trans. Rosette C. Lamont (New Haven, CT: Yale University Press, 1995), 267.

4. Primo Levi, *Survival in Auschwitz: The Nazi Assault on Humanity*, trans. Stuart Woolf (New York: Collier Books, 1976), 150.

5. Delbo, *Days and Memory*, 1–2.

6. Ibid., 3.

7. Ibid., 3–4.

8. Ebbo Demant, ed., *Auschwitz—"Direkt von der Rampe Weg..." Kaduk, Erber, Klehr: Drei Täter geben zu Protokoll* (Hamburg: Rowohlt, 1979), 100. My translation.

9. Samuel D. Kassow, *Who Will Write Our History? Emanuel Ringelblum, the Warsaw Ghetto, and the Oyneg Shabas Archive* (Bloomington: Indiana University Press, 2007), 141. The full text of Goldin's essay, "Chronicle of a Single Day," may be found in *The Literature of Destruction: Jewish Responses to Catastrophe,* ed. David Roskies (Philadelphia: Jewish Publication Society, 1989), 424–34.

10. Jean Améry, *At the Mind's Limits: Contemplations by a Survivor on Auschwitz and Its Realities,* trans. Sidney Rosenfeld and Stella P. Rosenfeld (New York: Schocken, 1986), 16.

11. Kassow, *Who Will Write Our History?,* 140.

12. Ibid., 141–42.

13. Ibid., 142–43.

14. Pierre Gascar, "The Season of the Dead," in *Beasts and Men & The Seed: Seven Stories and a Novel,* trans. Jean Stewart (New York: Meridian, 1960), 221.

15. Father Patrick Desbois, *The Holocaust by Bullets: A Priest's Journey to Uncover the Truth behind the Murder of 1.5 Million Jews,* trans. Catherine Spencer (New York: Palgrave Macmillan, 2008), 109.

16. Ibid., 30.

17. Ibid., 57–58.

18. Ibid., 65.

19. Gascar, "The Season of the Dead," 198.

Bibliography

Améry, Jean. *At the Mind's Limits: Contemplations by a Survivor of Auschwitz and Its Realities.* Trans. Sidney Rosenfeld and Stella P. Rosenfeld. New York: Schocken, 1986.

Delbo, Charlotte. *Auschwitz and After.* Trans. Rosette C. Lamont. New Haven, CT: Yale University Press, 1995.

———. *Days and Memory.* Trans. Rosette C. Lamont. Marlboro, VT: Marlboro Press, 1990.

Demant, Ebbo, ed. *Auschwitz—"Direkt von der Rampe Weg..." Kaduk, Erber, Klehr: Drei Täter geben zu Protokoll.* Hamburg: Rowohlt, 1979.

Desbois, Father Patrick. *The Holocaust by Bullets: A Priest's Journey to Uncover the Truth behind the Murder of 1.5 Million Jews.* Trans. Catherine Spencer. New York: Palgrave Macmillan, 2008.

Gascar, Pierre. "The Season of the Dead." In *Beasts and Men & The Seed: Seven Stories and a Novel*. Trans. Jean Stewart. New York: Meridian, 1960.

Goldin, Leyb. "Chronicle of a Single Day." In *The Literature of Destruction: Jewish Responses to Catastrophe*, ed. David Roskies, 424–34. Philadelphia: Jewish Publication Society, 1989.

Kassow, Samuel D. *Who Will Write Our History? Emanuel Ringelblum, the Warsaw Ghetto, and the Oyneg Shabas Archive*. Bloomington: Indiana University Press, 2007.

Levi, Primo. *Survival in Auschwitz: The Nazi Assault on Humanity*. Trans. Stuart Woolf. New York: Collier Books, 1976.

Naumann, Bernd. *Auschwitz: A Report on the Proceedings against Robert Karl Ludwig Mulka and Others before the Court at Frankfurt*. New York: Frederick A. Praeger, 1966.

Pendas, Devin O. *The Frankfurt Auschwitz Trial, 1963–1965: Genocide, History, and the Limits of the Law*. Cambridge: Cambridge University Press, 2006.

Sem-Sandburg, Steve. *The Emperor of Lies: A Novel*. Trans. Sarah Death. New York: Farrar, Straus and Giroux, 2011.

2

Witnesses and Witnessing

Some Reflections

ANNETTE WIEVIORKA

The Era of the Witness

Just like a personal experience, a testimony can communicate the discourse, or discourses, emerging in society about the events experienced by witnesses. Testimonies of the postwar period are different from those of today: different things are being said and there are diverging expectations. I have called an open period during the 1980s, when Jewish survivors who witnessed the genocide became a familiar sight in society,[1] the "era of the witness."[2] The success of this title can cause some confusion. I borrowed it somewhat mischievously from Nathalie Sarraute's *L'ère du soupçon*.[3] Yet, the two "eras" are antithetical: Sarraute raises doubts about characters and how their stories are told. A testimony is just a character and a story.

Some do not agree with this position. We should not call that period the "era of the witness," but the "era of the victim." Indeed, a book by Didier Fassin and Richard Rechtman titled *The Empire of Trauma* is an inquiry into the condition of the victim that is inscribed in the same timeframe as the era of the witness. But these victims, those who launch class-action suits in the United States, for instance, often remain silent. In my mind, the "era of the witness" begins when the historical narrative consists of first-person accounts. It is linked to a notion of democracy that envisions anybody's statements as equally worth considering, whether those of a historian, an expert, or a witness; it reflects the individualism that characterizes our societies.

Is the era of the witness doomed to end when the last Auschwitz survivor dies? Nothing is more uncertain. Still, a question remains: What happens to the memory of the genocide when those who lived through it are gone? This was a recurring theme in 2005 at the sixtieth anniversary of the liberation of the camps at Auschwitz, an anniversary that was commemorated internationally like no other: "How will the Shoah be remembered once there are no more witnesses?" At that time, I thought the question was insensitive: these witnesses were present and they had no intentions of dying and some even were, and are, my friends. The formulation lays out confusing parallels between memory and history, between witness and testimony. Even in terms of memory, when the last "poilus"[4] died out at the end of this last decade, the Great War was ever more present in the public sphere. In terms of history, the narrative of earlier periods is still being written without living witnesses.

Today, eight years later, we have to admit that the survivors are disappearing one after the other. Their disappearance strikes us as sudden, even shocking, when it was perfectly inevitable and predictable. While 1,500 survivors were present at Auschwitz for the sixtieth anniversary of the liberation, only 150 were around at the sixty-fifth commemoration. Until recently, high school students visiting the camp were guided by survivors. This is happening less and less. Soon, it will be over. This is the order of things: their vanishing confirms the passage of time. The grandparents of today's children and teenagers were born after the Second World War.

The End of the Witness

The passing of these witnesses poses a specific and unprecedented challenge, however, because the memory of the genocide was constructed with the survivors. At the trial of Adolf Eichmann, they were entrusted with being the messengers of history, in charge of a narrative that would inform later generations. Thus, the anxieties about their vanishing reveal the essential role of witnesses. Today, seemingly as a corrolary to their voices, the phenomenon of witness sites[5] are developing exponentially; Auschwitz-Birkenau is the first among them, where attendance is at an all-time high.

The growing specter of modern-day forms of witnessing says a lot about our own epoch. It lends credence to subjective speech and individual opinions. It may be characterized by what historian François Hartog calls presentism,[6] as described by Olivier Rolin in the novel *Tigre en papier*. In his youth, which was about the same time as mine, give or take a few years, he wrote, "The world before your eyes, in which you lived, was somehow transmuted by a power that linked every event, every person to a whole ancient chain of events and more tragic figures. Yet today, it seems that only the present or even the instant is left; the present has become a massive ant farm, an astounding network of nerves, an everlasting big bang."[7]

Here, we must define the term "witness." In the French language, the word "witness" can refer to the victim, as well as to a third party present during an event. In legal terms, the eyewitness is the person who saw something with her own eyes and can attest to it. Such testimony or declaration is seen as truthful because the person can say, "I was there." Yet the term "witness" has been stretched to mean people who "were there," but under very different circumstances. There are those "who saw," like the Ukrainian farmer who was around during the mass executions by firing squad: they would be defined in English as "bystanders"; then there are those who were victims and testify about what they endured in various situations, mostly in court appearances, in documentary films, or in autobiographical works. Also, there are those, some still children at the time, who simply explain the effects that these events had on their own lives. They would usually be referred to in English as "witnesses." Yet witnesses are sometimes also participants in historical developments, as Göring or Eichmann were witnesses at their own trials, or even the Jewish resistance militants, members of "MOI"[8] whom I interviewed for my book *Ils étaient juifs, résistants, communistes*.[9] What they did, then, was more important than what they saw.

In *Shoah*, Claude Lanzmann interviews Nazi officials like Suchomel who was operating at Treblinka. He belongs to a category that English speakers call "perpetrators" and German speakers "Täter" (related to the verb "tun" [do] and the noun "Tat" [deed]); the ones who do the deed, who perform the act, a role that is hard to define in the French language, in which perpetrators have to be referred to as either "torturers," "criminals," or "executioners." Lanzmann also interviews resistance militants like Antek Zuckerman and eyewitnesses like Polish resistance messenger

Jan Karski, who was smuggled into the Warsaw Ghetto by Jewish resistance fighters just so that he could describe to the allies what he saw there. He also talks with victims like Simon Srebnik and even with Polish country folk who were living close to the extermination centers. One of the characters in Lanzmann's film is historian Raul Hilberg, who may have taken the Shoah as a starting point when he conceptualized the three categories: "executioners," "victims," and "witnesses." Or is it the other way around?

Even if it sounds a little tautological, a witness is, in current parlance, the one who produces a testimony, a first-person narrative. Neither the context in which he or she testifies, nor his or her relation to the event, matters. In this case, testifying means delivering a narrative account of their own story, often in school classes in front of teenage audiences. These witnesses do not testify about specific facts, but their testimonies are acts in themselves, like walking. This stretching of the definition is the source of much confusion.

The first testimonies are concurrent with the event. We now know who belonged to the group of comrades enlisted by historian Emmanuel Ringelblum in the Warsaw ghetto and what they were working on thanks to Samuel Kassow's magnum opus *Who Will Write Our History?*[10] But other texts have been written in the ghettos, in the camps, and up to the threshold of the gas chambers. There are unrepentant diarists like the German philologist Victor Klemperer, who kept a lifelong diary from which only the two volumes covering the Nazi Era (1933–1945) have been published.[11] Starting from this diary, he built up his essay on LTI (*Lingua tertii imperii*), the Nazi language. Yet the urge to write, or the impulse to testify, stemmed from the realization of just how extensive the destruction really was, and how radical. Some writings were lost. During the Großaktion,[12] between July 22 and September 21, 1942, a total of around 300,000 Jews from the Warsaw Ghetto were killed—some murdered there, but most displaced to Treblinka to be exterminated.

Michel Borwicz, the first scholar to pore over testimonial writings as early as the 1950s, estimates that, as of 1942, a great wave of ghetto writings and a shift in subject matter are traceable. Until 1942, there was "a stubborn belief that defeat was imminent for Germany, which meant that it was still conceivable that at least some of the victims would be spared."[13] After the start of mass deportations from the ghettos to the extermination centers, this belief in a Nazi defeat did not abate, but it was accompanied by another certainty: that "the last Jewish survivors" would be eliminated.

The Traces of Memory

From then on, giving testimony meant leaving a trace of a people that would otherwise have been erased from world memory. These shipwrecked souls used all literary forms, journals, poetry, and even novels. Some of these writings were recovered and most are now translated into French. Some of the journals, as Saul Friedländer points out, stop in mid-sentence or even mid-word, when the authors are arrested before being deported or assassinated. Most of these texts have been hidden, most often buried like the dreadful writings found on various occasions in the main crematorium and gas chamber areas at Birkenau. They were sometimes called the "Auschwitz scrolls," a definition that gives them a sacred aura. Testimonies from the hub of the extermination process altogether found few readers in France, even if some of them (such as the "Auschwitz Scrolls" published for the sixtieth anniversary of the camps' liberation under the title *Voices under the Ashes)*[14] had a short-lived success in bookstores. Yet they never entered the "canon" like Primo Levi's *If This Is a Man* (published in the United States as *Survival in Auschwitz*).

Among the most popular testimonies is that of Anne Frank, whose diary has been translated into every language, and has also been the subject around the world of films, cartoons, theatrical performances, and more since the 1950s. Helen Berr's testimony follows the same path, if somewhat more tentatively. Her work's success as well as that of Frank's can be attributed to the quality of their writings (Frank had actually rewritten her diary so that it could be published as a book), but it also hinges on the fact that they are not utterances of despair, written at the heart of the catastrophe, but instead relate events happening at its periphery; they are the stories of teenagers, young women whose awakenings to life and love are disrupted by persecution.

The reader is transfixed by these lives rendered more intense by the looming tragic backdrop. None of the ghetto writings ever stirred up much interest, even though many of them are of outstanding literary quality. In a certain sense, they illustrate Primo Levi's remark in *The Drowned and the Saved*,[15] a thought that comes to him at the twilight of his life, almost forty years after *If This Is a Man*, where there is no trace of this idea: "We, the survivors are not the real witnesses.... We are a minority not only tiny but also abnormal: we are those who, through deceit, skill or chance did not hit rock bottom. Those who did it, who saw the Gorgons,[16] but could not come back to tell, or became mute, but yes it is them, the 'moslems,' the submerged beings, the full witnesses, those whose testimony would have had a wide-ranging meaning." Some survivors, echoing the title of one of Charlotte Delbo's works,[17] thought that the knowledge that they acquired in the camps was useless. What does "useful" mean? If it means a deeper investigation of man and society, of human interaction, the reading of great testimonies from the concentration camps (Primo Levi, Charlotte Delbo, Robert Antelme, and so on) or those written in the midst of the Shoah, then all are inexhaustible sources. Yet overall, it does not necessarily lead to optimistic conclusions. If the point is to learn in order to improve man and society, in order to prevent racism, war, antisemitism, genocide, and dictatorship, to foster justice, respect, and equality, and to discourage violence in human relations, then it is enough to look at the way the world is going to start doubting the usefulness of these testimonies.

The conditions in the camps[18] or in the ghettos were such that they gave rise to extremely violent behavior. Was this a specific kind of violence? Is it possible that once stripped of its context and considered in its essence, it could be compared with, or somehow related to, the violence we observe today in our society? The "useless" knowledge invoked by Charlotte Delbo is exactly what we—who did not know the camps—are striving to acquire but cannot quite understand.

It is hard to really say how the survivors were received when they settled in other countries, including Israel. They were sometimes assumed to have committed horrible deeds to save their lives. They faced contempt, indifference, or incredulity when they tried to tell their stories. Their loved ones could not stand to hear the stories of what they had just endured, and neither could those who had lost family members; and which Jewish family did not have deported relatives? During the years following his return, long after one of his sisters and his father had died at Auschwitz, Henri Borlant explains that when he tried to tell of his deportation, "it turned out to be unbearable to others." Fifty years after his return, during a quiet family reunion, he tried to say how astonished he was that they had never asked about their father's last moments. Odette, one of his sisters, fainted. "So," said Henri, "they did not ask questions; not just to spare me the pain, but also to keep their own suffering at bay. Those directly concerned by these stories cannot bear to hear them."[19]

The Eichmann trial restored dignity for the first time to those who had survived and inscribed their experiences into history. It helped integrate survivors into Israeli society. It marked what I have called the "advent of the witness." The Israeli prosecutor, Gideon Hausner, opted for a trial that would bring forward the entire narrative of persecution and destruction starting with Hitler's rise to power, a narrative spelled out by as many witnesses as could be called to the stand. That choice of strategy, as well as the selection of witnesses, was steered to a significant extent by Rachel Auerbach, one of the survivors of Oyneg Shabbos.[20] In Israel, she had been in charge of the testimonies division at Yad Vashem and so she embodied the link between Oyneg Shabbos and the trial.[21]

The Visual Archive

It has often been claimed that the act of testifying could free the witness from trauma. This, for example, is the assumption behind the collection of testimonies assembled by the Fortunoff Video Archive in New Haven, Connecticut. In fact, we do not really know much about the witnesses' state of mind, not even of those who gave testimonies in court: as far as I know, there is still no study on the effects that testifying has on witnesses. For his 1979 film *Memories of the Eichmann Trial*, which has just been rediscovered, director David Perlov trained the camera on Rivka Yosselevka as she listened to her own testimony.[22] At the trial, she had explained how her entire village was killed in a mass shooting, in particular her little girl, who understood everything. She somehow extricated herself from a pile of bodies. On her face, you can read an inscrutable sadness as she talks to Perlov. How did she live with this story once it had been made public? Israel was still a village then. Everyone would know whenever she went out on errands, left for work, or picked up her two sons from school. Everyone knew her story and I suppose that she could or believed that she could read the fact that they knew as she approached them. But, as she tells Perlov, many people in Israel have similar stories to tell.

After the Papon trial,[23] nobody worried about what happened to chief witness Esther Fogiel after she told of all the horrors inflicted upon her as a child. Except from those who testified of medical experiments, there were no closed-door depositions at such trials. Indeed, court testimonies were often broadcast in the media, which cannot remain without consequences on the witnesses' relations with their loved ones, especially their children. And we know nothing of these effects. Rivka Yosselevska came to bring justice to her family and continued testifying in spite of a heart seizure; the cause was precisely the stress involved in answering the call of duty, to talk about the deaths in her town, in her family. As an intended comforting remark, the prosecutor ended his deposition with the words: "You live in Israel, you are married and you have two children"—as if the very existence of the Jewish state had caused her to be reborn, to be saved. Today, when there is much emphasis on the "trauma" and its transmission from generation to generation, this kind remark sounds dated and leaves one baffled. Yet many were eager to talk as soon as they were let out of the camp: "Being interviewed was a unique and memorable occasion, an event that one had been awaiting ever since liberation day, an occasion that, in itself, gave meaning to our liberation."[24] Indeed: "In every deportee there is a slumbering humiliated being," explains Henri Borlant, who chose to call his book *Thanks for Surviving*. When ex-deportees know that they are perhaps not understood, but at least heard, their testimonies restore their dignity, repairing the very aspects of their identities that had been humiliated.

This focus on individual suffering erases the context in which it was endured and generates a mental picture of a world without a political dimension. American director Leo Hurwitz, who filmed the Eichmann trial,[25] was a Communist obsessed with what he called "fascism." He was distressed by the testimonies that he filmed day after day. Yet he deplored the fact that the trial failed to generate an explanatory narrative and that such a narrative was not even considered. In this regard, the developments that took place during the Eichmann trial were a preview of what was to come. Both past events and those happening before our eyes are no longer analyzed in political terms and do not produce a great collective narrative. Instead, they generate a succession or a juxtaposition of individual accounts. We feel. We identify. We experience empathy. But do we still really think? Do we still have this ambition that is at the core of the historian's craft—to understand?

To be sure, Shoah survivors will soon no longer be with us, but their disappearance will not end the mass phenomenon that was vastly accelerated by the Internet: events are no longer analyzed, they are told by individual "witnesses," in the rather vague general sense of the word, who give opinions. We live in the realm of an "I" who is not concerned with the collective story. When the memory of World War II, that of the Résistance, but above all that of the Shoah seemed to take over everything from commemorations to lectures in schools and even fiction films like Steven Spielberg's *Schindler's List* (released in France in 1995)[26] or Claude Berri's Lucie *Aubrac* (1997), some historians started to go on the warpath against memory and witnesses. When focusing on very recent contemporary events, historians face a dilemma with each testimony between two conflicting ethical positions. Everyone has a right to construct their own memory, to paste together what they remember and what they forgot. The right to memory is the right to identity, to being. But this right can conflict with the historian's work that entails an obstinate quest for truth.

Death and Survival

With Elie Wiesel's *Night* (1958), another image emerged, that of a survivor both dead and alive, both a martyr and a lucky person. François Mauriac, who wrote the preface to that text, stated: "A resuscitated Lazarus stranded in the dark borders where he strayed." We can learn something from Mauriac's words. They highlight the way a survivor can be perceived in our societies: a victim somehow sanctified by suffering in a Christian perspective. A split-personality, partly here, partly there, among the dead. Yet, there was no sanctification of suffering in Elie Wiesel's earlier version of this testimony written and published in Yiddish in 1954, *Und di Velt hot geschwingn* (And the World Remained Silent). For Wiesel, writing was an act of revenge, a drive against forgetting and against the rebirth of a not-quite-cleansed Germany. Early witnesses often manifested similar inclinations in their testimonies. Then, a new figure emerges, Lazarus, a figure already invoked by Jean Cayrol, a one-time Matthausen detainee, in his book *Lazare parmi nous* (Lazarus Among Us), published in 1950. That same vision is palpable in the graciously suffering face of Elie Wiesel and has been popularized by the phrase often heard from the mouth of so many witnesses: "I never got out of Auschwitz." This would not, then, be a case of survival, but of eternal presence, immune to the passage of time that usually breeds oblivion. As far as Claude Lanzmann and also Serge Klarsfed are concerned, time must be suspended. We are forever the contemporaries of these children who did not grow up, of all the dead people whose spokespeople are Shoah survivors. Inspired by Jules Michelet, Michel de Certeau said that researching history is like visiting dead people so that after that visit they may return somewhat less distressed to their graves. The historian's discourse redirects the dead and buries them: it is a deposition. "It turns the dead into separate entities. It honors them with rituals that have been missing." Michel de Certeau even adds that any historical endeavor strives to calm the dead who still haunt the present as if to build them "scriptural tombs." Both Claude Lanzmann and Serge Klarsfeld reject any separation between the dead and the living. They are not trying to keep them quiet. They want to keep them with us.

In *Shoah*, Podklebnick, a Chelmno survivor, is smiling constantly while narrating in Yiddish. We can see that smile again, this time filmed by Leo Hurvitz as Podklebnick recounts the same episode during the Eichmann trial, the moment when he discovers the body of his wife and two children and wishes he would die. Lanzmann asks what has died in him at Chelmno:

> Everything died; everything. But being only human you want to live. Then you have to forget. And thank god for what still remains and for what is forgotten. And you cannot talk about that.
> [Does he think that it could be a good thing to talk about it?]
> It's not good as far as I'm concerned; it's not good.
> [Did he survive as a living being or ... ?]
> When he was there he lived like a dead man because he never thought that he would survive; but he is alive.
> [Why does he smile all the time?]

What do you want him to do? Should he cry? Sometimes you smile and sometimes you cry.

And when you live it is better to smile ...

Podklebnick is alive. Rivka Yosselevska told Perlov the same thing, that she is alive.

History and Testimony

Historians are known to be wary of using testimonies obtained after the fact. Testimonies about the Shoah are no exception in this regard. If we choose to use them as a source, they should be examined rigorously with the historian's critical methods. These testimonies are indispensable if we are to write a history of both the destruction apparatus and of its victims. There is no shortage of red tape left from the Third Reich bureaucracies, and it constitutes a massive archive of testimonies. Meanwhile, Saul Friedländer's two-volume book *Nazi Germany and the Jews*[27] expands this perspective since all the testimonies he used, such as private diaries or letters, are also from the time of the events that they describe. Over the years, more and more of these testimonies have cropped up. The victims ended up leaving many traces of their existence even if their overall quantity is small when compared to the ocean of archives compiled by the Nazi administration or those of other states. Ultimately, only testimonies can retell this history. In order to write our work *Inside the Drancy Camps*,[28] Michel Laffitte and I used journals kept by various Jewish camp leaders, as well as vast amounts of mail distributed by corrupt gendarmes.

Today, historians consider that testimonies that were gathered later, during great collecting drives, such as those pioneered by the Fortunoff Archive, also provide a valuable source. Here, Christopher Browning's latest book *Inside a Nazi Slave-Labor Camp*[29] convincingly rises to the challenge of writing a history of the Starachowice labor camp almost exclusively based on testimonies. No study had ever been done on labor camps for Jews. He contends that as a veteran of archival research, you acquire "a very subjective form of intuition" which helps you appreciate the authenticity and reliability of testimonies.

The early testimonies, such as those used by director Eric Weiss in his film *Auschwitz, First Testimonies*, tend to have a different type of documentary weight from other testimonies. They are more concrete, more precise. They are not affected by any interference from what the survivor could have read or seen since being freed. As to later testimonies, historian Christopher Browning establishes a clear distinction between places like Auschwitz that have received extensive media coverage—including testimonies, documentary films, and works of fiction—and those that have never been discussed in the public arena. I agree with this point of view. Places in the first group have been plagued by "stereotyped characterizations" and "iconic depictions" that found their way into the testimonies. These images originate from films like *Holocaust* or *Schindler's List*. We can observe this phenomenon in Auschwitz testimonies when former detainees talk about walking into Birkenau under the portal inscribed with the words *Arbeit macht frei*, which is actually located at Auschwitz-I; but of course it shows up in so many films. Many also describe the selection process upon entering the camp or in the Blocks, and they almost invariably mention that it was led by Doctor Mengele, as if he had been on duty around the clock on the arrivals' ramp.

The effects of *Schindler's List* have been fairly noticeable, especially those of the controversial sequence in which female workers at the enamel factory walk into the bathrooms, expecting gas to come out of the shower heads. It turns out to be water. While collecting testimonies for the Fortunoff Video Archive, we interviewed a woman who had been deported from a Polish ghetto to Birkenau. She told of walking through the front gate where the inscription was not *Arbeit macht frei* [work makes you free], but *Arbeit macht freude* [work makes you happy]. Then she described the showers, how they expected gas to come out of the showerheads, the arrival of an SS officer saying that these women could still work, and the fact that it actually was water pouring out instead.

This description is especially interesting. It reveals the effects that a film can have on memory and the desire to give meaning to what has remained obscure. Why was this woman along with her co-detainees spared the gas chamber? She finds the answer in Spielberg's film. In the method developed by the Fortunoff Video Archive for collecting testimonies, interviews are always conducted by two people. One leads the conversation, while the other sits back, observes the unfolding interview, and intervenes only if he or she feels that something has been forgotten. I was in the position of the second interviewer. When the conversation ended, I asked a single question: "Do you ever go and watch films about this subject?" She replied: "Yes, I actually was invited to a preview screening of *Schindler's List*." And it ended there. We are not there to criticize witnesses, to put them in tight spots, or to restore some historic truths, but to listen to someone's words. I thought that by asking this question, I was paving the way for a future historian to detect the influence of *Schindler's List* on what Browning calls the "iconic and stereotyped visions" of Auschwitz. Many more examples could be found. Some witnesses have lived through experiences that they never got a chance to fully explain, they are unknown to the media, and they have not been exposed to other testimonies, lectures, or films. Those testimonies are somehow "encapsulated," they have remained intact. They are particularly interesting to historians when they research unknown aspects of the persecutions. Yet the value of a testimony should not be evaluated solely on its documentary value. Some late testimonies may not always tell us much about the facts, but they can reveal other things. In addition, there is more to a testimony than just establishing facts.

Since time immemorial, historians have tracked and sometimes analyzed errors in testimonies. The first scholar to systematically log testimonies, to try and establish a typology, and the first to reflect on them as a totality, was Jean Norton Cru after World War I. In his fascinating tome, *Witnesses,* and a short essay, "On Testimony,"[30] Cru hunts for historical truth, for pertinent detail. In this regard, we can talk of a hypercritical stance. Among historians of World War I, some admire him and some outright reject his approach. Because of the "Norton Cru model," which is centered on factual errors, there is a tendency to bypass, as a judge might do, any testimony that contains errors. But in fact, no testimony is ever exact in its entirety and in all details. Cru has been a role model to Paul Rassinier, a survivor of Buchenwald and Dora, and the father of negationism, who before denying that there were gas chambers had published his own testimony, *Crossing the Line*, before launching an attack in *Ulysses Betrayed by His Own*[31] against the "errors" committed, and against the denunciations of the Communists for their role in the camps.

Jean-Claude Pressac has envisaged a history without witnesses. This is to say, he writes a history of killing as a technical process. He places himself in the shoes of the camp's commanding officer, Rudolf Höss, who was essentially working on fixing technical problems and breakdowns in gas chambers and cremation systems. And the most challenging, it seems, was not gassing but cremation. Pressac works from archival material, in particular from the Topf & Söhne archives. In 1989, he wrote a large-scale work published by Serge and Beate Klarsfeld. The book focused on the cremation ovens installed in the camps with all the technical specifications.[32] There was something mind-boggling about the experience of reading such a technical history of killing methods. Still, this was much appreciated by some historians, among them Pierre Vidal-Naquet, for example, because they thought the notes constituted a barrage against negationists, confronting them with the ultimate proof. They may well have been right. Pressac insisted that all testimonies describing smoke coming out of the cremation chambers were false because, technically, there could be no smoke. This is not at all certain. In many concentration camps with cremation ovens similar to those in Birkenau, where the detainees could secretly draw (which was otherwise impossible at Auschwitz), many drawings depicted the smoke mentioned in the testimonies.

Something can be learned even from false testimonies, such as that of Benjamin Wilkomirski on his childhood, which was a great success in the 1990s until its author was unmasked. We learn about the expectations of readers, what story they would like to hear, and what one should say at any given moment to get the attention of an audience. And in this respect, Wilkomirski responded exactly to the public's expectations in the 1990s, a time when the emphasis was on trauma.

Nobody suspected the falsification. Simone Veil gave a speech for the prize-giving ceremony *Memory of the Shoah*, when Wilkomirski won, saying: "We always wondered what happened to the children but now we know." He obtained every prize from the Foundation for the *Memory of the Shoah* around the world. The only person to suspect a falsification was the son of a deportee, Daniel Ganzfried. Once you have heard that it may have been false and you reread the text, everything becomes obvious, including the author's behavior. For example, every time he was interviewed, he cried profusely. I am among those who failed to notice that.

Yet if you look at the interviews of survivors, they never cry. They can be caught in an emotional rapture, but only by chance, unexpectedly.

Claude Mouchard has come up with the concept of authored testimonies.[33] The literary quality of the text determines the dividing line between authored testimonies and documentary testimonies. To a historian, this dividing line is at once meaningful and meaningless. Most testimonies, whether they show great or little talent, are constructed on the same model. Their factual content is approximately identical, but some are written in a tedious speech and flat narrative and they literally fall out of one's hands as one tries to read them, and one feels slightly ashamed at finding them so difficult to get through. Others have the power of making us sense something, of pulling us away from ourselves, of getting us to think differently, of transporting us. Sometimes, the writer finds a brilliant, concise formulation that is worth pages. So does Paul Celan in "Death Fugue,"[34] in one particular verse: "In the sky we are digging a tomb where we are less tightly packed together."

Testimony and Silence

It has often been said that the experience of the camps was impossible to recount. I went against this contention in *Deportation et génocide*.[35] I judged it to be a lazy assumption just like the commonplace notion of "the silence of deportees" which essentially rested on the fact that nobody wanted to hear them. Yet the one who gives a testimony does not tell everything. And what he/she does not say is not necessarily a repressed memory that could have surfaced in the course of psychoanalysis or during a testimony. There are taboo subjects and the survivors' taboos are those of the period in which they live. One of the most difficult questions, which is another taboo, hovers around the "gray area" occupied by those detainees who were in charge of other detainees, the "kapos," the block leaders, or those who worked in the Judenräte, the Jewish police in the ghettos. In the camps and in the ghettos, there were all sorts of different behavior patterns, from the cynical collaborator to the sheer victim. The ghettos and the camps were human societies where the veneer of civilization had largely broken down. There were fights to settle arguments that went on in court proceedings after the war. Traces of these can be found in early witness accounts. "Kapo trials" took place in Israel and in France. The law at work in the Eichmann trial was designed to bring to justice the Jewish police, the kapos, and all those who had been accused by the Jews themselves of "collaboration" (this was the word used). Since witnesses had become exemplary figures, sanctified by suffering, and presented as role models to young people, those sinister aspects were brushed aside even though they were well documented. This all sometimes resurfaces, as recently with the publication of Agata Tuszyńska's novel dedicated to Wiera Gran,[36] a singer in the Warsaw ghetto. This woman was singing at Café Sztuka before July 1942, before the great deportations of Warsaw; she was accompanied by Władysław Szpilman, the title character in Roman Polanski's film *The Pianist*. She was tried after the war by the Committee of Polish Jews who cleared her of all suspicion of collaboration. She later lived in France and has been one of the witnesses in the first film to tell their story, *Le temps du ghetto*,[37] by Frédéric Rossif. The accusations of collaboration stuck to her, fueled by rumors both in France and in Israel, and they ruined her life. Agata Tuszyńska's book spells out very serious accusations against Szpilman, the pianist. He was a policeman in the ghetto and Wiera Gran was his "hidden face." The work caused a stir in Poland but remained ignored. Some survivors from France underwent sterilization in the camps and their children are adopted; their fellow detainees know it and talk about it in private. Yet in the course of testimonies gathered for the archives they never mention it. Similarly, sex and money have most often remained taboo subjects. Questions related to sexuality are beginning to emerge because society today is ready to hear them. Simone Veil never addressed them in her numerous testimonies. She explains why in a conversation with Esther Mujawayo, who herself survived the genocide in Rwanda.

There were many rapes and countless Tutsi women were infected by the AIDS virus through Hutu rapists. This is perhaps the very situation that motivated Simone Veil to speak out: "There are facts that are completely obscured, that are never talked about. They are exceptional situations but they actually happened. I lived for a few months in a small camp, a few miles away from Auschwitz, which was a very atypical situation.

The accounts that I read about this camp hardly ever mentioned this. I talked about it once without having planned to do it. That's all." Souad Belhaddad, who moderated the talk, urged her to specify these situations. "No," Simone Veil answers. Then, after a brief hesitation:

> Actually, yes, I can say it. It was during the very long evacuation march from the camps at Auschwitz. We found ourselves together in a vast camp, a few dozen women and thousands of men, some of whom had been detained for years. And there, it became like some sort of Dante's *Inferno*. Most of us were exhausted if not dying.... We all thought that we would die. But some had managed to keep in better shape, especially some kapos and leaders. At that point, they would have done anything to embrace a woman in their arms or even kiss her. This is the only time when the question of a possible rape arose. It took this specific situation to lead some to yield to the temptation. In the camps the question did not come up because most people were in such a dire state.... Yet there even some SS men and some deportees.... Those who, for one reason or another had had some responsibilities at the camp or still had some strength would start to launch into a bit of blackmail: "I have not seen a woman in years...." Meanwhile in another part of the camp a selection was taking place and the SS were continuing their deadly task.... There was something frightening about it. This is why we cannot talk about it, because it was a very specific situation, with a particular ratio of men to women and where death was present. Few of us lived through the experience but it did take place and it is very difficult to talk about it.

Simone Veil won't be saying any more. And we may never know anything else about it.

Notes

1. Didier Fassin and Richard Rechtman, *The Empire of Trauma: An Inquiry into the Condition of Victimhood*, trans. Rachel Gomme (Princeton, NJ: Princeton University Press, 2009). Originally published as *L'Empire du traumatisme. Enquête sur la condition de victime* (Paris: Flammarion, 2007).

2. Annette Wieviorka, *The Era of the Witness*, trans. Jared Stark (Ithaca, NY: Cornell University Press, 2006). Originally published as *L'Ère du témoin* (Paris: Plon, 1998).

3. Editor's note: The French title is translated as *The Age of Suspicion* in English-language editions, but it could also be understood as *The Era of Doubt*. Nathalie Saurrate, *L'ère Du Soupcon* (Paris: Flammarion, 2007).

4. Editor's note: During the First World War or Great War (1914–1918), when millions died as cannon fodder, "poilu" (pronounced ['pwaːluː]) was a term of endearment for fearless soldiers, the last of whom died in 2008.

5. Editor's note: "Witness site," a location or space that bears witness to history, is a memorial site where specific events took place, an almost literal translation of the French phrase *lieu-témoin* coined by Wieviorka.

6. François Hartog, *Régime d'historicité. Présentisme et expérience du temps* [Historicist Approaches: Presentism and the Experience of Time] (Paris: Seuil, 2002).

7. "Le monde que vous aviez sous les yeux, dans lequel vous viviez, était comme transfiguré par une puissance qui reliait chaque événement, chaque individu, à toute une chaîne ancienne d'événements et d'individus plus tragiques. Or aujourd'hui il semble qu'il n'y ait plus que du présent, de l'instantané même, le présent est devenu un collossal fourmillement, une innervation prodigieuse, un big bang permanent." Olivier Rolin, *Tigre en papier* (Seuil: Paris, 2003), trans. William J. Cloonan as *Paper Tiger* (Lincoln: University of Nebraska Press, 2007).

8. Editor's note: MOI is an acronym for *main d'œuvre immigrée*, foreign labor.

9. Annette Wieviorka, *Ils étaient juifs, résistants, communistes* [They Were Jews, Resistance Fighters, Communists] (Paris: Denoël, 1984). This book is mainly based on testimonies from former resistance fighters of the MOI.

10. Samuel Kassow, *Who Will Write Our History? Emanuel Ringelblum, The Warsaw Ghetto, and the Oyneg Shabes Archive* (Bloomington: Indiana University Press, 2007). Reprinted as *Who Will Write Our History? Rediscovering a Hidden Archive from the Warsaw Ghetto* (New York: Vintage, 2009).

11. Victor Klemperer, *I Will Bear Witness: A Diary of the Nazi Years, 1933–1941*, trans. Martin Chalmers (New York: Random House, 1998), and *I Will Bear Witness: A Diary of the Nazi Years, 1942–1945*, trans. Martin Chalmers (New York: Random House, 1999).

12. Großaktion Warschau (Great Warsaw Sweep), a mass extermination campaign against the Jews of the Warsaw Ghetto in 1942.

13. Michel Borwicz, *Écrits des condamnés à mort sous l'occupation nazie (1939–1945)* (Paris: Idées/Gallimard, 1973), 49.

14. *Des voix sous la cendre: Manuscrits des Sonderkommandos d'Auschwitz* [Voices under the Ashes: Manuscripts from Auschwitz's Sonderkommandos] (Paris: Calmann-Lévy, 2005).

15. Primo Levi, *The Drowned and the Saved*, trans. Raymond Rosenthal (New York: Summit Books, 1988), 83–84. Originally published in Italian as *I sommersi e i salvati* (Torino: Einaudi, 1986).

16. Editor's note: Gorgons are terrifying and partly reptilian figures in Greek Mythology.

17. Charlotte Delbo, "Useless Knowledge," in *Auschwitz and After*, trans. Rosette C. Lamont (1995; reprint, New Haven, CT: Yale University Press, 2013).

18. Editor's note: Here, the author uses the German word *Lager* (camps) in the original French text.

19. Henri Borlant, *Merci d'avoir survécu* [Thanks for Surviving] (Paris: Seuil, 2011), 164–65.

20. Oyneg Shabbos is a group of professional and volunteer historians and chroniclers founded by Emanuel Ringelblum around 1942 to document life in the Warsaw Ghetto.

21. About the Eichmann trial, see in particular Annette Wieviorka, *Eichmann. De la traque au procès* [Eichmann: From the Chase to the Trial] (Paris: André Versaille, 2001), and Hanna Yablonka, *The State of Israel vs Adolf Eichmann* (New York: Schocken, 2004).

22. Rivka Yosselevska's testimony can be read, like all other testimonies at the Eichmann trial, on the following site: www.nizkor.org/hweb/people/e/eichmann-adolf/transcripts/.

23. Editor's note: Maurice Papon was convicted in 1998 of crimes against humanity for his participation in the deportation of 1,600 French Jews during World War II.

24. Primo Levi, *Intervista a Primo Levi ex deportato di Anna Bravo e Federico Cereja* (Torino: Einaudi, 2011); Primo Levi, *Le devoir de mémoire* [The Duty of Memory], interview with Anna Bravo and Federico Cereja (Paris: Mille et une nuits, 1995), 75.

25. On Leo Hurwitz and the filming of court proceedings, see Sylvie Lindeperg and Annette Wieviorka, "Les deux scènes du procès Eichmann" [The Two Stages of the Eichmann Trial], *Annales ESC* 63 (June 2008): 1249–74.

26. Editor's note: The film *Schindler's List* was based on a novelistic treatment (by Thomas Keneally) of a true story.

27. Saul Friedländer, *Nazi Germany and the Jews: Volume 1: The Years of Persecution, 1933–1939* (New York: HarperCollins, 1998), and *Nazi Germany and the Jews: The Years of Extermination, 1939–1945* (New York: HarperCollins, 2007).

28. Annette Wieviorka and Michel Laffitte, *A l'intérieur du camp de Drancy* [Inside the Drancy Camps] (Paris: Perrin, 2012).

29. Christopher Browning, *Remembering Survival: Inside a Nazi Slave-Labor Camp* (New York: Norton, 2010).

30. Jean Norton Cru, *Temoins: Essai d'analyse et de critique des souvenirs de combattants édités en français de 1915 à 1928* (Paris: les Etincelles, 1929); Jean Norton Cru, *Du Témoignage* (Paris: La Nouvelle Revue française (NRF), 1930); Jean Norton Cru, *War Books: A Study in Historical Criticism*, trans. Jean Norton Cru, ed. Ernest Marchand and Stanley J. Pincetl Jr. (San Diego: San Diego State University Press, 1988).

31. Paul Rassinier, *Le passage de la ligne* [Crossing the Line] (Paris: Editions Bressanes, 1950); Paul Rassinier, *Ulysse trahi par les siens* [Ulysses Betrayed by His Own] (Paris: La Librairie Francaise, 1961).

32. Jean-Claude Pressac, *Auschwitz: Technique and Operation of the Gas Chambers* (New York: Beate Klarsfeld Foundation, 1989).

33. Claude Mouchard, *Qui si je criais . . . ? Œuvres-témoignages dans les tourmentes du XXe siècle* [Who If I Cried? Authored Testimonies in Twentieth-Century Upheavals] (Paris: Laurence Teper, 2007).

34. Editor's note: Todesfuge, in the original German, was published in several anthologies, but first in a Romanian translation, *Tangoul Mortii*, in 1947. Paul Celan, *Death Fugue*, trans. Jerome Rothenberg (Greensboro, NC: Unicorn Press, 1967).

35. Annette Wieviorka, *Déportation et génocide: Entre la mémoire et l'oubli* [Deportation and Genocide] (Paris: Hachette, 1995).

36. Agata Tuszyńska, *Wiera Gran: The Accused*, trans. Charles Ruas (New York: Alfred A. Knopf, 2013). Originally published in Polish as *Oskarżona Wiera Gran* (Kraków: Wydawnictow Literackie, 2010). Originally published in French as *Wiera Gran, l'accusée*, trans. Isabelle Jannès Kalinowski (Paris: Grasset & Fasquelle, 2011).

37. *Le temps du ghetto* [Times in the Ghetto], dir. Frédéric Rossif, Les Films de la Pléiade, 1961.

Bibliography

Borlant, Henri. *Merci d'avoir survécu* [Thanks for Surviving]. Paris: Seuil, 2011.

Borwicz, Michel. *Écrits des condamnés à mort sous l'occupation nazie (1939–1945)*. Paris: Idées/Gallimard, 1973.

Browning, Christopher. *Remembering Survival: Inside a Nazi Slave-Labor Camp*. New York: Norton, 2010.

Cayrol, Jean. *Lazare parmi nous* [Lazarus among Us]. Paris: Editions la Baconnière, 1950.

Celan, Paul. *Death Fugue*. Trans. Jerome Rothenberg. Greensboro, NC: Unicorn Press, 1967. Originally published as *Tangoul Mortii*, 1947.

Cru, Jean Norton. *Du Témoignage*. Paris: La Nouvelle Revue française (NRF), 1930.

———. *Temoins: Essai d'analyse et de critique des souvenirs de combattants édités en français de 1915 à 1928*. Paris: les Etincelles, 1929.

———. *War Books: A Study in Historical Criticism*. Trans. Jean Norton Cru. Ed. Ernest Marchand and Stanley J. Pincetl Jr. San Diego: San Diego State University Press, 1988.

Delbo, Charlotte. "Useless Knowledge." In *Auschwitz and After*, trans. Rosette C. Lamont. 1995. Reprint, New Haven, CT: Yale University Press, 2013.

Des voix sous la cendre: Manuscripts des Sonderkommandos d'Auschwitz [Voices under the Ashes: Manuscripts from Auschwitz's Sonderkommandos]. Paris: Calmann-Lévy, 2005.

Fassin, Didier, and Richard Rechtman. *The Empire of Trauma: An Inquiry into the Condition of Victimhood*. Trans. Rachel Gomme. Princeton, NJ: Princeton University Press, 2009. Originally published as *L'Empire du traumatisme. Enquête sur la condition de victim*. Paris: Flammarion, 2007.

Friedländer, Saul. *Nazi Germany and the Jews: Volume 1: The Years of Persecution 1933–1939*. New York: HarperCollins, 1998.

———. *Nazi Germany and the Jews: Volume 2: The Years of Extermination 1939–1945*. New York: HarperCollins, 2007.

Hartog, François. *Régime d'historicité. Présentisme et expérience du temps* [Historicist Approaches. Presentism and the Experience of Time]. Paris: Seuil, 2002.

Kassow, Samuel. *Who Will Write Our History? Emanuel Ringelblum, The Warsaw Ghetto, and the Oyneg Shabes Archive*. Bloomington: Indiana University Press, 2007. Reprinted as *Who Will Write Our History? Rediscovering a Hidden Archive from the Warsaw Ghetto*. New York: Vintage, 2009.

Klemperer, Viktor. *Je veux témoigner jusqu'au bout, 1942–1945*. Paris: Seuil, 2000.

Klemperer, Viktor. *Mes soldats de papier, 1933–1941*. Paris: Seuil, 2000.

Le temps du ghetto [Times in the Ghetto]. Dir. Frédéric Rossif. Les Films de la Pléiade, 1961.

Levi, Primo. *The Drowned and the Saved*. Trans. Raymond Rosenthal. New York: Summit Books, 1988. Originally published in Italian as *I sommersi e i salvati* (Torino: Einaudi, 1986). Originally published in French as *Les naufragés et les rescapés* (Paris: Gallimard, 1989).

———. "Intervista a Primo Levi ex deportato di Anna Bravo e Federico Cereja." Torino: Einaudi, 2011.

———. *Le devoir de mémoire* [The Duty of Memory]. Cereja, Paris: Mille et une nuits, 1995.

Lindeperg, Sylvie, and Annette Wieviorka. "Les deux scènes du procès Eichmann" [The Two Stages of the Eichmann Trial]. *Annales ESC* 63 (June 2008): 1249–74.

Memories of the Eichmann Trial. Dir. David Perlov. 1979. Israeli Television.

Mouchard, Claude. *Qui si je criais . . . ? Œuvres-témoignages dans les tourmentes du XXe siècle*. [Who If I Cried? Authored Testimonies in Twentieth-Century Upheavals]. Paris: Laurence Teper, 2007.

Mujawayo, Esther, and Souad Belhaddad. *Survivantes. Rwanda-Histoire d'un génocide* [Survivors. Rwanda-History of a Genocide]. Avignon: L'Aube/poche essai, 2005.

Pressac, Jean-Claude. *Auschwitz: Technique and Operation of the Gas Chambers*. New York: Beate Klarsfeld Foundation, 1989.

Rassinier, Paul. *Le passage de la ligne* [Crossing the Line]. Paris: Editions Bressanes, 1950.

———. *Ulysse trahi par les siens* [Ulysses Betrayed by His Own]. Paris: La Librairie Francaise, 1961.

Rolin, Olivier. *Tigre en papier*. Seuil: Paris, 2003. Trans. William J. Cloonan as *Paper Tiger*. Lincoln: University of Nebraska Press, 2007.

Saurrante, Nathalie. *L'Ere Du Soupcon* [The Age of Suspicion]. Paris: Flammarion, 2007.

Shoah. Dir. Claude Lanzmann. 1985. New Yorker Films.

Tuszyńska, Agata. *Wiera Gran: The Accused*. Trans. Charles Ruas. New York: Alfred A. Knopf, Random House, 2013. Originally published in Polish as *Oskarżona Wiera Gran*. Kraków: Wydawnictow Literackie, 2010. Originally published in French as *Wiera Gran, l'accusée*. Trans. Isabelle Jannès Kalinowski. Paris: Grasset & Fasquelle, 2011.

Wieviorka, Annette. *Déportation et génocide: Entre la mémoire et l'oubli* [Deportation and Genocide]. Paris: Hachette, 1995.

———. *Eichmann. De la traque au procès* [Eichmann: From the Chase to the Trial]. Paris: André Versaille, 2001.

———. *The Era of the Witness.* Trans. Jared Stark. Ithaca, NY: Cornell University Press, 2006. Originally published as *L'Ère du témoin*. Paris: Plon, 1998.

———. *Ils étaient juifs, résistants, communistes* [They Were Jews, Resistance Fighters, Communists]. Paris: Denoël, 1984.

Wieviorka, Annette, and Michel Laffitte. *A l'intérieur du camp de Drancy* [Inside the Drancy Camps]. Paris: Perrin, 2012.

Yablonka, Hanna. *The State of Israel vs. Adolf Eichmann.* New York: Schocken, 2004.

3

Halakhic Witnessing

The Auschwitz Memoir of Berish Erlich

HENRI LUSTIGER THALER

> This is a short description of the camp Auschwitz-Birkenau. Many more pages can be written about that, however, all would not grasp the reality, because it was yet worse, than all, which a man could be capable of comprehending.
>
> Berish Erlich, 1946

Primo Levi was a chronicler of things seen at close hand. He sensitized us to the complex and serrated mnemonic landscapes of the Holocaust. Levi resituated an act of witnessing by directing our attention to the proverbial "first witness" embodied in the drowned, the perished. Scholars would later locate Levi's insights about the ineffable *a priori* space of death—before physical death—as a state of consciousness beyond language and representation.[1] For Levi, witnesses, or the layered subject-positions of witnessing, must commence with the brutal and devastating core of the Holocaust: the drowned and the voiceless. Rabbi Yitzchok Avigdor captured this interstitial moment of co-presence between life and death in his memoir about life in Mauthausen.

> After many days of rain, today is the first day we see sky. We feel nothing. Our bodies are either burning with heat, fever, and from millions of bites from lice; or they're frozen, ice cold—dead. The living and the

dead lay together, one next to the other. From day to day the dead increase. The living scream, argue, but every day it gets quieter, colder, (as) the dead increase. We are jealous of the dead, wishing death would approach rapidly. Already three days without eating! Better not to eat then to need to get up from our place and stand on a line, despite the rain, something permeates the air. What? No one knows. We know nothing. We don't know where we are. We don't know what we're doing or what they're doing with us. We feel nothing. Today is a good day. Restful. Today, the SS haven't chased us out of the barracks. Why? No one knows. It doesn't matter. At least it is peaceful. Don't need to get up. No *appel*, no food, just peace.... It is so close. Death is approaching—finally.[2]

The moment that Rabbi Avigdor was describing, "despite the rain, something permeates the air. What? No one knows. We know nothing," was the day of the liberation of Mauthausen on May 5, 1945. Rabbi Avigdor captured the subjective sense of co-presence—life and death—that was the experience of liberation for many prisoners. In his description, we hear an embodied "acultural moment," a sense of absolute resignation that could have been expressed by an "everyman" or women regardless of identity or beliefs. Rabbi Avigdor was an Orthodox Jew (see Esther Farbstein's discussion of Rabbi Avigdor in this volume). His archival collection is replete with religious and halakhic (Jewish Law) references. Yet this moment of oncoming death is how one might imagine a drowning: an interstitial space. In Primo Levi's universe of witnessing, the central ghostly figures were the majority of victims who never put pen to paper and those who wrote diaries but did not survive. These are the originary roots of witnessing for Levi: the lost voices of missing narratives.

Today, we add to these origins through institutionalized collections of Holocaust survivor testimony in their spatial, cultural, gendered, and religious differentiations. These accounts provide unique gateways to the experiential knowledge of the Holocaust, but also insights into the critical aesthetics of how we listen and how listening has come to frame the changing thematics of survivor testimony.[3] These interrelated narratives, mnemonic imaginaries, chronologies, and subjectivities are most importantly relational, in view of the meaning(s) they generate for the future of Holocaust memory and representation. Still, in a consideration of origins as distinct from representations, they demand an existential emplotment that leads inevitably to relying on those who speak in another's stead. As Primo Levi explains:

> We who were favored by fate tried, with more or less wisdom, to recount not only our fate but also that of the others, indeed of the drowned; but this was a discourse 'on behalf of third parties,' the story of things seen at close hand, not experienced personally. The destruction brought to an end, the job completed, was not told by anyone, just as no one ever returned to describe his own death. Even if they had paper and pen, the drowned would not have testified because their death had begun before that of their body. Weeks and months before being snuffed out, they had already lost the ability to observe, to remember, to compare and express themselves. We speak in their stead, by proxy.[4]

Shoshana Feldman and Dori Laub have offered perhaps the closest synoptic and analytical analogy to Levi's "first" witness, by referring to the Holocaust as "an event without a witness."[5] By this, they mean that the experience of mass murder described in survivor testimony unfolds inevitably under the umbrella of a dual conundrum, composed of witness experiences that struggle with meaning in the face of an event at the limit. Survivor testimony cannot present itself as a descriptor that testifies from the inside (one cannot bear witness from the inside of death) nor from the outside (as the individual is, by definition, excluded from the event). The philosopher Giorgio Agamben has argued that Feldman and Laub bring attention to the central paradox of survivor testimonies; in their close yet distanced relationship to the perished, "there is no voice for the disappearance of voice."[6]

These antinomies reveal the shredded debris of tragic signifiers that characterize the existentially incomplete history and memory of the Holocaust. Holocaust survivor and artist Sam Bak describes this incompleteness as "encountering something that is basically broken and put together again. This breaking apart and putting back together in an incomplete form is the main subject of the memory of the Holocaust."[7] These definitions of witnessing are not inconsequential to how we might understand what constitutes an act of witness, then, and the multiple representations of the Holocaust today, so many decades later. To borrow an amended expression from Lawrence Langer's *portmanteau*, "the afterdeath of the Holocaust,"[8] we may similarly think about the "afterlife of witnessing" as a relational form of cultural memory steeped in changing representations and generational subjectivities of those who are now in the situation of address; listeners. The latter are a backdrop to the increasingly cumulative collective memory of the Holocaust. Yet the question that Primo Levi poses of "relying on those who speak in another's stead" is not sufficiently mined when one considers the variable of cultural affiliation.

At the core of Levi's work rests the thesis of "unspeakability" of the Holocaust experience. It is present as well in Adorno's admonition regarding the incapacities of poetry after Auschwitz or Agamben's insistence that there can be "no voice for the voiceless." In *Witnessing Witnessing*, Thomas Trezise has provocatively examined each of these claims as the subjective stance of listeners, not survivors. He argues that the trope of unspeakability dispossesses survivors of their own stories. Trezise brings attention to the act of receiving witness as a form of subjective re-representation, wherein the conditions of address are themselves responsible for framing traumatic experiences, as something beyond language. The trauma contained in the "otherness of listening" structures the perceived trauma of the telling. Trezise argues that understanding the survivor's experience has become dependent on the relational effects of listening. The interlocutor as interpretive listener creates the aesthetic and philosophical paradigm of what is deemed unspeakable. Trezise's analytical shift from the speaker to the listener unfolds through a critical analysis of theories of trauma, buttressed by an influential history of ideas about the very nature of an event at the limit that defies description in its horror. Trezise's shift in emphasis is critical in understanding the lost narratives of diversity within testimony and the aesthetic effects of listening. This is particularly the case in the reception of Orthodox forms of subjectivity.

In this cumulative mnemonic process, the cultural dimension of meaning making through religious beliefs—about the "drowned and the saved" during and immediately after the Holocaust—has received short shrift. In the search for a perspectival overview that stands outside the aforementioned and influential history of ideas of the Holocaust—from Theodor Adorno to Dori Laub and Georgio Agamben—as well as the psychology of trauma—Cathy Caruth (1995)[9]—one would do well to consider an alternate cultural epistemology. Orthodox and faith-based

Jewry during the Holocaust allows us to consider "the relationality of being" and its resonance within a community of speakers, enacted through what can be referred to as "halakhic witnessing," as an important conduit for "speaking in another's stead." Halakhah or Jewish law, literally "the way of walking and behaving," structures moments of everyday life. In a world turned upside down during the Holocaust, comportment and agency were captured in discursive relations between prisoners and rabbis. Indeed, rabbis spoke in the place of prisoners as evidenced in documented *shailos* and *teshuvas* (questions and rabbinic responsa related to halakhah). However, contrary to the many genres of survivor subjectivity, sourced through testimony, diaries, and memoirs, the exchanges between rabbis and faith-based victims acquired a manifestly relational form. The question is posed to the rabbi, he considers all the jurisprudential implications and consequences, a response is given, negotiation from the questioner arises, and an action is taken in regard to comportment and behavior. The rabbi, if he survived, documented the *shailos* and *teshuvas* in his scholarly postwar writings.[10] In contradistinction to the singular intent of voice to tell the story—within testimony, memoir, and diaries—the "relationality of being" between rabbis and Jews is captured through the pen of the rabbi, recounting the dilemma of a fellow survivor framed within halakhic (identitarian) concerns, humanizing both as individuals replete with questions about their objective situations. The halakhic questions posed can only be answered by an authoritative figure, hence placing "halakhic witnessing"—the victim as understood through an identitarian question and the rabbi through his knowledge of halakhic reasoning—in the same subjective genre, not unlike testimonies, memoires, and diaries. Yet it is also deeply intersubjective.

Confronting the lost voice of the perished in the Holocaust—*pace* Primo Levi's insight of "speaking in their stead"—takes us to an appreciation of deeply held perspectives of the victims when read from different cultural scripts. As mentioned, in exchanges known as *shailos* and *teshuvas*, Jews in ghettos and concentration camps posed questions to rabbis about what to do in the unprecedented circumstances of the Holocaust (again, see Farbstein's chapter herein). The "way of walking" can be understood in a first instantiation of "Halakhic Man,"[11] asking, "What is the 'way' to walk, to deal with the situation that I am confronted with?" It is a question of action that will determine a reconciled place in this world and beyond. In the second instance, "Halakhic Man" is ignited in moments of behavior or singular comportment, as we shall see in the memoir of Berish Erlich.

This is critical in understanding Orthodox Jewish perspectives on the Holocaust, wherein Giorgio Agamben's specter of the *muselmann* might have descriptive value but holds little ontological sway[12] as the physical embodiment of what lies beyond language. The allusion to the *muselmann*—the walking dead as in the case of Rabbi Avigdor at the liberation of Mauthausen—and the survivor as witness confront each other from an Orthodox perspective through halakhic exegetical interpretations. This juncture is historical, meta-historical, and existential in its revisionist understanding of what Lawrence Langer has referred to as the realm of "choiceless choices."[13] Halakhah structures the subjective voice/identity of the prisoner and therefore invites intersubjective choices (via questions and responsa). Indeed, it is a relational search for choice through biblical/ mnemonic references and allusion to community (*Klal Yisroel*).

Quoting from the work of Meir Dvorzeski, Pesach Schindler argued that in the annals of Jewish martyrology there was an option when confronting death: die or choose life by rejecting Judaism.[14] The lack of "objective choice" in the mass murder of Jews during the Holocaust became the existential catalyst for new interpretive meanings about "arrogated choice." The transition/extension from *Kiddush Hashem*, "sanctification of the name [of God]" in the face of death—the traditional Jewish response to catastrophe—toward *Kiddush Hahayim*, "sanctification of life in confronting death," marks a watershed moment in faith-based understandings and action during the Holocaust, and the beginning of a protracted rabbinic discourse on death with dignity, as well as spiritual and physical resistance.[15] Schindler argues:

> The martyr of the Holocaust without life options and in full expectations of being murdered also had a choice: the manner in which they would accept and prepare for death. Freedom to choose between life and religious faith was converted from the option of going to one's death degraded and dejected as opposed to confronting death with an inner peace, nobility, upright stance, without lament and cringing to the enemy.... This new option ... became another attribute of *Kiddush Hashem* (i.e., its transition towards *Kiddush Hahayim*) during the Holocaust.[16]

In order to mine the Orthodox Jewish memoirist of the Holocaust, it is therefore necessary to consider the subjective landscape of *mentalités* and its religious significance within the context of humiliation, brutality, and finally death.[17] Rabbinic discourses on *Kiddush Hashem* and *Kiddush Hahayim* are in this regard portals into realms of Orthodox praxis in the villages, ghettos, and camps. Primo Levi argued that if Auschwitz had lasted any longer, a new language would have emerged to describe the atrocities of everyday life. *Kiddush Hahayim* is indicative of discursive meaning given to death and survival amongst the Orthodox in that it reclaims the sanctity of life central to Jewish law, in a situation that militated against it at every turn. The interpretive transformation of *Kiddush Hashem* into *Kiddush Hahayim* has been attributed to Rabbi Isaac Nissenbaum in the Warsaw ghetto. *Kiddush Hahayim* describes a lexicon developed specifically for the Jewish subjective faith-based experience of the Holocaust. Central to the emphasis upon sanctity of life is the concept of *hithazut* (the strengthening of the will to live) against *ye'ush* (despair). Survivor testimonies that explore expressions of faith during the Holocaust have often referred to the rebbes' refrain *Yidden zeit sich nisht meya'esh* (Jews do not despair), imploring their followers to recline existentially on their faith in the face of death, so not to "feel void or corrupt and thus reflect the persecutors actions."[18]

Recognizing the unprecedented scope of the annihilation, Rabbis Menachem Ziemba and Kalonymus Kalman Shapira shared in Rabbi Nissenbaum's effort to redefine the religious response parameters of what they halakhically defined as an unprecedented condition, the Orthodox version of an event at the limit: in Rabbis Ziemba and Nissenbaum's case this took the call for spiritual *as well as* physical resistance. The latter was an exceptional response from an Orthodox perspective. Many rabbis in the Warsaw ghetto saw Rabbi Nissenbaum's neologism as a logical continuation of the traditional response of martyrdom. Others vehemently opposed it.

The rabbis' and their authoritative function in the interpretation and the discourse of suffering is captured in the dilemma of Rabbi Zvi Hersch Meisels in the immediate postwar period. A survivor of Auschwitz, Rabbi Meisels served as the head of the religious court in the Bergen-Belsen displaced persons camp. His task was to create a platform for halakhic witnessing after liberation, indeed speaking for the dead, not unreminiscent of Primo Levi's admonition against "speaking in another's stead."

Rabbi Meisels's travail was to find a witness whose testimony could release women from the status of an *aguna,* literally "a woman chained" in marriage. The halakhic process demands absolute certainty of the death of the spouse, traditionally confirmed by two witnesses. The following is recorded in Rabbi Meisels's *sefer* (work of rabbinic literature), *Kuntres Takanas Agunos,* written in the Bergen-Belsen displaced persons camp after 1945. As a survivor of Auschwitz, he used the specific lexicon of camp internees to determine whether one lived or died. Meisels wrote: "In Auschwitz, if the individual was last seen going to the left, we might assume that they are dead, but we cannot be certain. They may have been taken to a labor camp thereafter. It must finally be left to the moral character of a witness who either saw the actual death, or last saw the individual in a condition that would rule out recovery."[19] Rabbi Meisels therefore situated the knowledge of particular witnesses within the framework and context of the general acknowledgment of a camp full of witnesses, the majority of whom did not survive to bear witness. Rabbi Meisels described the context as follows: "Every time transports came into the camp, soon afterwards there were flames from the crematoria. When the transports stopped, the flames stopped. This is clear knowledge. This is knowledge without dispute. Yet [to establish] a particular death, in a situation where the difference between going to the left or the right determined survival, it takes one witness to confirm precisely what everyone witnessed generally." Rabbi Meisels's halakhic deliberations underscore the tensions and linkages between subjective and collective interpretive experiences, coupling the rigorous strictures of the *agunot* to both juridical and moral witnessing, all prerequisites for allowing the widow to finally remarry. Rebirth from the Orthodox standpoint is therefore halakhically achieved through a dual prism which requires knowledge of the exact circumstances of the death of the "first witness" (which allows a release from the *agunot*, allowing the widow to remarry), and finally the renewal of the collective (*Klal Yisroel*, the sacred crust, the community). Meisels's search for a moral witness to free the widow from the death of her husband (to be read as a trope for all postwar Jewish widows) holds an important key to understanding the centrality of rabbis and authoritative religious figures in acts of witness within faith-based European Jewish communities during and immediately after the Holocaust.

Memory and Meta-History:
The Auschwitz Memoir of Berish Erlich

Rethinking the core experiential categories of a limit event from a cultural perspective—and engaging different ways of explaining choices and actions—allows for a fruitful commingling of meta-historical and historical approaches to meaning-making during the Holocaust. Not unlike Samuel Kassow's[20] emphasis on Emanuel Ringelblum's prewar life in Poland as key to deciphering the meaning of his work with the *Oyneg Shabbos* archives in the Warsaw Ghetto, reading Berish Erlich's memoir demands similar considerations and commingling of meta-historical and historical approaches.

Berish Erlich was born in Warsaw on August 25, 1925, the seventh of eight siblings, the scion of a well-known Orthodox family. His father, Rabbi Nusyn Pinchus Erlich, was a respected talmudic scholar in Poland.[21] The Erlich household at 30 Nowolipie Street was located in what would become the Warsaw Ghetto. He was fifteen years old on November 16, 1940, when the Germans closed the ghetto to the outside world. With a keen sense of foreboding, his father built a concealed entryway leading from one of the rooms in the house into the attic. This became the family's hiding place. Twenty-six individuals hid in the attic. Amongst them were Rabbi Shlomo Chanoch Rabinowitz, the revered Radomsker Rebbe and his family.[22] In spite of the fatal consequences of being caught on the streets of the ghetto, the young Berish Erlich accompanied the Radomsker Rebbe every morning to the mikvah (ritual bath), after which both careened the alleys of Warsaw back to the attic.

In August 1942, a Jewish policeman whose father was a Radomsker *hasid* (a follower of the Rebbe) notified the Rebbe that the Gestapo was searching for Jews on Nowolipie Street. The residents of the Erlich family's apartment left to hide in another location. When the sabbath came, the families, feeling more secure, returned to the apartment on Nowolipie Street. This second phase of their hiding would end tragically. An informant betrayed them. The Gestapo stormed the house. The Erlich and Rabinowitz families, including the Radomsker Rebbe, were brutally murdered in the middle of prayer. Berish Erlich and his father were at the back of the room. The Gestapo left them alive to carry out the corpses. Four days later, Nusyn Pinchus Erlich was sent to Treblinka, where he was murdered.

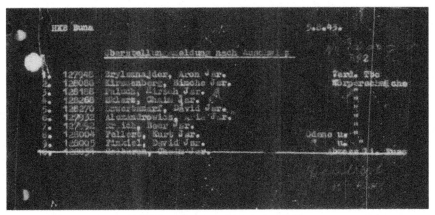

Berish Erlich's registration at HKB Buna sub-camp of Auschwitz, 1943.

International Tracing Service records[23] indicate that Berish Erlich was in the Warsaw ghetto from November 1940 to May 7, 1943. He was deported from Warsaw to Majdanek after the ghetto revolt. Following Majdanek, he was deported to Auschwitz, arriving on July 8, 1943, as part of a transport of 750 Polish Jews (prisoner number 127992).[24]

From Auschwitz, he was taken to Sachsenhausen (prisoner number 109308). He arrived in Ohrdruf, a sub-camp of Buchenwald, on January 12, 1945 (prisoner number 102870), where he was liberated in S3 south camp Ohrdruf.[25] After liberation, he was taken to the Landsberg displaced persons camp to recover.[26]

Josef Friedenson first met Berish Erlich in the Warsaw Ghetto. The next time their paths crossed was on a transport wagon leaving Auschwitz on route to the Sachsenhausen concentration camp in Oranienburg, Germany. They lost contact before meeting again in Ohrdruf, a sub-camp of Buchenwald. On Berish Erlich's arrival in Ohrdruf, he quickly became an assistant to the camp electrician. While doing lighting repairs, he discovered Friedenson in the camp infirmary. Josef Friedenson describes conditions in the Ohrdruf hospital: "The Germans practically did not appear

Berish Erlich's Buchenwald card indicating his new prisoner number, 102870, and previous Sachsenhausen prisoner number, 109308. ITS Collection / USHMM Collections.

there. But for that reason, they barely gave us even the smallest bit of food. It was very easy there to die, in only a short time. R' Berish, just as soon as he saw me, searched for a way to rescue me from the danger of hunger." Evening curfews in Ohrdruf did not allow Berish Erlich to return to the infirmary and bring soup to Friedenson. He told him to do whatever he must to sneak out and come to his barrack later that night. Josef Friedenson describes his arrival in Erlich's barrack and meeting the barrack house-servant. "Just then, R' Berish was called away to some sort of work, and instead of soup, I received a blow to the head with a soup ladle from the house-servant. At the last minute, as I was beginning to leave, R' Berish ran over, panting, and brought me a few spoonfuls of soup, which I suspected was part of his personal portion, because when I was leaving, I saw that the soup kettle was empty."[27]

The timing of his visit to Erlich's barrack could not have come at a more propitious moment. It saved Josef Friedenson's life. During his absence, a selection took place. As he returned to the infirmary he observed: "Nearly all of the patients were undressed down to their shirts (it was December, 1944), and they were led away to some sort of stable at the edge of the camp to die."[28]

Berish Erlich and Josef Friedenson were to meet again in the Landsberg displaced persons camp after the liberation. Josef Friedenson went on to found the Orthodox Jewish newspaper *Dos Yiddishe Vort*.[29] Berish Erlich, through the help of his mentor Rabbi Alexander J. Rosenberg, director of the Joint Distribution Committee (JDC) for Religious Activities for the American Zone, soon established himself as a valued mediator between the Jewish displaced persons and the American military authority.

Postwar identity card in Landsberg displaced persons camp, indicating prisoner number 109308, a Sachsenhausen concentration camp serial designation.
ITS Collection / USHMM Collections.

The Klausenberger Rebbe, an important postwar figure in the revival of Jewish religious life in the displaced persons camp, appears at center right in this photograph of the Landsberg rabbinical council. At center left is Rabbi Hillel Lichtenstein, Rabbi of Krasna, and the head of the Landsberg Rabbinical Council of displaced persons. Berish Erlich, fourth from the left on the bottom row, is referred to as the *askan* of *pidyon shvuyim*, "one who devotes himself to bringing about the release of a fellow Jew."

Berish Erlich was known in the Landsberg displaced persons camp as a *melitz yosher*, a defender of the Jews. He was particularly active on behalf of Jewish prisoners incarcerated in displaced person jails. Most were there because of activities in the black market. Berish Erlich's functions in the camp were polyglot. He was secretary to the religious liaison between the Joint Distribution Committee in Landsberg and the American military authorities. In preparation for immigration to the United States, he solicited reams of supporting documents from key American military figures in the Landsberg.[30] Hillel Seidman, archivist of the prewar Warsaw Jewish community, and later the archivist and secretary of the Warsaw *Judenrat*, wrote that Berish Erlich spent his days in "Landsberg hospital taking care of the sick, as well as those in prison, as he himself suffered hunger and coldness."[31] The Landsberg displaced persons camp had a large faith-based and Orthodox Jewish population.³² Berish Erlich was a member of the Rabbinical Council of Landsberg.

The Halakhic Witness and the Annulment of the First-Person Voice

The Auschwitz memoir of Berish Erlich is excerpted here for the first time, having remained in private hands for the past 70 years.³³ He completed it in January 1946 in the Landsberg displaced persons camp, a year after liberation. The memoir is in three languages: German, English, and Yiddish, all tightly written together side by side on single pages of an American Army–issued accounting ledger. The memoir had its origin in an English class at Landsberg. Berish Erlich thanks his teacher on the inside cover page of the memoir for encouraging him to record his experiences at Auschwitz. The green memoir cover is embossed in faded gold lettering with Berish Erlich's name. But there is a proviso that comes with the memoir that adds significantly to its historical as well as metaphorical value. Berish Erlich did not write it. His children hold that the handwriting in the memoir is not their father's. Yet the story is entirely his. He recounted bits and pieces of it to them throughout his life. The first part of the memoir details his life in the Warsaw Ghetto. The second part narrates the time he spent in Auschwitz. The writing of the memoir likely transpired in the English class at Landsberg. The presence of another writer sheds light on why the memoir was written in three languages, two of which presumably all the students in the class understood (Yiddish and German) and the third, English, was the subject matter of the class and is prominent in the middle of the page. One can also assume that the personal and traumatic significance of the memoir was such that Berish Erlich wanted as much accuracy and grammatical consistency as possible in the actual writing; hence, deductive reasoning would suggest that the displaced person ghostwriter is likely his English teacher whom he thanks at the very beginning of the memoir.

The contextual circumstance of writing the memoir, wherein the actual narrator does not take pen to paper but speaks it, allows for a further level of mediation, distanciation, and annulment of the first-person voice to that of a halakhic witness guided by lawful codes: to evaluate an event under the rubric of halakhah. Berish Erlich's memoir presents, in this regard, both a recounting and a cultural perspective, when viewed through the grid of a faith-based reading of the individual and the collective. The halakhic concepts of *ahavas Yisroel* (love, devotion, and empathy for fellow Jews) and *bittul atzmi* (the dissolution and nullifying of self) allows entry into a spiritualistic causal reading of intentionality and halakhic witnessing—not necessarily verifiable by empirical historical methodologies.[34]

In contrast to Primo Levi's personal account of *l'univers concentrationnaire* or Filip Muller's disturbing recollections of three years as a Sonderkommando in Auschwitz,[35] Berish Erlich's memoir is written in detached prose, as if he is preparing a witness statement for a *bet din* (religious court): as a halakhic witness to a cataclysmic destruction, reminiscent of Rabbi Zvi Hersch Meisels's relational understanding of a witnessing discussed earlier. There are no references to his personal experiences, even as he is describing barbarous events that clearly included his own suffering. There is no recounting of words or actions by victims that betray any faith-based sentiments.[36] He surveys events, steadily, unfalteringly. He recounts the story of the Jewish dancer Franceska Mann, from Warsaw, and her fatal shooting of SS Major Josef Schillinger and wounding of SS trooper Emmerich in crematorium 4 in October 1943.[37] Berish Erlich's account differs from all others of this incident. He asserts that Franceska Mann took her own life. Erlich writes:

> Something must be said about Report Leader Schillinger. He has many human lives on his conscience. He killed and murdered many prisoners with his own hands. He lost his life in the following way: From a newly arrived transport of Jews of Warsaw, 80% were selected for gassing. Among the persons selected for death was a famous Jewish dancer (a woman), who refused to undress and advocated for the other women. The SS called Schillinger and he came to make order. When he appeared, the dancer befell him, dragged his revolver away from him, and killed him on the spot. She wounded another SS man by the same weapon and then killed herself.

For a contrary emphasis upon narration, rich in detail within the Holocaust memoir genre, consider Filip Muller's description of a selection for members of the *Sonderkommando,* as they were lined up in the yard of crematorium 2, before their deaths. Muller was not a religious Jew.

> Suddenly from out of the ranks of doomed prisoners stepped the young rabbinical student who had worked in the hair-drying team. He turned to the Oberscharfuhrer Muhsfeld and with sublime courage told him to be quiet. Then he began to speak to the crowd: Brothers! He cried, it is God's unfathomable will that we are to lay down our lives. A cruel and accursed fate has compelled us to take part in the extermination of our people, and now we are ourselves to become dust and ashes. No miracle has happened. Heaven has sent no avenging bolts of lightning. No rain has fallen strong enough to extinguish the funeral pyres built by the hand of man. We must submit to the inevitable with Jewish resignation. It will be the last trial sent to us by heaven. It is not for us to question the reasons, for we are as nothing before Almighty God. Be not afraid of death! Even if we could, by some chance, save our lives what use would that be to us now. In vain we would search for our murdered relatives, without friends, without place we might call our own, condemned to roam the world aimlessly. For us there would be neither rest nor peace of mind until one day we would die in some corner, lonely and forsaken. Therefore, brothers, let us now go to meet death bravely and with dignity.[38]

The Auschwitz memoir of Filip Muller is replete with individual references to both the terror as well as the subjective and spiritual succor at the door of the gassing station. In Berish Erlich's memoir, we confront the depths of the abyss, the murdered and the murderers, face to face, as a preparatory recounting for judgment.

The Auschwitz Memoir of Berish Erlich
   I. Auschwitz Camp (documents the arrival procedure at the camp)
   II. Report about Those Who Arrived in the Camp for Labor
   III. The Military and Administrative Direction of Auschwitz-Birkenau
   - The Military Direction

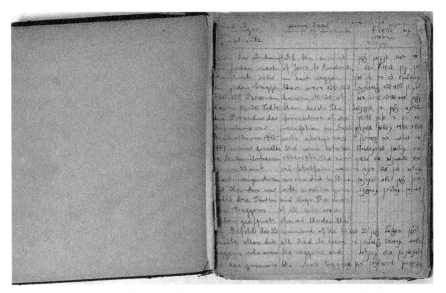

The Auschwitz Memoir, 1946. Ber Erlich Collection, Amud Aish Memorial Museum. Photo: Shoshana Greenwald.

IV. The Interior Order of the Camp
- The Jewish Czech Camp
- How the SS Celebrated Christmas of 1942

I. Auschwitz Camp

At the arrival of Jews to Auschwitz, in each wagon, there were 120–150 persons, 10–20 of them dead. The procedure of the reception was always the same. The arrival platform was surrounded by SS men with machine guns and dogs. The doors of all cars were opened. Under the command of the SS, all had to leave the wagons and all their baggage had to enter separately, likewise the women and children. At the separation of families, tragic things happened. Then came the SS men and counted the men. They pointed who had to stand to the right side and who to the left one. The young healthy ones were separated and the weaker and old ones separated too. The same happened with the women and children, young, healthy women separated and older and weaker, as well as young women with children were separated. From each transport about 20–25% men and 15–20% women were considered healthy and were brought into the camp. All other men, women, and children were transported to Birkenau.

Birkenau is about 2 km from Auschwitz. Near a small forest there was a white house without windows. All men, women, and children had to completely undress. Then, they were forcibly moved into the white house. When the house was full, the doors were shut hermetically. An SS man made steam gas flow through a hole on the roof and 10 minutes later all in that house were dead. The gas chamber contained about 3,000 persons. After being gassed the corpses were removed from the killing room and searched for golden teeth. These were extracted at once. Barbers had cut the long hair of all women and children. Thereupon all the dead were brought into a nearby mass grave. The mass grave was soaked with gasoline. Corpses were thrown and burnt on it. The killing duration of the various transports was different. Those who did not know what awaited them, and therefore went silently into the gas chamber, got a lot of gas and were dead in the course of a few minutes. But those who had the sentiment that horror awaited them and had to be forcibly moved into the gas chamber got very little gas, and were dead only after some hours and under terrible pain.

This kind of annihilation lasted till March 1943. At this time four large crematoriums were built. These were erected so that those appointed for killing by gas did not know their fate till the end. The crematoriums looked like little factories or bathing establishments. The incoming transports were led into a large barrack. There it was written, that everyone shall bind together their shoes and articles of dress to get them back after "bathing." Everyone got a towel and a piece of soap. They went naked from the barrack into a subterraneous shelter. On the door was written "To Bathing." The arrangement of the shelter was done in such a way that you could suppose it was a bathing room. When the shelter room was filled all doors were shut and the gas was poured in from the top.

In the course of some minutes all were dead. The gas was "Zyklon B." It arrived by massive wagons from Hamburg to Auschwitz. From the bathing room all corpses were pulled into the crematorium by an electric lift. The temperature in the stoves was so high that the bodies were burnt to ashes, in the course of minutes. In each crematorium, there were 12 stoves. The ashes of the burnt Jews were buried into mass graves, and so it lasted till August 1944. When the Red Army began its advance in the direction of Warsaw-Cracow, the ashes were dug out, to wipe out the traces, and poured into the Vistula River.

All the work assigned to gassing and burning was done by a command of Jewish prisoners. This command was called the Sonderkommando (special-command). In summer 1944 Russians were allotted to this command, too. Prisoners, who were active in this command, did not live long. After a certain time they were murdered and replaced by others. No prisoner voluntarily announced himself for the "special-command." The prisoners of that command were catered and dressed well. The activity of the "special command" was the following: The movement of transports into the barracks, supervising the undressing and moving the people into the gas chamber. After the gassing, the same personnel had to extract teeth and to cut off the hair of the corpses of the women and children, and last the transportation into the stoves. All that took place under the supervision and compulsion of the SS. Some prisoners of Birkenau reproached the members of the Sonderkommando. Those who joined them had nothing to lose. Some tried to destroy the crematorium and disarm the SS.

In August 1944 the camp leader selected 300 weak prisoners of the Sonderkommando for a transport. There were about 1,000 Sonderkommando in Auschwitz. The high number of Sonderkommando was a consequence of the extreme and massive Hungarian transports, which arrived chiefly in the months of April, May, and June 1944 and became less in the later months.

When they transported the first 100 Sonderkommando into another camp, and would fetch the remaining 200, those prisoners set themselves against the SS, and set on fire the crematorium Nr. 3. When the 150 prisoners of the crematorium Nr. 1 noticed the burning of the crematorium Nr. 3 they disarmed more SS men, cut through the hedge electrically loaded, and escaped from the camp armed by guns.

The whole team of the SS of Auschwitz was alarmed at once, the fugitive prisoners were persecuted, surrounded, and shot down till the last person. At this battle about 10 SS people were killed and wounded. On that day, 300 Sonderkommando were exterminated. Among the abovementioned 150 prisoners of the crematorium Nr. 1 were also 19 Russians.

The other command that was employed with the transportation was called "Canada." The labor of this command was the following: to empty the wagons of the arrived transports; the unloading the corpses from the wagons; to place the baggage on trucks and to send off to the warehouses. This command consisted of only Jewish prisoners. It is impossible to describe all that has happened at Auschwitz between 1942 and 1944. Each transport had its particularities and occurrences. Hundreds of children were thrown alive into the stoves by Oberscharfuhrer Moll, the chief of all the crematoriums; he shot thousands by himself. Once a three-year-old child was found alive, after the gassing at the very opening of a gas shelter, lying on 3,000 corpses. Thereupon, the child was thrown alive into the fire by Moll.

II. Report about Those Who Arrived in the Camp for Labor

Of the healthy men and women selected from the transports, about 20–25% came into the concentration camp for labor. All they possessed was taken away from them. After being bathed, they received bad prisoner dresses and uncomfortable clogs. Every prisoner got tattooed his current number on his forearm. Then, all were distributed into the blocks. The block-leaders and room servants and prisoners behaved very brutally. The people were struck by thick cudgels. There was only a little to eat. From the small quantity, which the SS apportioned, much was stolen by the room servants and the block leaders. At the beginning, the prisoners had to sleep on blank boards, without coverlets. The labor was very hard. It lasted from the early morning till the commencement of darkness. Prisoners were struck and ill treated during labor by the SS, capos, and foremen. Because of this treatment and of hard work almost 50% of them became sick in course of some weeks and were delivered to the hospital. But they were not long there, because every two days a motorcar came and took those who were more ill to the crematorium. They were gassed there. In this manner, 90% of those, who came into the camp for labor died, in course of some months.

This was the fate of Jews from Greece and the Netherlands. They were less capable of resistance to the bad climate and the bad treatment. By the end of 1943, treatment in the camp grew a little better. It was caused probably because of the Red Army's advance. The Russian prisoners of war organized themselves and soon controlled the block leaders and the capos, and did much to help in the easing of camp life. In the women's camp, the conditions were worse with frequent selections. The camp doctor ordered them to undress completely, and the ones who looked weak and meager or had wounds were selected and transported for gassing on the same day. One of the biggest and most serious selections took place on January 20, 1944. The SS camp doctors Mengele and Tito selected almost 50% of all the Jews for gassing on this day. Among them there were many strong and healthy men.

III. The Military and Administrative Direction of Auschwitz-Birkenau

The first prisoners were Germans and Poles. At the second half of 1941, Russian prisoners of war arrived too. Then, several camps were erected around Auschwitz by those prisoners. The so-called Bauabschnitt II (building sector II) was erected. This consisted of 6 camps. Each camp contained 35 large barracks without windows, the so-called Pferdebaracken (horses' barracks). The barracks dwelt about 300 to 400 prisoners. When great transports arrived, this number grew up to 800 to 1000. To the right of the 6 camps were 4 large crematoriums, 1 large bathing establishment and a camp for effects and a number of warehouse stores were erected. Each camp was surrounded by a hedge, loaded with electricity and guarded by SS guards. In this area was also the so called F.K.L Frauenkonzentrationslager (women concentration camp), which imprisoned about 30,000 women. The SS began erecting the "Bauabschnitt III" (buildings' sector III) near these camps. The barracks were already erected, but the quick advance of the Red Army destroyed the Germans' plans.

The Military Direction

At the commencement of 1943, there was a camp leader, an SS officer named Palitsch, a very bad man, who was the fright of the whole camp. He was degraded on account of abuses. His successor was the SS man Schwarzhuber. This one was not so brutal. Another camp leader in Birkenau ordered the shooting 15,000 Jews on September 21, 1943.

Something must be said about Report Leader Schillinger. He has many human lives on his conscience. He killed and murdered many prisoners with his own hands. He lost his life in the following way: From a newly arrived transport of Jews from Warsaw, 80% were selected for gassing. Among the persons selected for death was a famous Jewish dancer (a woman), who refused to undress and advocated for the other women. The SS called Schillinger and he came to make order. When he appeared, the dancer befell him, dragged his revolver away from him, and killed him on the spot. She wounded another SS man by the same weapon and then killed herself.

There were simple SS men in a great number in the camp, so-called Blockfuhrer (block leaders). For this job they purposefully brought in brutal and sadistic murderers. At work, and in the camp, they only had one task: to torment the prisoners. There were also some among them who played the role of "good" men. Those never struck the prisoners; sometimes they even helped them. But this happened to win the confidence of the prisoners to betray them. Such a type was the block leader Schneider, who had befriended some prisoners. So he promised to help them escape from the camp. Of course for good payment. But instead of liberating them, he delivered them in the hands of the Gestapo (state secret police) and these were shot. They were thrown into the fire alive.

IV. The Interior Order of the Camp

The prisoners were under the supervision of the SS at the camp and at work. Each camp had its camp leader. In 1943 there was a camp leader, a certain man, then a prisoner but not a political one, but a criminal by profession. He ruled at the camp as a criminal. His follower was a Dane, a Reichs-German from Litzmannstadt, likewise not a political prisoner but a convict who was not much better than his predecessor. The camp leader's task was to keep order at the camp and the supervision over the camp personnel. Each block had its block leader, secretary, and several room servants, whose task was to keep order at the block, to distribute the food, etc.

From 1941 to 1942 those posts could only be had by such prisoners who were murderers. They were recruited from all nations. Only at the end of 1943 the conditions changed for better. From this time on these posts could be occupied by non-criminals. Things also changed for the better with the capos and foremen.

The SS made medicinal experiments with healthy prisoners. Many hundreds of Jews, young, healthy men and women, were selected for various experiments. Yet before being fully recovered, they were sent for hard labor again. Once a group of young, healthy, and strong men and eight women were selected. They were fastened naked on tables with their faces covered by clothes. Then their necks were cut through with sharp knives, their blood was caught up into glasses and different experiments were done with the same.

The Jewish Czech Camp

In the autumn of 1943 great transports of Jews from Theresienstadt arrived. They were better treated than other Jewish transports, they were not struck, not selected, the baggage were not taken away from them, even their hair was not cut off. These transports got a separate camp, where whole families were allowed to live together. So they lived six months. Suddenly, in the spring holiday, the entire transport, without exceptions was gassed and burnt.

How the SS Celebrated Christmas of 1942

In December 1942 all Jews of the camp were called to an *Appel* (roll call). Thereupon, a command was heard for everyone to put on their jackets, but reversed, and to place sand in them. The way the Jews had to pass was surrounded by SS men, Capos, etc. who were equipped with thick cudgels. Every prisoner had to pass this way in a running pace. They got violent slaps on his head and his whole body. After the course of one hour several hundred Jews were dead.

This is a short description of the camp Auschwitz-Birkenau. Many more pages can be written about that, however, all would not grasp the reality, because it was yet worse than all which a man could be capable of comprehending.

Notes

1. Shoshana Feldman and Dori Laub, *Testimony: Crises of Witnessing in Literature, Psychoanalysis and History* (New York: Routledge, 1992).

2. Yitzchok Avigdor, *The Auschwitz Memoir*, Amud Aish Memorial Museum Archival Collections, Brooklyn, NY, n.d.

3. Thomas Trezise, "Unspeakable," *Yale Journal of Criticism* 14 (Spring 2001): 38–63; Thomas Trezise, *Witnessing Witnessing: On the Reception of Holocaust Survivor Testimony* (Bronx, NY: Fordham University Press, 2013).

4. Primo Levi, *The Drowned and the Saved,* trans. Raymond Rosenthal (New York: Summit Books, 1988), 84.

5. Feldman and Laub, *Testimony,* 324–25.

6. Giorgio Agamben, *Remnants of Auschwitz: The Witness and the Archive* (New York: Zone Books, 1999), 35.

7. Sam Bak, interviewed in the documentary film *Memory after Belsen* (time stamp 0:58–1:02), Henri Lustiger Thaler and Ed Sonshine, executive producers (Stories to Remember, 2014).

8. I defer to Lawrence Langer, in chapter 1 of this volume, in explaining this succinct term: "When dealing with the Holocaust, the difficult challenge before us is to identify with the target of deep memory, that intellectual and emotional terrain where the clear borders between living and dying merge and we are faced with the condition of being what I call 'deathlife' (the Afterdeath of the Holocaust), a territory we instinctively flee because it is uninhabitable by reasonable creatures like ourselves."

9. Cathy Caruth, *Trauma: Explorations in Memory* (Baltimore: Johns Hopkins University Press, 1995).

10. See Esther Farbstein's chapter in this volume.

11. Joseph B. Soloveitchik, *Halakhic Man* (Philadelphia: Jewish Publication Society, 1991).

12. See Agamben, *Remnants of Auschwitz,* on the *muselmann.*

13. Lawrence Langer, "The Dilemma of Choice in the Concentration Camps," *Centerpoint: The Holocaust* 4, no. 1 (Fall 1980).

14. Pesach Schindler, *Hasidic Responses to the Holocaust in the Light of Hasidic Thought* (Hoboken, NJ: KTAV, 1990).

15. Ibid., 60. Schindler quotes Meir Dvorzeski, *Ha'amidah Behaye Yom Yom Bergeta'ot U'vemahanot*, 128.

16. Ibid., 61.

17. By cultural, I do not refer to the study of institutions, mores, and conventions, but the ways in which meaning is produced through constantly changing personal and collective experiential frameworks.

18. I. Tishby, "*Hasidut,*" in *Haenziklopedia Ha'ibrit*, 17:818, quoted in Schindler, *Hasidic Responses to the Holocaust*, 167.

19. Quoted in Henri Lustiger Thaler, "History and Memory: The Orthodox Experience in the Bergen-Belsen Displaced Persons Camp," *Holocaust and Genocide Studies* 27, no. 1 (Spring 2013): 31.

20. Samuel D. Kassow, "Vilna and Warsaw, Two Ghetto Diaries: Herman Kruk and Emmanuel Ringleblum," in *Holocaust Chronicles: Individualizing the Holocaust through Diaries and Other Contemporaneous Personal Accounts*, ed. Moses Shapiro (Hoboken, NJ: Yeshiva University Press/KTAV, 1999), 171–216.

21. Nusyn Pinchus Erlich was also a philanthropist and chairman of the prewar Jewish charity in Warsaw known as *Kupath Rabbi Meyer Baal Hanes*.

22. The Radomsker Rebbe was a first cousin to Nusyn Pinchus Erlich. The Rebbe had a network of thirty-six yeshivas throughout Poland, known as *Keser Torah*.

23. I wish to thank Jo-Ellyn Decker of the United States Holocaust Memorial Museum for her diligent research through the International Tracing Service Records of the International Red Cross in reference to Berish Erlich.

24. Danuta Czech indicates the name of Berish Erlich among 749 prisoners, nos. 127913 to 128662, on a transport to Auschwitz from Majdanik. See Danuta Czech, *Auschwitz Chronicle, 1939–1945*, 1st American ed. (New York: Henry Holt & Company, 1990).

25. Dates of arrival in Ohrdruf tend to vary because the documentation system collapsed in the final three months of the war, and variations of prisoner chronologies at Ohrdruf differ from that recorded at the main administrative center in Buchenwald.

26. See Angelika Eder, *Fluchtige Heimat: judische displaced persons in Landsberg am Lech 1945 bis 1950* (Munchen: Kommissionsverlag UNI-Druck, 1998), and Atina Grossmann, *Jews, Germans and Allies: Close Encounters in Occupied Germany* (Princeton, NJ: Princeton University Press, 2007), on the history of the DP camp.

27. Josef Friedenson, "Rabbi Erlich: A Pillar of Righteous Persecution in the Ghetto and the Camps," *Dos Yiddishe Vort*, 1962.

28. Ibid.

29. The newspaper was first established in the Landsberg displaced persons camp in 1945, and published continuously in Brooklyn until Friedenson's death in February 2013.

30. Letters attesting to Berish Erlich's work on behalf of Jewish displaced persons in Landsberg, as well as Jewish prisoners in the displaced persons jail, are documented in letters from American military commanders: Military Government Liaison Major, August 20, 1946; Dr. Walter Linden, Prison Office, May 20, 1946, American Joint Distribution Committee, Rabbi Rosenberg; Major Carl Rein Military Government, Marshall L. Mott, March 6, 1946. The Kleinman Family Holocaust Education Center (KFHEC), archival collections, Brooklyn, NY.

31. Letter from Hillel Seidman, the Berish Erlich Collection, KFHEC archival collections, Brooklyn, NY.

32. Landsberg displaced persons camp was located sixty kilometers west of Munich on the grounds of a former German military compound. It was the second-largest displaced person camp in the American zone. Landsberg housed the field headquarters for ORT (Organization for Reconstruction and Training) in the American zone. It had an educational system from preschool to college, a Talmud Torah, and a yeshiva. Holocaust survivor and artist Sam Bak worked and lived there. The camp was closed on October 15, 1950.

33. The Berish Erlich memoir is currently archived in the Amud Aish Memorial Museum, Brooklyn, NY.

34. Berish Erlich's memoir, in this regard, has the discursive cadence of rabbinic responsa of the time, characterized by measured composure. Emotion is reserved in the responsa of the period to biblical incantations for vengeance from the hand of the divine: "Earth cover not the blood shed on thee."

35. Filip Muller chronicles how he might have succeeded in his attempt to end his own life had it not been for a group of Jewish girls in the gas chamber who pushed him out the chamber door.

36. In this regard, Berish Erlich's memoir presents a counterpoint to the martyrological victim of the Holocaust in Orthodox counter-historiography texts by writers such as Yechiel Granatstein, Moshe Prager, and Moshe Schoenfeld. See Kimmy Caplan, "How Many Lies Accumulated in History Books: The Holocaust in Ashkenazi Haredi Historical Consciousness," Yad Vashem, Shoah Resource Center, 2003.

37. Accounts of Franceska Mann's death in Auschwitz on October 7, 1943, vary. Eberhard Kolb states that she was gassed. Auschwitz Commandant Rudolf Höss, in his disposition, states that Mann and the other Jewish women who attacked the guards were executed. Martin Gilbert's account,

decades later, indicates that Franceska Mann was executed. Gilbert's account is based on Jerzy Tabau's report, "The Polish Major's Report," that entered the Nuremburg International Tribunal as document L-22. In yet another report, titled "Jewish Resistance in Nazi-Occupied Germany" by Ainsztein, and also quoted by Gilbert, Franceska Mann was executed. The writer Tadeusz Borowski in his short story "The Death of Schillinger" recounts that Franceska Mann was gassed. The depositions to the Nuremburg Trials, which have served as the basis for the majority conclusion that Franceska Mann was executed, is contradicted by Berish Erlich's memoir. Erlich arrived in Auschwitz on July 8, 1943. Mann was murdered in October 1943. The memoir is likely one of the firsthand accounts of this event, written in January 1946, along with the Nuremburg International Tribunal depositions. The Nuremburg Trials commenced on November 20, 1945, and ended on October 1, 1946.

38. Filip Muller, *Eyewitness Auschwitz: Three Years in the Gas Chambers* (Chicago: Ivan R. Dee, in association with the United States Holocaust Memorial Museum, 1999), 161–62.

Bibliography

Agamben, Giorgio. *Remnants of Auschwitz: The Witness and the Archive*. New York: Zone Books, 1999.

Avigdor, Yitzchok. *The Auschwitz Memoir*. The Amud Aish Memorial Museum Archival Collections. Brooklyn, NY, n.d.

Caruth, Cathy. *Trauma: Explorations in Memory*. Baltimore: Johns Hopkins University Press, 1995.

Czech, Danuta. *Auschwitz Chronicle, 1939–1945*. 1st American ed. New York: Henry Holt, 1990.

Eder, Angelika. *Fluchtige Heimat: judische displaced persons in Landsberg am Lech 1945 bis 1950*. Munchen: Kommissionsverlag UNI-Druck, 1998.

Feldman, Shoshana, and Dori Laub. *Testimony: Crises of Witnessing in Literature, Psychoanalysis and History*. New York: Routledge, 1992

Friedenson, Josef. "Rabbi Erlich: A Pillar of Righteous Persecution in the Ghetto and the Camps." *Dos Yiddishe Vorte*, 1962.

Goldberg, Amos. "The History of the Jews in the Ghetto." In *The Holocaust and Historical Methodology*, ed. Dan Stone. New York: Berghahn, 2015.

Grossmann, Atina. *Jews, Germans and Allies: Close Encounters in Occupied Germany*. Princeton, NJ: Princeton University Press, 2007.

Kassow, Samuel D. "Vilna and Warsaw, Two Ghetto Diaries: Herman Kruk and Emmanuel Ringleblum." In *Holocaust Chronicles: Individualizing the*

Holocaust through Diaries and Other Contemporaneous Personal Accounts, ed. Moses Shapiro. Hoboken, NJ: Yeshiva University Press/KTAV, 1999.

Kavon, Eli. "The Last Rabbi in the War Ghetto—Zionist?" April 30, 2013.

Langer, Lawrence. "The Dilemma of Choice in the Concentration Camps." *Centerpoint: The Holocaust* 4, no. 1 (Fall 1980).

———. *Holocaust Testimonies: The Ruins of Memory*. New Haven, CT: Yale University Press, 1993.

Levi, Primo. *The Drowned and the Saved*. New York: Summit, 1988.

———. *Survival in Auschwitz*. New York: Simon and Schuster, 1958

Lustiger Thaler, Henri. "History and Memory: The Orthodox Experience in the Bergen-Belsen Displaced Persons Camp." *Holocaust and Genocide Studies* 27, no. 1 (2013): 30–56.

Muller, Filip. *Eyewitness Auschwitz: Three Years in the Gas Chambers*. Chicago: Ivan R. Dee, in association with the United States Holocaust Memorial Museum, 1999.

Schindler, Pesach. *Hasidic Responses to the Holocaust in the Light of Hasidic Thought*. Hoboken, NJ: KTAV, 1990.

Seidman, Hillel. Letter a2: The Ber Erlich Collection. The Amud Aish Memorial Museum Collections. Brooklyn, NY, n.d.

Soloveitchik, Joseph B. *Halakhic Man*. Philadelphia: Jewish Publication Society, 1991.

Thaler, Henri Lustiger, and Ed Sonshine, executive producers. *Memory after Belsen* (documentary film). Stories to Remember, 2014.

Trezise, Thomas. "Unspeakable." *Yale Journal of Criticism* 14 (Spring 2001): 38–63.

———. *Witnessing Witnessing: On the Reception of Holocaust Survivor Testimony*. Bronx, NY: Fordham University Press, 2013.

4

Memoirs Not Forgotten

Rabbis Who Survived the Holocaust

ESTHER FARBSTEIN

> Just one volume of Holocaust writings should be enough to cause our bookshelf to collapse under the weight of the losses described therein. But apparently, there is no limit to the oak tree's tolerance. The shelves may sag, but they endure, and do not give way. Neither do they agree to relinquish even one story from those tragic times, for these are truly the sacred memories of that era.
> Yishaya Avrech, "A Train Car Full of Women's Hair"

The publishing of memoirs of Holocaust survivors, and the testimonies they have submitted to various institutions, have become a widespread phenomenon since the 1980s. The singular voice of the individual, in the context of the Holocaust, opens a door into the complex layers of human history that no cold, factual documentation can ever capture. Without these works, we cannot understand human actions. Nor can we comprehend the influence of the heritage that was passed down from generation to generation, before and after the Holocaust: the effects of culture,

---

This essay was translated from the Hebrew by Jessica Setbon and Shira Leibowitz Schmidt. The epigraph is taken from Yishaya Avrech, *Pirkey Yotam*, "A Train Car Full of Women's Hair," *Mahanayim* 1, no. 66 (Tel Aviv: Am Oved, 1996).

education, and values, and the ways individuals perceived and reacted to what was unfolding before their eyes. For historians, who mean to reconstruct the facts "as they were," the points of view of individuals represent a raw slice of life, which enable us to understand the multi-faceted nature of the reality victims and survivors were facing. As Raz Segal has argued, "The personal dimension is what offers us an opening to understanding the past, the possibility of understanding history and learning from history."[1]

From a linguistic viewpoint, testimonies and memoirs best express the manner in which survivors perceived reality.[2] Over the years, this phenomenon has grown among survivors from the Orthodox sector,[3] and some researchers have identified those aspects that in particular characterize Orthodox memoir genres, both oral and written.[4]

For these reasons, the absence of rabbis who were Holocaust survivors—the elite group in the Orthodox world—has been conspicuous in the literature. Some of them lived through the Holocaust in active service as rabbis, others as rabbinic judges [*dayanim*], educators, and yeshiva directors, while still others were young men who became rabbis many years later. While some authors were already well known for their works,[5] they were few in number. This paucity of rabbinic memoirs created a sense that rabbis self-consciously repressed the topic of the Holocaust and avoided struggling with its memory.[6]

However, contrary to the aforementioned assumption, rabbis did write and record their Holocaust experiences. This body of work presents us with a new genre of "memory writings" with very unique characteristics. These consist of writings of a large number of rabbis who survived the Holocaust. While a few rabbis wrote *in situ*, during the Holocaust itself,[7] the majority began to write with the period of liberation and rehabilitation, continuing to the present day. But these memoirs were not published *qua* memoirs. Rather, they were included as prefaces to rabbinic works. In their visual appearance and main content, they seemed to be the usual tomes of Jewish sacred literature. However, sequestered within the autobiographies of these authors, there were their discourses on the experience of the Holocaust.

Why did rabbis and Torah scholars choose this genre in order to record their memories and reflections on the Holocaust? In the rabbinic world, writing a book, in particular a book of traditional scholarship (whether it be Jewish law, Torah commentary and interpretation, or philosophy), has always been considered the peak of accomplishment, unlike the publication of an autobiographical work, which is not valued in the rabbinic cultural milieu. It is no wonder, therefore, that Torah scholars would view the pages of their scholarly works as the appropriate medium within which to embed their memories of the central events of their lives. This element of Jewish historiography,[8] the writing of autobiographical material, usually took place in the wake of tragedies.[9] After the Holocaust, we find a significant expansion of this practice, such that hundreds of Torah scholars chose this genre, found in prefaces, in order to write about their experiences.

Because most of these books are unavailable to the general public, Zachor, the Center for Holocaust Research and Education at the Michlalah–Jerusalem College, initiated a project to gather over 150 of these writings, within prefaces to religious books that were published between 1945 and 2006. These prefaces were published on a CD-ROM and on the Zachor website.[10] Some were accompanied by research and annotations, in Hebrew and in English.[11] The English anthology, *The Forgotten Memoirs*, made these previously inaccessible writings available to researchers and interested readers.

This collection includes texts written in a variety of styles. Although each recounts a unique and personal story, they share common characteristics, in content and structure. In this chapter, I discuss innovative avenues of research that this database of memoirs makes available to the public. I also explain the significance of these memoirs for understanding Jewish life—before and during the Holocaust—and finally, we examine what this represents as a contribution to the new Orthodox historiography and the study of Holocaust commemoration within the Orthodox community.

Before, During, and After the Holocaust: The Vitality of the Jewish World

From childhood onward, the authors of the memoirs were profoundly grounded in religious practices within their communities, whether they were from Eastern or Western Europe. In short, they were born in the very heart of traditional Jewish life. The Holocaust struck many of them when they were at the apex of their creativity in terms of Torah scholarship. Afterward, like many Holocaust survivors, they longed to memorialize the prewar Jewish life that was lost. In their writings, they depict a world of robust Jewish activity in all its diversity.

The authors weave into their memoirs the values of home and family life, their studies in yeshivas, their experiences in Hasidic courts and communities, and descriptions of scholars and rabbinic dynasties. They also write of antisemitism, economic distress, and confrontations with ideologies and religious tendencies that developed around them. Although this genre of writing has a nostalgic component, it does not prevent the reader from gaining insight into foundational concepts that structured religious life before the war.

For example, the son of Rabbi Avraham Abba Reznik describes the shtetl of Pilvishki in Lithuania. Rabbi Yaakov Avigdor describes the rich Torah activity in Drohobycz-Boryslaw, Poland, while Rabbi Yehoshua Grunwald takes us through the streets of Chust, Hungary. Rabbi Chaim Ephraim Zaichyk leads the reader into the Novardok yeshiva, Rabbi Moshe Rothenberg into the Chachmei Lublin yeshiva, and Rabbi Yechiel Yaakov Weinberg leads us to the Orthodox Rabbinical Seminary of Berlin.[12] The many names mentioned throughout the memoirs are part of an important database of Holocaust victims and a source for further genealogical research.

Within the writing styles of these genre-driven texts are further reflections of the Jewish world from which the authors came.[13] They express their manner of coping with the events of the Holocaust. Their language is interwoven with expressions from religious sources, and at times it seems as if authors were holding a dialogue with these sources in order to give meaning to the terrible events transpiring before their eyes.[14]

The cultural precepts of the authors, as reflected in the memoirs, take the form of Torah interpretations, Hasidic stories, and family values. C. Hendler researched Hasidic stories within the rabbinic texts. She writes, "It appears that even in the Valley of Death, the vitality of Hasidic interpretation and story do not fade. For many religious Jews, these texts continued to serve as a basis for faith and a wellspring for spiritual renewal. These stories, drawing from the depths of memory, brought attention to the reality of the Holocaust and the individual immersed within it."[15]

Continuity within the Crisis

These memoirs provide rich sources for understanding the lives of religious Jews during the Holocaust. In most of the texts, first-person singular and plural, "I" and "we," are intertwined, especially when the author served as a community rabbi, and thus as the spokesperson for a lost community. Although the writing is usually chronological, and includes many descriptions of events during the Holocaust, we must recall that this work is not historical writing, recounted in a sequential manner with exact dates. Rather, the genre draws our attention to the conditions of life that the writer considers significant. The texts contain a high level of subjectivity.

The main axis is faith and struggles around Jewish identity. However, devotion to their faith and way of life (as far as conditions permitted) is not emphasized as a separate topic; rather, it is an inherent part of their daily lives. This devotion is expressed with modesty and sincerity. The dilemmas they faced are self-sketched against the reality of the genocide, thus enabling the reader to understand individual actions and depictions of the Holocaust period.

Faith and the Meaning of the Holocaust

The issue of faith infuses these writings, as does attention to religious and philosophical questions on the ascribed meaning of the Holocaust. Rabbinic scholars emphasized their inability to explain the enormity of the loss, and expressed fear that discussing it could cause fissures in faith. For example, in the memoirs of Rabbi Moshe Nosson Nota Lemberger of Makó, Hungary, we find an unusual description of Rabbi Yechiel Michel Schlager of Galicia, who was apprehensive when reflecting about the future. When asked about this, he replied that he was worried. He wondered how he would reply if asked after the Holocaust why this unprecedented disaster took place. How could questioners preserve their faith in the future?[16] Most of the authors' writings in this genre of Holocaust reflections emphasize the importance and value of pure faith, without asking the "why and wherefore."

In keeping with this approach, we note that questions dealing with reward and punishment—and the attempt to identify those guilty, amongst errant Jews, for the Holocaust—are not issues which are conspicuous in these writings. This stands in contrast to the prevalence of these claims in the polemical writings in post-Holocaust Orthodox print media and didactic writings. The framing of Zionism as the source of the disaster served as a weapon with which to fight the movement.[17] Rabbis who were Holocaust survivors, we find, relate to it as an unsolved riddle that remains hidden and undeserving of simplistic answers. In general, the writers do not ignore the negative phenomena of Jews against Jews, from *Judenrat* leaders to simple folk, but they do emphasize the Jewish environment as supportive and moral, through empathy and shared fate. They do criticize the tendency of liberal Judaism to adhere to humanistic thinking. They emphasize the gap between the Germans' advanced level of culture and the personal and collective nadir to which they sank during the Holocaust. The subject of faith is mainly found in the emphasis on God's presence even under the most severe circumstances. The sense of "I am with him in distress" (Ps. 91:15) has two aspects. The first aspect is the response of the Torah-faithful Jew, in his most difficult hour in the struggle to survive. The second is the description of Divine Providence, when the author understands his story of individual survival (described as if it were a natural, chronological sequence of events) as one in a chain of miracles.

Throughout the memoirs, descriptions of the wavering between discouragement and hope, between erasure of identity and its preservation, between danger to life and the chance to live, are grounded in faith. Examples of the attachment to Torah and prayer, remembering the holidays, and performing a limited number of mitzvot, which are described in the memoirs, represent a database on their own, as they are reflections of life and hope.

In these contexts and others, the texts enable us to revisit the status and role of rabbis in the Holocaust, first and foremost in their efforts to strengthen the spirit and in their battle against gnawing despair. Rabbi Tzvi Hersch Meisels writes:

> When we were in Auschwitz ... the Jews were beaten and oppressed and many fell into the depths of despair.... When we returned each day from forced labor, exhausted and crushed, we used to sit on the floor in a circle to give thanks to the Creator ... that we had returned from work and remained alive.... It was my practice then to say a few words, to comfort broken hearts ... by telling them that our days of oppression were numbered. Our redemption was not far off, our liberation was close, our eyes would witness our salvation, and our hearts would rejoice.[18]

Rabbi Yosef Greenwald of Pupa took upon himself a similar role:

> During the period of forced labor ... we were together with friends who were Torah-observant and God-fearing. Thus we were able to support each other—"Each man would help his fellow and to his brothers he would say, 'Be strong!'" (Isa. 41:6)—so that our spirits did not fall completely.[19]

The rabbis' roles as halakhic adjudicators also remained relevant during the Holocaust, although they differed in character and direction from previous positions. The database of texts enables us to correct a number of one-dimensional views that the rabbinic leaders were considered to have held, including views in the realm of Jewish law.

The texts reflect a dualistic attitude on the part of rabbis and ordinary Jews to the halakhic dilemmas that faced them. In the rabbinic memoirs, we find significant emphasis on the approach taken by rabbis who enjoined individuals and the public not to observe halakhah when it put lives at risk. In most cases, the rabbis themselves behaved as the public, sometimes serving as personal examples showing that saving lives was the highest, most sacred value in Judaism, and in cases where lives were in danger, the halakhic ruling is "transgress to avoid death," meaning one must transgress all mitzvot except the three cardinal sins (idolatry, murder, and sexual prohibitions) in order to live.

For example, Rabbi Pinchas Asher Goldberger of Slovakia faced a dilemma when he was deported to a gathering point:

> From there they took us like sheep to the slaughter to the nearby city of Komárno [Komaros, in northwest Hungary], where the Jews from the environs were gathered. There were men, women, and children whose lives were truly endangered to an extent that cannot be described in writing. Warming a little milk for the children meant saving lives, but they avoided doing so on Shabbat. Although I was the youngest of the rabbis, I worked up my courage and cut branches from the trees in order to make a fire with which to warm the milk. I said that Maimonides, in his commentary to the Mishnaic chapter *M'fanin* [Shabbat, chap. 18], says that in circumstances of danger, Torah scholars should explicitly instruct people to violate the Shabbat. Then the rabbis discussed it, and among them were Torah scholars who wept and said that the young scholar [referring to myself] was correct, and they had the responsibility to act as he did.[20]

Rabbi Alter Weinberger of Turka described traveling on Shabbat in order to save lives, as well as hiding under a Christian identity.[21] Rabbi Yaakov Avigdor emphasized that the battle for life was the battle against the Germans, and any other action, including strict observance of severe halakhic prohibitions involving mortal danger, aided Hitler in his goal.[22] As opposed to the uniform image often expressed in Orthodox historiography about religious leaders and ordinary Jews who sacrificed their lives for mitzvot, even for the most seemingly minor ones, the rabbinic prefaces actually reveal another reality: rabbis made halakhic decisions based on the precept of "v-chai bahem" [live by them, i.e., the mitzvot, Lev. 18:5] because there is a halakhic requirement to disobey certain mitzvot when saving lives is involved.[23]

On the other hand, despite the life-threatening situations, the halakhic questions, the responses, and the investigation of each matter on its own merit continued. There was no desire to receive a blanket exemption from observing the mitzvot. Thus, for example, Rabbi Weinberger of Turka, who as stated above violated the Shabbat in order to save lives, attempted to recite the Shabbat kiddush according to halakhah, even under disastrous circumstances, and went to great lengths to observe *seudah shlishit* (the third Shabbat meal).[24] Jews held onto the mitzvot even in the concentration camps. In the camps, most were forced to relinquish observance of *kashrut* and the symbols of the holidays. It involved struggle and mental suffering. But when they could observe a mitzvah, even if only partially or symbolically, they regarded it as an expression of defiance and victory, as if they had observed each one of the 613 mitzvot to completion:

> While we were imprisoned by the evil ones, it was not realistic for us to observe God's mitzvot, except for a small number which we observed with the utmost dedication. We felt that this small number was considered in Heaven as if we had observed all 613 mitzvot to completion. If it had been possible to observe all of them, certainly we would have done so, just as we observed the small number with utmost dedication.... Observing a few [under oppression] is like observing many in times of comfort.[25]

As noted above, at the same time as there was a call to *relinquish* observance of mitzvot, we also find a trend to *preserve* and *observe* what was possible without endangering life. This included utilizing existing leniencies and finding ways to perform the prohibited acts with certain changes that would result in the avoidance of Torah-based transgressions. This duality was an integral part of the rabbis' lives as leaders during the Holocaust.

In writing their personal memoirs, the rabbis opened windows into their deliberations and considerations regarding halakhah under various circumstances. For example, when someone found enough oil to light Hanukkah wicks in the Strasshof camp, Rabbi Lemberger wondered whether by taking a risk and lighting them they were indeed doing the correct thing vis-à-vis halakhah. He gave a psychological-emotional explanation for permitting the lighting: "But in those situations we felt an inner impulse to do a mitzvah without giving a thought as to whether halakhah required us to endanger ourselves."[26] Similarly, other rabbis describe the observance of mitzvot during the Holocaust as an emotional phenomenon that was "outside the realm of halakhah." Some of the writers describe weighty moments in which they deliberated unprecedented questions, without being able to consult their books or other rabbinical authorities. They express doubt whether someone not in their position could understand their decision-making methods. Rabbi Yaakov Avigdor describes the *beit din* meetings in Drohobycz, when the rabbis were asked whether it was permitted to hide with Christian families, or even with priests:

> Our intuition told us we were dealing with the three cardinal sins that are in the category of "better to give up one's life than to commit them." My colleagues and I on the *beit din* spent much time on these issues, and spent entire nights discussing the relevant sources. But now [1949] it is best to keep quiet [about those deliberations].[27]

One year later, in 1950, he broke his silence, and explained that as the war progressed they came to a deeper understanding of the uniqueness of the Holocaust, which called for unprecedented halakhic responses. Since the goal of the Nazis was to destroy every Jew, every act that preserved life, including hiding under a Christian identity, was an act of bravery and rebellion against the Germans. Thus, the *beit din* decided they should encourage every act that would lead to saving lives, although this was contrary to the accepted practice.[28]

In that extraordinary 1950 essay on Jewish bravery, Rabbi Avigdor defines and expands the term "resistance" in a most original manner to include such acts as restraint from reactions that might endanger the public. He subsumed under the rubric of "resistance" any act that protected life (such as digging bunkers) and any attempt to defend ethical principles. These were definitions that preceded Holocaust research on the phenomenon of resistance:

> Despite our pitiful situation, despite the fact that we had reached the nadir and lived in darkness, we still searched for some meaning and purpose in the suffering and punishment. Thus from our miserable existences would rise a spark of hope, a flicker of optimism, and an inexhaustible source of heroism . . . of the kind of valor that allowed us to withstand all our trials and tribulations for the sake of eternal moral, ethical principles.[29]

In their memoirs, the rabbis addressed their relationship with the *Judenrat* and expressed a wide range of opinions about its members. On the one hand, they level sharp criticism. For example, Rabbi Avigdor refused to accept their assistance even when he was in danger, because they did not heed his ruling against handing Jews over to the Germans.[30] On the other hand, they praised ethical decisions and also shared the burden of decision making and leadership in the ghettos, as Rabbi Weinberger of Turka describes.[31] The variety of opinions reflects the fact, confirmed today from research, that the *Judenrat* councils were not homogenous, and that they varied from place to place.

Aid, Rescue, and Mutual Responsibility

Efforts for survival and rescue form another axis in the memoirs. In this realm as well, the memoirs offer us new facts and understanding. For example, we learn how the Hungarian yeshivas operated to absorb refugees from Poland and Slovakia before the occupation of Hungary.[32] We read about the support system of community rabbis and Jews in forests on the borders of Slovakia and Romania,[33] and the Budapest rescue operation of Rabbi Baruch Rabinowitz of Munkacs for refugees from Poland.[34] Several of the memoirs describe the story of the wanderings and rescue of the Novardok yeshivas. Most significant of these is the description by Rabbi Chaim Zaichyk of their peripatetic travels and also the students' spiritual resilience in difficult situations.[35]

Rabbi Michael Dov Weissmandel's activities as a rescuer are portrayed not only on the macro level, in his attempts to save huge groups of Jews, but also on the micro level, in his personal commitment to save every last Jew. For example, the teenaged Avraham HaCohen describes how Rabbi Weissmandel instructed his students and their companions at the Nitra yeshiva to prepare a shelter for themselves and to practice how to escape from trains:

> I remember well how Rabbi Michael Dov Weissmandel, may he rest in peace, insisted that each person must do whatever need be done in order to survive and to rescue any Jew whom it was possible to save from the cursed oppressors, may their names be blotted out. He was very active and did his utmost so that people would not be discouraged or give up. To this end he insisted again and again that everyone hide a small razor

or metal cutting edge in his shoe so that if he would be caught and sent to Auschwitz he could cut a hole [while] in a train through which to escape. He even had us practice how to jump off a moving train. He told people to practice jumping off the train in Pressburg while it was traveling so that they would become adept at it.[36]

Demonstrations of solidarity, assisting others, and group unity are expressed in the rabbis' memoirs. Their approach is reminiscent of what Elie Wiesel wrote: "The Jewish soul was a target of the enemy. He sought to corrupt it, even as he strove to destroy us physically. But despite his destructive force, despite his corrupting power, the Jewish soul remained beyond his reach."[37] They do not refrain from descriptions of negative actions of Jews who harmed others in the madness of the struggle for their lives, but they view them as a marginal phenomenon. In almost all the writings, they portray the Jews' acts of kindness. In the preface to his book, *Mekadshei Hashem* [Sanctification of the Name], Rabbi Meisels describes the ethical resoluteness of religious boys with him in Auschwitz, and the courage of a father who refused to ransom his son because it would likely be at the expense of another's life.[38] Rabbi Yehoshua Grunwald of Chust writes about his being rescued by friends,[39] while Rabbi Moshe N.N. Lemberger of Makó illustrates the ethical system organized in the family camps in Austria, which were intended to protect the women, children, and elderly:

> We managed to produce so much that we could meet our quotas while allowing the weak and the sick to stay behind [and not to have to go to work].[40]
>
> The elderly men and women recited Psalms every day. We worked particularly assiduously, and took upon ourselves to complete their daily quota, so that they could all stay behind in the camp.... We arranged for the children who did not go out to work to study Mishnah and the weekly Torah portion [with the elderly].[41]

When Rabbi Weinberger expressed doubts about permitting forbidden foods to people who were deathly ill, he sent his question to Rabbi Yerucham of Stary Sambor, Altstadt, and received an innovative answer saying it was permissible to give them the non-kosher food, citing the phrase in Tractate Berachot of the Talmud which says that even when a sharp sword dangles at one's throat, we must not despair of mercy. The rabbi interpreted "mercy" not as Divine mercy, but rather as mercy for one's fellow man.[42]

The Holocaust: A Unique Event or Part of a Continuum?

The memoirs enable a novel examination of the rabbis' approach to a series of historiographic issues. One of the questions is whether we should view the Holocaust as a unique event in Jewish history, or as one link in a chain of disasters that resulted from the antisemitism that they considered embedded in the nations of the world. Should we isolate the Holocaust or view it as part of a continuum?

In the rabbinic writings, we find a significant sense of continuity with the Jewish past. The terminology used to describe the Holocaust is drawn from biblical and historic events such as the binding of Isaac, the war against Amalek, the silence of Moses' brother Aaron when confronted with the sudden death of two sons, the book of Job, the ten martyrs killed by the Romans, the destruction of the Temples, and the pogroms of the Diaspora.[43] But emphasizing continuity does not negate the understanding of the Holocaust as a decidedly unique, incomparable event. This is stated directly in most of the texts.[44] For example, Rabbi Israel Shabbtai Schepansky wrote, "We must emphasize that we cannot compare the Holocaust of our times to any other tragedy. This is a period that defies comparison in terms of its dimensions, cruelty, and the number of families and Torah scholars who were completely destroyed in it."[45]

An additional question is this: how aware of the Final Solution were the leaders? Opinion is divided on this. Similarly controversial are some rescue efforts, about which the verdicts are not final, such as the Kasztner train.[46] Another facet of the Holocaust illuminated by the rabbinical memoirs is the Jewish world's reaction to and relationship with the survivors, especially addressed by Rabbi Avigdor's memoirs published in 1950:

> Our present generation is not shocked and horrified at the terrible tragedy. On the contrary: our contemporaries have no complaints against Divine Providence, and do not even rail against the Amalekites of our

generation who invented cruel, unusual and . . . ghastly deaths that have not been recorded since the day of Creation. Rather, our contemporaries find fault with *our* behavior—we who were slaughtered, who were led to the gas chambers, who were killed by electrified fences, who were buried alive. They dare to ask: Why did the Jews stretch out their necks willingly to the executioner, without any effort at self-defense? Why did they not organize themselves to fight the torturers? Why did they not unite to rise up actively against the murderers? These kinds of questions can only come from Jews who lived in the free world, far from the Vale of Tears in which we lived and far from the torture, distress, and anguish to which our enemies subjected us.[47]

The Survivors' View of Survival and Memorialization

Many survivors were awash with guilt feelings and questions (for example, "Why did I survive and others did not?" and "What does my survival require of me?"). The rabbis who survived were no exceptions. In general, they, too, vacillated between the pain of mourning and the joy of survival; between silence and speech; between the burying of memories and the need to publicize their experiences.[48] In addition to these responses, familiar from the general memoir literature, there were spiritual and religious facets.

In their writings, the rabbis felt the need to explain the motives for their writings and the ways they related to their survival. One central motive was the felt obligation to describe the series of miracles, which in their view, accompanied or enabled their survival, despite the fact that their narrative is told factually (e.g., escapes, counterfeit documents, hiding, and so on). The memoirs are considered by the rabbis as thanksgiving offerings, and relate to three distinct phenomena: (a) their personal rescue and the survival of the Jewish people who were on the verge of disappearance; (b) the spiritual survival of the Jewish religion and faith after the Shoah, and the revival of Torah study; and (c) the possibility of publishing a religious text after everything they had been through.

> I am the man who has seen my people's affliction in the days of the Shoah and I have seen everything that was done. He has driven me into

darkness, and yet in His boundless compassion has saved me from the teeth of the lion, and freed my soul from confinement [to acknowledge Him].... He has been generous to me so that I am privileged to see this essay to completion, part one of *Beit Aharon*.[49]

In these descriptions, despite the severe suffering, the Holocaust is viewed not only as a period of extreme "concealment of the Divine" (*hester panim*) but also, somewhat paradoxically, as a period of Divine revelation (*gilui panim*). The latter is due to the dimensions of the catastrophe which some experienced as Divine manifestations. Rabbi Ephraim Zaichyk, among the surviving remnant of the Novardok yeshiva movement, explains this view:

In our generation we have merited witnessing the revelation of all the qualities of the Holy One, Blessed is He, both the quality of judgment and the quality of mercy, more so than the earlier generations witnessed. Let us stand in awe and respect before our God. You "conceal Yourself and [yet] save people" [Isa. 45:15], and were so kind as to rescue us so that we may recount Your glory throughout the world.[50]

Rabbi Zaichyk found support for his view in the midrash about King David (Midrash Rabba, Lekh Lekha), in which the coins that were minted were engraved on one side with a stick (symbolizing suffering and wandering) and on the other side with an image of Jerusalem (symbolizing rescue, hope, and faith).[51] But the miraculous aspect of the survival does not dull the pain of the suffering, because it requires a return to the past and raises again the question:

What is the point of returning to revisit that hellish suffering? Will we find balm for our souls and peace for our spirits? By doing so we will not subdue the ghoulish nightmares that frighten us, nor will it heal the wounds etched so deeply in our souls that our hearts tremble from sorrow.[52]

Oscillation between the poles of thanksgiving and mourning, between Divine compassion and Divine justice, were intrinsic to the attitudes of the rabbis *vis-à-vis* their survival. Rabbi Yehoshua Grunwald captured this dichotomy in the title he gave his memoirs: "*Ein Dim'a*," a term comprising the last words of the verse from Psalm 116, "For You have delivered my soul from death, my eyes from tears." This expressed his ambivalent feelings, thankfulness juxtaposed with sorrow, as he explained: "You have delivered my soul from death ... *but* my eyes are still full of tears."[53] Rabbi Yaakov Pester wrote: "If you wish to understand the tears in my eyes, then you must also understand the sigh of relief emanating from them, because the two are intertwined; they come from the same Divine source."[54] Rabbi Yitzchak Yaakov Weiss of Grosswardein, who subsequently became the head of the rabbinical court of the Eida Haredit in Jerusalem, deliberated about the appropriate halakhic way to remember his own survival. Following Maimonides, he took upon himself observance of two consecutive days each year, a day of fasting followed by a festive day of thanksgiving.[55]

The rabbis who survived were a minuscule remnant of the pre-Holocaust rabbinic world and therefore they felt an impetus, as one reason for their survival, to preserve the spiritual heritage of their people. They undertook this difficult challenge, building an infrastructure to restore the survivors' faith, and to strengthen religious life on the ruins of the Holocaust. Still shattered by their private grief, they threw themselves into the building of prayer minyans and synagogues, kosher kitchens, ritual immersion pools (*mikvaot*), as well as educational institutions.

Rabbi Tzvi Hersch Meisels likened the post-Holocaust rabbis to the post-diluvian Noah.

> "Go forth from the ark" [Gen. 8:16] can be interpreted as follows. When Noah saw the terrible destruction, he despaired of being able to rebuild a new world. Thus God had to command him, "Go forth from the ark" because it was not for nothing that the Holy One Blessed be He kept Noah alive after the destruction. It was only for the purpose of rebuilding everything anew.[56]

Rabbi Avraham Izrael of Hunyad Vármegye wrote:

> I thought that I had lost all hope, because I saw no possible way out of the awful destruction around me. No ray of light, no hope that the dry

bones [vision of Ezek. 37] would come to life and the brands plucked from the fire [Zech. 3:2] would regenerate. But when I was asked ... to lead a community of survivors to rehabilitate the broken spirits, I said to myself [as Joseph in Egypt said to his brothers], "Maybe it was to be a provider that the Lord has designated me for this mission" [Gen. 45:5]; "this has emanated from the Lord" [Ps. 118:23] and it may be the reason God left me alive.... So I acquiesced and, thank God, I fulfilled the task with respect to rehabilitating the community and its institutions. I saw to it that the unfortunate orphaned young people who survived and had no parents would marry.... I took care of them as if they were my own children, my own flesh and blood.[57]

The call to remember and to memorialize the Holocaust is emphasized in these writings as a religious imperative, whether along the lines of "remembering Amalek"[58] or as a gesture of thanksgiving for a miracle, or for other reasons. In the preface to his book *Mada v-Ha-Hayim*, Rabbi Zaichyk wrote an essay titled "Remembering the Miracle" specifically on this subject.[59] Rabbi Avigdor objected to the silence of the survivors and maintained that the attempt to forget is a sign of lack of faith, does an injustice to the victims (*kedoshim*), dulls the connection with the past, and weakens the sense of obligation for the future.[60]

There are segments where rabbis lament the losses. But in general, the rabbinic memoirs are characterized by a spirit of thankfulness for rescue and of defiance. They express pride that despite the attempts of the Nazis to put an end to Jewish families and to undermine the chain of the generations, continuity has been maintained, as has the unique spiritual character of the writers and the Jewish people.

Recording their Holocaust experiences in the prefaces to books filled with Torah content is in itself part of the above-mentioned defiance. The ability to regain their stature and publish books in Jewish scholarship represents a victory over the attempts by Nazism to destroy the Jews not only physically, but also to wage a bitter war against the spirit of the Jewish people, its Torah, and its values. During the Holocaust, the destruction of Jewish books was one of the goals of Nazism, and the Jewish bookshelf was an intended victim. Thus, the survivors were adamant in expressing their spiritual survival by publishing books of Torah scholarship:

Those Amalekites wanted to blot out the name of Israel, to erase any remnant of the Jew and Judaism. To defy this I am publishing my book, a protest against their evil attempt. I proclaim loud and clear in public: the chain has not been broken.[61]

Notes

1. Raz Segal, *Yemei Hurban: ha-Merkaz ha-Yehudi be-Munkacs bi-Tkufat ha-Shoah* [Days of ruin: The Jews of Munkacs during the Holocaust] (Jerusalem: Yad Vashem Publications, 2011), 19.

2. This approach is exemplified by Ilana Rosen. See her works: *Sho'ah be-merkaz ha-hayim—nituah folkloristi shel sipure hayim mi-pi nitsole sho'ah dovre hungarit* [The Holocaust at the center of life: A folkloristic analysis of life histories told by Hungarian-speaking Holocaust survivors] (PhD diss., Hebrew University, 1994); *Sister in Sorrow—Life Histories of Female Holocaust Survivors from Hungary* (Detroit: Wayne State University Press, 2003); *Be-Auschwitz takanu be-shofar—yotsey Karpatorus mesaprim al ha-Shoah* [In Auschwitz we blew the shofar—Carpatho-Rusyn Jews remember the Holocaust] (Jerusalem: Yad Vashem and the Institute for the Study of Contemporary Jewry at the Hebrew University, 2004).

3. The concept "Orthodox" in our context means the strictly Orthodox, those Jews for whom the study and practice of Jewish law are the center of their lives. I refer here to those who were religious before the war, survived, and remained Orthodox. There are, indeed, many subdivisions and different nuances among the Orthodox, but this is irrelevant for our purposes.

4. See, for example, Amos Goldberg, "The Holocaust in the Ultra-Orthodox Press–Between Memory and Rejection" [Hebrew], *Yahadut Zemanenu—Contemporary Jewry* 11–12 (1998): 155–206; Kimmy Caplan, "Have 'Many Lies Accumulated in History Books?' The Holocaust in Ashkenazi *Haredi* Historical Consciousness in Israel," *Yad Vashem Studies* 29 (2001): 321–78. See as well Henri Lustiger Thaler, "History and Memory: The Orthodox Experience in the Bergen-Belsen Displaced Persons Camp," *Holocaust and Genocide Studies* 27, no. 1 (Spring 2013): 30–56.

5. For example: Rabbi Ephraim Oshry, *Responsa min ha-ma'amakim*, rev. ed. (1983; reprint, New York: Judaica Press, 2001); Rabbi Tzvi Hersch Meisels, *Responsa Mekadshei Hashem* (Chicago, 1955); Rabbi Yehoshua Grunwald, preface to *Chessed Yehoshua* (New York, 1948); Rabbi Yehoshua Moshe Aronson, *Alei Merorot* [Leaves of bitterness] (Bnei Brak, 1996) and

the chapter on him in Esther Farbstein, *Hidden in Thunder* (Jerusalem: Mossad Harav Kook, 2007), chap. 6.

6. See, for example, the research by Rosen, cited in note 2.

7. For example, Rabbi Avraham Yosef Pesah, *Mei ha-be'er* (New York, 1944); Rabbi Eliezer Dunner, *Zikaron Avraham Moshe* (Jerusalem, 1945).

8. Among writers of autobiographical material were Don Isaac Abrabanel (d. 1508), Rabbi Moshe Isserles, the *Rema* (d. 1572), Rabbi Yaakov David Wilovsky, the *Ridbaz* (d. 1913), and Yaakov Yehoshua Falk, the *Pnei Yehoshua* (d. 1756). See Esther Farbstein, *The Forgotten Memoirs: Moving Personal Accounts from Rabbis Who Survived the Holocaust* (New York: Mesorah Artscroll, 2011), 16–17.

9. Such tragedies could be on individual or public levels, such as after a plague or after the Chmielnicki massacres of 1648–49.

10. *Korot ha-Shoah ba-mevo'ot la-sifrut la-rabanit* [History of the Shoah in the prefaces to rabbinic literature], CD-ROM database compiled by Esther Farbstein (Jerusalem: Michlalah, and Tel Aviv: Tal Systems). See the Zachor-Michlalah website http://zachor.michlalah.edu.

11. In Hebrew: Esther Farbstein, Asaf Yedidya, and Nathan Cohen, eds., *Zikaron ba-sefer: korot ha-Sho'ah ba-mevo'ot la-sifrut ha-rabanit* [Memories in a book: History of the Shoah in the prefaces to rabbinic literature] (Jerusalem: Rubin Mass, 2008). Fifteen memoirs were annotated by Esther Farbstein, and translated into English by Jessica Setbon and Shira Leibowitz Schmidt. See Farbstein, *Forgotten Memoirs*.

12. See the annotated English translations in *The Forgotten Memoirs* of these six memoirs, which are only a few examples of descriptions of the hundreds of pre-Holocaust Jewish communities mentioned in various rabbinic memoirs. The English was translated from the following sources, respectively: Rabbi Avraham Abba Resnick, *Klei sharet* (Netanya, 1957); Rabbi Yaakov Avigdor, *Chelek Yaakov* (New York, 1950); Rabbi Yehoshua Grunwald, *Chessed Yehoshua* (New York, 1948); Rabbi Chaim Zaichyk, *Ha-mada ve-ha-chaim* (New York, 1952); Rabbi Moshe Rothenberg, *Bikurei aviv* (St. Louis, 1942); Rabbi Yechiel Yaakov Weinberg, *Seridei eish* (Jerusalem: Mossad Harav Kook, 1999).

13. See the above-cited research by Rosen, note 2.

14. See Esther Farbstein, *Pesukim ve-zichronot* [Verses and memories], in *Be-seter ha-madrega* (Jerusalem: Mossad Harav Kook, 2013).

15. Channah Hendler, "Use of Hasidic Stories and Homilies in Prefaces to Rabbinic [Holocaust] Literature" [Hebrew], in Farbstein, Yedidya, and Cohen, *Zikaron ba-sefer*, 96–97.

16. Rabbi Moshe Lemberger, *Klei golah* (New York, 1996), 31. In English, Rabbi Moshe Nosson Notta Lemberger, "In the Merit of Our Holy

Forefathers," in Farbstein, *Forgotten Memoirs*, 225; Rabbi Avraham Schlager, *Afikei yam* (Montreal, 1987), 25.

17. Kimmy Caplan, "Have 'Many Lies Accumulated in History Books'? The Holocaust in Ashkenazi *Haredi* Historical Consciousness in Israel," *Yad Vashem Studies* 29 (2001): 321–75, esp. 326; also, Michal Shaul refers to this as a "surprising phenomenon" in "Ultra-Orthodox Holocaust Survivors Confront Their Survival" [in Hebrew], in Farbstein, Yedidya, and Cohen, *Zikaron ba-sefer*, 38–62, esp. 49.

18. Rabbi Tzvi Hersch Meisels, "Sanctifying His Name," in Farbstein, *Forgotten Memoirs*, 259.

19. Rabbi Yosef Grunwald, "So That Our Spirits Did Not Fall Completely," in Farbstein, *Forgotten Memoirs*, 128; for a general discussion see Havi Dreifuss (Ben-Sasson), "Like Sheep without a Shepherd? Rabbis and Their Status during the Shoah" [Hebrew], in Farbstein, Yedidya, and Cohen, *Zikaron ba-sefer*, 143–67.

20. Rabbi Asher Pinchas Goldberger, *Minhat Asher* (Brooklyn, 1989), 12. The author, head of the yeshiva and rabbinical court in Nagymegyer (present-day Velky Meder), Slovakia, was a student of Rabbi Chaim Elazar Shapira, the rabbi of Munkacs. His father, wife, and children were murdered during the Holocaust.

21. Rabbi Alter Yitzchak Isaac Weinberger, "My Eye, Eye Sheds Tears," in Farbstein, *Forgotten Memoirs*, 500 and 518ff.

22. Rabbi Yaakov Avigdor, "Our Heroism," in Farbstein, *Forgotten Memoirs*, 54ff.

23. Esther Farbstein, *Hidden in the Heights: Orthodox Jewry in Hungary during the Holocaust* (Jerusalem: Mossad Harav Kook, 2014), 675.

24. Rabbi Alter Yitzchak Isaac Weinberger, "My Eye, Eye Sheds Tears," in Farbstein, *Forgotten Memoirs*, 481, 489.

25. Rabbi Tzvi Hersch Meisels, *Zer zahav*, in *Responsa Mekadshei Hashem* [Sanctifying his name], sec. 72. The expression "613 mitzvot" refers to the enumeration of positive and negative precepts totaling 613, a number that symbolizes total commitment to observance of Jewish law.

26. Rabbi Moshe Nosson Notta Lemberger, "In the Merit of Our Holy Forefathers," in Farbstein, *Forgotten Memoirs*, 214–16.

27. Rabbi Yaakov Avigdor, "Our Heroism," in Farbstein, *Forgotten Memoirs*, 55–56n.25.

28. Ibid.

29. Ibid., 59.

30. Ibid., 55n.25.

31. Rabbi Alter Yitzchak Isaac Weinberger, in ibid., 463ff.

32. Avraham HaCohen, *Brit Avraham HaCohen* (New York, 1993), 336–451.

33. Rabbi Alter Yitzchak Isaac Weinberger, "My Eye, My Eye Sheds Tears," in Farbstein, *Forgotten Memoirs*, 463–530; Rabbi Kalman Landau, *Menat ḥelki* [Hebrew] (Jerusalem, 2004).

34. Rabbi Baruch Rabinowitz, "Miracle upon Miracle," in Farbstein, *Forgotten Memoirs*, 318–43; HaCohen, *Brit Avraham HaCohen*, 345.

35. Rabbi Chaim Ephraim Zaichyk, "Remembering the Miracle, in Farbstein, *Forgotten Memoirs*, 572–609; Rabbi Israel Shabbtai Schepansky, preface to "From the Vale of Tears," in *She'eirit Israel* (New York, 1997), esp. 25–31.

36. HaCohen, *Brit Avraham HaCohen*, 362.

37. Elie Wiesel, *All Rivers Run to the Sea: Memoirs*, trans. Jon Rothschild (New York: Knopf, 1995), 87.

38. Rabbi Tzvi Hersch Meisels, "Sanctifying His Name," in Farbstein, *Forgotten Memoirs*, 266–71.

39. Rabbi Yehoshua Grunwald, in Farbstein, *Forgotten Memoirs*, 64–117.

40. Rabbi Moshe N.N. Lemberger, in Farbstein, *Forgotten Memoirs*, 201.

41. Ibid., 218.

42. Rabbi Alter Yitzchak Weinberger, in Farbstein, *Forgotten Memoirs*, 477.

43. See Sara Kaplan, "The Memory of the Holocaust and Its Memorialization by Ultra-Orthodox Jews" [Hebrew], (Master's thesis, Hebrew University, 1998), esp. 49. The biblical precedents referred to are the binding of Isaac, Gen. 22; Amalek, Exod. 17, Deut. 25; and the silence of Aaron, Lev. 10. The martyrology is found in the liturgy of Yom Kippur and Tisha B'av.

44. Rabbi Alter Yitzchak Isaac Weinberger, "My Eye, My Eye Sheds Tears," in Farbstein, *Forgotten Memoirs*, 468, "A slaughter that the world has never before seen." The uniqueness of the Holocaust in Jewish history is also discussed in *Forgotten Memoirs* on pp. 44, 50, 439, 479, and 535. Nathan Cohen analyzes this approach in "'My Eyes Weep and Weep': Memoirs of Rabbi Alter Yitzchak Isaac Weinberger of Turka," in Farbstein, Yedidya, and Cohen, *Zikaron ba-sefer*.

45. Rabbi Schepansky, preface to "From the Vale of Tears."

46. See the memoirs of two rabbis who survived on the Kasztner train: Rabbi Shalom Kraus, *Divrei Shalom* (New York, 1964), and Rabbi Akiva Glasner, *'Ikvei Ha-Tzon* (London, 1958). See also a lengthy discussion of the Kasztner train in Esther Farbstein, "Talks with the Devil," chap. 4 in *Hidden in the Heights: Orthodox Jewry in Hungary during the Holocaust* (Jerusalem: Mossad Harav Kook, 2014), 330–72.

47. Rabbi Yaakov Avigdor, "Our Heroism," in Farbstein, *Forgotten Memoirs*, 51.

48. Shaul, "Ultra-Orthodox Holocaust Survivors," 38–62.
49. Rabbi Aharon Maggid, *Beit Aharon* (New York, 1962), 49.
50. Rabbi Chaim Ephraim Zaichyk, "Remembering the Miracle," in Farbstein, *Forgotten Memoirs*, 593.
51. Ibid., 590.
52. Rabbi Avraham Gustman, preface to *Panim Masbirot* (New York, 1966).
53. Rabbi Yehoshua Grunwald, "Wellspring of Tears," in Farbstein, *Forgotten Memoirs*, 65.
54. Rabbi Yaakov Pester, introduction to *Birkat Yaakov* (Chicago, 1981), 1.
55. Rabbi Yitzchak Yaakov Weiss, "Publicizing the Miracle," in Farbstein, *Forgotten Memoirs*, 536.
56. Rabbi Tzvi Hersch Meisels, *Sha'ar Mahmadim, Zer Zahav*, in *Responsa Mekadshei Hashem* (Chicago, 1955).
57. Rabbi Avraham Izrael, *Imrei Avraham* (New York, 1960), 7.
58. Deut. 25:17–19, "Remember what Amalek did to you . . . you shall not forget."
59. Rabbi Chaim Ephraim Zaichyk, "Remembering the Miracle," in Farbstein, *Forgotten Memoirs*, 577–80.
60. Rabbi Yaakov Avigdor, in Farbstein, *Forgotten Memoirs*, 41–61.
61. Rabbi D. Tz. Halperin, *Hilula d'Pascha* (New York, 2001), 6–7.

Bibliography

Aronson, Rabbi Yehoshua Moshe. *Alei Merorot* [Leaves of bitterness]. Bnei Brak, 1996.
Avigdor, Rabbi Yaakov. *Chelek Yaakov*. New York, 1950.
Caplan, Kimmy. "Have 'Many Lies Accumulated in History Books?' The Holocaust in Ashkenazi Haredi Historical Consciousness in Israel." *Yad Vashem Studies* 29 (2001): 321–78.
Dunner, Rabbi Eliezer. *Zikaron Avraham Moshe*. Jerusalem, 1945.
Farbstein, Esther. *The Forgotten Memoirs: Moving Personal Accounts from Rabbis who Survived the Holocaust*. New York: Mesorah Artscroll, 2011.
———. *Hidden in the Heights: Orthodox Jewry in Hungary during the Holocaust*. Jerusalem: Mossad Harav Kook, 2014.
———. *Hidden in Thunder: Perspectives on Faith, Halakhah and Leadership during the Holocaust*. Jerusalem: Mossad Harav Kook, 2007.

———, comp. *Korot ha-Shoah be-mevu'ot le-sifrut rabbanit* [History of the Shoah in the prefaces of rabbinic works]. CD-ROM database (Jerusalem: Michlalah, and Tel Aviv: Tal Systems).

———. *Pesukim ve-zichronot* [Verses and memories]. In *Be-seter ha-madrega*. Jerusalem: Mossad Harav Kook, 2013.

Farbstein, Esther, Asaf Yedidya, and Nathan Cohen, eds. *Zikaron ba-sefer: korot ha-Sho'ah ba-mevo'ot la-sifrut ha-rabanit* [Memories in a book: History of the Shoah in the prefaces to rabbinic literature]. Jerusalem: Rubin Mass, 2008.

Glasner, Rabbi Akiva. *Ikvei Ha-Tzon*. London, 1958.

Goldberg, Amos. "The Holocaust in the Ultra-Orthodox Press—Between Memory and Rejection" [Hebrew]. *Yahadut Zemanenu—Contemporary Jewry* 11–12 (1998): 155–206.

Goldberger, Rabbi Pinchas Asher. *Minhat Asher*. Brooklyn, NY, 1989.

Grunwald, Rabbi Yehoshua. *Chessed Yehoshua*. New York, 1948.

Gustman, Rabbi Avraham. Preface to *Panim Masbirot*. New York, 1966.

HaCohen, Avraham. *Brit Avraham HaCohen*. New York, 1993.

Halperin, Rabbi D. Tz. *Hilula d'Pascha*. New York, 2001.

Izrael, Rabbi Avraham. *Imrei Avraham*. New York, 1960.

Kaplan, Sara. "The Memory of the Holocaust and Its Memorialization by Ultra-Orthodox Jews." [Hebrew]. Master's thesis, Hebrew University, 1998.

Kraus, Rabbi Shalom. *Divrei Shalom*. New York, 1964.

Landau, Rabbi Kalman. *Menat helki* [Hebrew]. Jerusalem, 2004.

Lemberger, Rabbi Moshe Nosson Notta. *Klei golah*. New York, 1996.

Lustiger Thaler, Henri. "History and Memory: The Orthodox Experience in the Bergen-Belsen Displaced Persons Camp." *Holocaust and Genocide Studies* 27, no. 1 (Spring 2013): 30–56.

Maggid, Rabbi Aharon. *Beit Aharon*. New York, 1962.

Meisels, Rabbi Tzvi Hersch. *Responsa Mekadshei Hashem*. Chicago, 1955.

Oshry, Rabbi Ephraim. *Responsa min ha-ma'amakim*. 1983. Reprint, New York: Judaica Press, 2001.

Pesah, Rabbi Avraham Yosef. *Mei ha-be'er*. New York, 1944.

Pester, Rabbi Yaakov. Introduction to *Birkat Yaakov*. Chicago, 1981.

Resnick, Rabbi Avraham Abba. *Klei sharet*. Netanya, 1957.

Rosen, Ilana. *Be-Auschwitz takanu be-shofar—yotsey Karpatorus mesaprim al ha-Shoah* [In Auschwitz we blew the shofar—Carpatho-Rusyn Jews remember the Holocaust]. Jerusalem: Yad Vashem and the Institute for the Study of Contemporary Jewry at the Hebrew University, 2004.

———. "*Sho'ah be-merkaz ha-hayim—nituah folkloristi shel sipure hayim mi-pi nitsole sho'ah dovre hungarit*" [The Holocaust at the center of life: A folkloristic analysis of life histories told by Hungarian-speaking Holocaust survivors]. PhD diss., Hebrew University, 1994.

———. *Sister in Sorrow—Life Histories of Female Holocaust Survivors from Hungary*. Detroit: Wayne State University Press, 2003.

Rothenberg, Rabbi Moshe. *Bikurei aviv*. St. Louis, 1942.

Schepansky, Rabbi Israel Shabbtai. Preface to "From the Vale of Tears," in *She'erit Israel*. New York, 1997.

Schlager, Rabbi Avraham. *Afikei yam*. Montreal, 1987.

Segal, Raz. *Yemei Hurban: ha-Merkaz ha-Yehudi be-Munkacs bi-Tkufat ha-Shoah* [Days of ruin: The Jews of Munkacs during the Holocaust]. Jerusalem: Yad Vashem Publications, 2011.

Weinberg, Rabbi Yaakov Yechiel. *Seridei Eish*. Jerusalem: Mossad Harav Kook, 1999.

Wiesel, Elie. *All Rivers Run to the Sea: Memoirs*. Trans. Jon Rothschild. New York: Knopf, 1995.

Zaichyk, Rabbi Chaim Ephraim. *Ha-mada ve-ha-chaim*. New York, 1952.

5

"Solidarity and Suffering"

Lager Vapniarka among the Camps of Transnistria

LEO SPITZER

Transnistria and the Romanian Concentration Camps

Early in the summer of 1941, as a reward for Romania's material support and military alliance with Nazi Germany in the war against the Soviet Union, Adolf Hitler promised his counterpart Führer, the Conducator Marshal Ion Antonescu, Romanian control of conquered territory east of the Dniester River in southern Ukraine. On August 30, that verbal promise was formalized in an agreement signed at Tighina (then in Bessarabia, now in Moldova) granting Romania political, military, and administrative command of what came to be known as Transnistria ("across the Dniester [Nistru]"), a territory nearly 65,000 square kilometers between the Dniester and the Bug Rivers, west to east, and the Black Sea and Lyadova River, south to north.[1] The Tighina Agreement also permitted the German military to set up naval and air bases in Transnistria, and allowed German units to continue to enter the region "to perform special jobs"—this, in the aftermath of the wave of genocidal "cleansing" operations in which nearly one-third of the area's Jewish population of approximately 300,000 were murdered during the initial weeks following Germany's invasion of the Soviet Union by the Einsatzgruppe D, an SS mobile death squad, and by members of the German Eleventh and Romanian Third and Fourth Armies. The agreement, moreover, allowed German-owned companies that built roads and bridges for the German military to operate in the area.[2]

The Tighina document left unstated that some of the "special jobs" performed by the German military would eventually be undertaken on behalf of or in conjunction with the Todt Construction Company: periodic raids or "actions" across the Bug River (which separated Romanian from German occupied territory)[3] to "recruit" surviving Jews for forced labor. These occasional German intrusions into Transnistria, however—especially when they followed notification of Romanian officials—hardly fazed Romanian authorities. Indeed, they fit well into Marshal Antonescu's vision for the future of the territory. He and other Romanian leaders viewed Transnistria as a long-term acquisition—as a new province of Greater Romania—into which ethnic Romanian settlers would eventually be introduced after the defeat of the Soviet Union and the removal of the region's Jewish inhabitants. He appointed a civilian governor for the new territory, Professor Gheorghe Alexianu, and issued orders dividing Transnistria into thirteen administrative districts, each governed by a prefect—an army officer or gendarmerie colonel—and into sixty-four (later sixty-five) subdistricts headed by pretors: military officers, jurists, or government officials from the Romanian heartland.[4] The Todt intrusions and the German military raids on the company's behalf reduced the number of Jews on Transnistrian soil further and thus advanced Antonescu's long-term goal. But they were hardly sufficient to eliminate Jews from the province, especially after the reconquest and Romanian reacquisition of Bessarabia and the northern Bukowina province following the German-Romanian invasion of the Soviet Union in June 1941, and the decision on the part of Antonescu and the Civilian-Military Cabinet under his authority to deport hundreds of thousands of Jews from these so-called lost provinces (as well as from the southern Bukowina) to the east.[5]

Initially, underlying these eastward deportations was the assumption that Jews surviving their brutal displacements would eventually be transferred out of Romanian territory altogether—across the Bug River into German-controlled Ukraine, where they would be subjected to "special handling," the euphemism for annihilation.[6] Transnistria, in this supposition, was to be nothing more than a large-scale temporary "holding" or "containment" place for deported Jews. The Tighina Agreement, however, stipulated that Bessarabian and Bukowinan Jews deported to Transnistria, as well as the local Ukrainian Jews who had survived the initial Einzatzgruppe D and Romanian executions, were to be transferred across the Bug only "following the completion of military operations."[7] In the meantime, they were to be kept in the province in ghettos and labor concentration camps.

It was to implement this stipulation that the Romanian authorities established large and small ghettos—temporary in intent—in towns and villages throughout Transnistria, both for local Jews and for the masses of incoming Jewish deportees. Moghilev on the Dniester and Bershad, by the Bug, were the largest of these ghettos. They also created numerous concentration camps, of which Lager Vapniarka, the central focus of this essay, was one of the most notorious and distinct.

Unlike the Nazi camps in Germany, Austria, Latvia, Lithuania, occupied Poland, or near the eastern bank of the Bug in occupied Ukraine, which were organized and were generally operated as part of a centralized network and planned system, the Romanian camps were, for the most part, set up in a very improvisatory manner.[8] The Nazi camp network included detention camps, labor camps, reeducation camps, transit camps, prisoner-of-war camps, and, with the implementation of the Final Solution, extermination camps. A number of them—such as Auschwitz-Birkenau, the most infamous among these—combined two or more of these functions and were equipped with gas chambers and crematoria. All of the Nazi camps, guarded by SS sentries, contained housing barracks for their prisoners, as well as buildings in which items of clothing, valuables, and other possessions brought into the camps by arriving inmates were "mined," sorted, and sent off to the Reich to further the war effort. In lieu of their own clothing, prisoners were made to wear striped uniforms marked with identifying insignia categorizing them according to national or "racial" origin and the grounds for their incarceration. They were provided with minimal daily amounts of food and water by camp authorities, and were organized hierarchically within their own ranks so that more privileged inmates—barrack heads, kapos, and other "special" kommandos—would battle to defend and enlarge their advantages over the less fortunate others.

Romanian camps in Transnistria, on the other hand, shared no such organizational and operational uniformity. Although identified with terms similar to those used in the Nazi network—"detention," "holding," "internment," "political," "labor," and "death camps"—the differentiation among them, as well as between them and some of the more restrictive Transnistrian ghettos—like in Shpikov and Tulchin—was quite fluid, if not blurry.⁹ A brief comparative examination of three dozens of these Romanian concentration camps—Bogdanovka, Pechora, and Cariera de Piatră—as a prelude to a more detailed examination of Vapniarka—should illustrate the range of practices characterizing the Romanian camp "system," or, perhaps more accurately, the lack of a system.

Three Camps

Located in northeastern and east-central Transnistria, close to or directly on the western bank of the Bug River—Bogdanovka in Golta, Cariera de Piatră in Tulchin, and Pechora in Vinnitsa district—these camps reflected the generally haphazard and crude efforts by Romanian Transnistrian authorities to concentrate, dispossess, extract labor by force, and eliminate both the remaining Ukrainian Jews in the province and the thousands of incoming Jewish deportees from Bessarabia and the Bukowina. All three camps were, in effect, dumping grounds—places improvised to receive Jews forcibly displaced from Odessa and southern Transnistria in the case of Bogdanovka, or, as with Cariera de Piatră and Pechora, to alleviate overcrowding and pressures on shelter and food in larger ghettos like Moghilev and Tulchin. All three were places where masses of Jews starved or froze to death, or died as victims of beatings, robberies, rapes, and executions by Romanian gendarmes and gangs of Ukrainians and ethnic Germans allied to them.¹⁰

The Bogdanovka camp, established in October 1941, near the town by that name on the Bug, on a large state farm (sovkhoz) that had been abandoned after the Soviet retreat, was the biggest Romanian concentration camp in Transnistria and the one, following the horrific annihilation of its inmates, with the briefest existence. Some 48,000 Jews from Odessa and approximately 7,000 from Bessarabia were deported there, allegedly to await further transport eastward, across the Bug into German territory, as soon as the military conditions for such a transport (a stipulation in the Tighina Agreement) were in existence.¹¹ Like in Domanevka and Akmechetka, two smaller Golta district camps in what came to known as the "Kingdom of Death," or in camps established further north in

Transnistria, the Romanians made no preparation to receive and maintain the hordes of deportees they amassed there. They took no responsibility for any of their most basic needs, not even minimally in order to keep them alive and to thus extract their labor. They built no barracks or latrines, and forced the inmates to seek shelter in whatever abandoned structures or ruins that existed within the camp's perimeter. Abandoned pigpens, stables, and bombed-out houses without floors or roofs served this purpose for thousands.[12] The authorities, moreover, neither fed nor provided the Jews with a regular supply of water. Food was only available to inmates able to make contact with local Ukrainian peasants and able to pay or barter for it. By thus severely restricting or denying nourishment and shelter, the Romanian government's objective for Jews there, as well as in other Transnistrian camps, was (as Jean Ancel indicated) their "'natural' extermination."[13] Vapniarka, as we shall see, differed in this regard.

But mass starvation did not occur fast enough among the tens of thousands of Jews squeezed into Bogdanovka. In mid-December 1941, two months after the camp was established, typhus broke out among inmates, posing a threat of contagion to Romanian gendarmerie guards and the inhabitants of the surrounding areas. Preemptively, Romanian officials settled on a radical action: to kill the entire population of the camp. This decision was made at the highest levels of authority: by Transnistrian provincial government officials, and with Marshal Antonescu's approval.[14] On orders from Modest Isopescu, the Golta district prefect, Romanian troops and gendarmerie, Ukrainian policemen, and local ethnic Germans and civilians undertook the mass murder of the Jews imprisoned in the camp. Starting with children, the elderly, and the disabled on December 21, 1941, the last day of Hanukkah, and continuing with the others until January 3 or 4, 1942 (only taking a break for the Christmas holiday), they slaughtered nearly 48,000 inmates by shooting or incinerating them. The carnage was then continued in the two other, smaller, camps in Golta district, Domanevka, and Akmechetka. Ultimately, a total of well over 100,000 Jews were liquidated in this region—the entire Jewish community of southern Transnistria. The "Jewish problem" in the Golta district was thus, to all extents and purposes, resolved.[15]

Further north, however, this was not at all the case. Transnistrian Jews that had survived the initial German-Romanian "cleansing," as well as thousands of deported Bessarabian and Bukowinan Jews, continued to exist in the province and, in the estimation of Romanian officials, had excessively strained the limits of available resources in the already established and overpopulated ghettos. Both Pechora and Cariera de Piatră concentration camps were thus established during the summer of 1942 as sites of deposit for recent deportees, as well as for Jews from the resource-pressured surrounding regions.

These concentration camps were much smaller than their Golta antecedents, but, like them, evidenced little practical infrastructural or longer-range planning for the inmates they would contain. The majority of Jews incarcerated in the Pechora camp were no doubt brought there to perish from exposure and starvation by the "natural extermination" process that had been employed in Bogdanovka and other "Kingdom of Death" camps. They were thus, essentially, deposited there and abandoned to fend for themselves. The pastoral site of this camp on the banks of the Bug—on the wooded grounds of a large, graceful, two-storied columned neo-Classical private estate that had become a tuberculosis sanatorium after the Russian Revolution—was perhaps incongruous with the horrors the Romanians perpetrated there.[16] But accounts by Jews that survived the camp after its liberation by the Red Army in March 1944 consistently highlight the fact that the Romanians provided neither food nor water at Pechora, and that "people fell like flies from starvation and illness." A number of survivor testimonies also tell of desperation so great that they led to instances of human cannibalism.[17]

The nearby camp at Cariera de Piatră differed somewhat from Pechora in the functions it was intended to perform. Located some fifteen kilometers north of the Ladijin ghetto, on an elevated plateau a short ascent from the banks of the Bug, it had once been an active rock quarry that the Soviets, before the war, had turned into a punitive camp for criminals. After the Romanians acquired Cariera de Piatră, they initially used the ruins of that camp to relocate hundreds of Jewish inmates who had been deported from Cernăuți's asylum for the mentally ill in the first transport in the summer of 1942. Those among these unfortunate inmates who managed to remain alive did so by finding shelter in wrecked guard and storage sheds that had partially been built into the rock, and by scrounging for whatever edibles they could find. They were joined on the upper plateau level of the Cariera by some 4,000 Jewish deportees from

Bessarabia and Bukowina, including the parents of Paul Celan, the poet Selma Meerbaum-Eisinger with her parents, the artist Arnold Daghani, and the future psychoanalyst Dori Laub together with his mother. The inmates were told that this camp was a transit camp from which they would be transferred to work destinations elsewhere.[18]

Although many of the Jews sent to Cariera de Piatră died there or in its vicinity—the physically impaired and mentally disturbed inmates were shot in late August 1942, by Ukrainian guards working for the Romanians—the camp did indeed serve as a transit point from which deportees were dispersed, for the most part to places like Mikhailowka on the eastern side of the Bug that were run as slave labor supply camps by the Germans for the Todt Construction Company. On August 18, 1942, for example, German soldiers came to the Cariera and, with the approval of the Romanian district prefect Colonel Loghin, selected some 1,400 inmates for forced labor in German-controlled territory.[19]

The Romanian willingness to supply the Germans with inmate workers, most of whom were shot after their labor was forcibly extracted, and their willful neglect and starvation of prisoners were, of course, complimentary in terms of their deadly end results. Both satisfied the desire of Marshal Antonescu and others to bring about a Jew-free Transnistria. That such German "recruitment" of workers also happened in a "natural extermination" camp like Pechora, however, and that it took place in Bogdanovka as well, despite the ghastliness of conditions there, indicates that even in the worst of the camps some inmates appeared fit enough to be taken and used as laborers. Certainly, the fact that some Jews managed to extend their life chances for a while in these camps, or that a sizeable minority of them survived the camps and the Transnistria deportation altogether, highlights the interstices that existed in the Romanian treatment of Jews during these years, not only in Transnistria, but throughout the Romanian realm. The very qualities that defined the Romanians as disorganized, unsystematic, improvisatory, haphazard, and venal in contrast to the Germans also provided Jewish deportees and camp inmates some small spaces and possibilities to barter for food, to bribe for favors, to communicate, and even to organize in order to resist and continue to live.

A more detailed examination of the Vapniarka concentration camp perhaps illustrates this point most effectively.

LEO SPITZER

Lager Vapniarka

From Nathan Simon's account:

> On the 16th of September 1942 we arrive in Vapniarka. It is a small town, between the Dniester and the Bug, located nearly mid-point on the rail-line between Lvov and Odessa.
>
> After everyone had left the train, we are compelled to line up in eight files and placed under the control of Romanian gendarmes. A gigantic human snake, whose tail-end I could no longer see, then creeps along the few kilometers separating the train-station from the lager. Ukrainian peasants stare at us during that march, and women throw bread into our midst. But these expressions of pity are quickly halted with club and rifle-butt blows from the gendarmes who guard us—by blows and shouts that they also unhesitatingly direct at anyone who, out of wariness or weakness, is unable to keep up with the pace. Faint prisoners have to be carried by others; weak ones, supported by their companions.
>
> In this manner, because we were all nearly totally worn out by hunger, thirst, and the ordeal of our horrendous journey in primitive cattle-cars, it takes some hours until we reach the lager. There, outside its gates, we are once again given over to military authorities. A sergeant, sitting by a table, notes down the name, age, and last previous residence of every single one of us prisoners....
>
> I look around. Three massive two-story brick buildings and a large yard surrounded by a high barbed-wire fence with only a single gateway. On one of its sides, on a raised wooden platform, stands a shed where guards keep strict track of everyone who passes by them. Watchtowers, manned by sentries guarding the entire lager with machineguns, are located along the perimeter of the fencing. A smaller, partially destroyed, house stands opposite the brick buildings—the former kitchen and its storage rooms....[20]

From Arthur Kessler's memoir:

> At the moment the camp is inhabited by only a few people from ghettos in the surrounding area, arrested for diverse violations, and a few

hundred Ukrainians. But preparations have been made for the several thousand that are expected. We walk as far as the first large building and see an immense hall, with small rooms off to the sides. We deposit our belongings in the first of these rooms and sit on them. More and more newcomers arrive and do likewise.... This continues until evening, until everyone has been moved from the station to the camp. There we lie, a gray, dirty mass of humanity. Looking at us, you cannot tell male and female apart, old or young. Nor distinguish our faces. Gray on gray, people and bags, tired bundles of flesh and rags.[21]

Vapniarka was first established as a detention camp in Transnistria's Zugastru district in the early fall of 1941. It had been located on the grounds of an ex-Soviet cavalry training base—a place whose structures, furnishings, and equipment had largely been dismantled and taken, or sabotaged and destroyed, when the Red Army withdrew in the aftermath of the July 1941 German-Romanian invasion of the Soviet Union. Despite the ruins and reigning chaos at the site, however, around one thousand deportees were brought there not long afterward: some minor bureaucrats who had been Soviet employees in Odessa and Tiraspol, and Jews from Bessarabia and the Bukowina who had failed in their efforts to flee to Russia in advance of the German-Romanian onslaught. Within a few months of their arrival, about half of these inmates died from starvation, the freezing winter, or a typhus epidemic. The remaining prisoners were then forced to abandon the camp, marched to the outskirts of the village of Koslova, and shot by Romanian gendarmes.[22] But Vapniarka was again employed not long afterward to imprison individuals accused of various "economic crimes" (such as blackmarketeering) and to fulfill what was to become its main purpose: to hold and punish suspected Communist sympathizers, Trotskyists, Socialists, and political dissidents. Officially, as proclaimed in the February 1942 decree signed by the Governor of Transnistria, Gheorghe Alexianu, it was to serve as a "Lager for Communists of Christian descent," and it was to be set up to receive and house approximately 5,000 inmates.[23] Despite this specific religious stipulation, however, the vast majority of persons deported to the camp were Jews. About twenty percent of the inmates were women—among them, a few were interned along with their children.

In August and September 1942, around 1,200 Jewish deportees were brought there—from Bucharest and other core areas of "Old Romania" (the Regat), but also from Bukowina, Bessarabia, and other Romanian annexed areas.[24] Although for the most part arbitrarily arrested, all were considered "politicals"—persons who had been active Communists or suspected of Communist leanings.

From Arthur Kessler's memoir:

Next morning the doors are opened at dawn and we take our first look around. There are no soldiers inside the camp compound. The three buildings [in which we sleep] are derelict. There are no window frames or panes, the floors are dirty and defective, some doors are missing and those still in place are without locks.... In the small house, opposite the three large ones, that was once a kitchen, big vats remain. But doors and windows, banisters, and everything else that is easily removable have disappeared.... On the other side of the yard, is a latrine, professionally dug and covered with wooden boards, which provides 40 holes. There are water pipes in two places in the yard, but no water.

... Summoned for roll call for the first time, we line up somewhat orderly, first women, then men.... The gate is thrown wide open, and the commandant of the internment area, Colonel Murgescu, appears with a following of officers and non-coms.... In Napoleonic fashion he clutches his right hand between the lapels of his coat and, with feet planted far apart and heavy-jowled head thrown back on a fat neck—a martial specimen, indeed—he turns his attention to us.... His speech is short: "On the slope behind the camp you can see the graves of 550 people who were in the camp before you. They died of typhoid. Try to do better if you can...."

From Nathan Simon's account:

As a welcoming speech, Colonel Murgescu hammers us with the rules of the camp, replete with threats, warning us for example that anyone attempting to escape will be executed by firing-squad. He finishes with these words: "You entered the Lager on two legs. But if you are still alive, you will leave it on all fours!"[25]

The first of the three residential buildings ("blocks" or "pavilions," as the inmates and camp officials referred to them) housed the women and children on the second floor, and the infirmary—of which Dr. Kessler was put in charge—on the ground level. Most of the men lived in the smaller rooms and the large dormitory space of the middle building and the third pavilion held some three hundred Ukrainians who had preceded the arrival of the Jewish inmates by a few months—men and women who included partisans, Seventh Day Adventists, and common criminals among their numbers. The buildings were locked in the evening after the lineup and roll call, and pails were placed near their staircases in each to serve the after-curfew need for nighttime relief. Throughout the night, at regular intervals and from tower to tower, the guards called out to each other in Romanian: "Poooost Number One: Aaall is well...," "Poooost Number Two, Aaall is well...."[26]

But despite such assurances, conditions at Vapniarka Lager were initially atrocious. "The place looked as though it had suffered through a storm from Hell," Nathan Simon recalled.[27] The pavilions did not contain any beds, chairs, tables, or storage cubicles. For some time after the inmates' arrival in the fall of 1942, cold and wind raged through the paneless window frames. Miraculously, two tile stoves did remain functional on opposite walls of the large rooms in each of the buildings. But there was little burnable material to heat them at first, other than what could be salvaged from odds and ends trashed within the buildings themselves.

Inmates were subjected to extremely harsh, forced physical labor and deprivation. Their water supply was shut off at the whim of the camp commander—a single valve controlled the waterflow into the two pipes inside the campgrounds. Thirst was induced as a punishment.

On a daily basis, inmates carrying whatever containers and implements they could manage to acquire—bowls, small pots, discarded cans, partially broken glass dishes—fetched a thick greenish-yellow soup made from chickling peas, approximately four hundred grams per person, from the old kitchen building. Each person also received a two-hundred-gram slice of bread made from a mix of barley and moistened straw—bitter tasting, according to Nathan Simon ("soapy," in Arthur Kessler's recollection), and difficult to digest.

Lathyrismus Sativus: Vapniarka's Disease

The chickling peas used in the soup had originated in a warehouse that had belonged to the Soviet cavalry school contingent that had inhabited the site before the Vapniarka Lager was set up. The Russians had occasionally used them as a horsefeed supplement in a blend with oats, chaff, and other fibrous ingredients—but never alone, in pure form, because of their known toxicity. When the Red Army cavalry soldiers abandoned Vapniarka, they allegedly poured gasoline near the warehouse in order to make its contents unusable to the incoming Germans and Romanians. But the latter salvaged much of the feed and began to use chickling peas as the main ingredient in the soup fed to Vapniarka's inmates.[28]

At the end of December 1942, almost five months after the Ukrainian prisoners in Pavilion III and some three and a half months after the others had been introduced to this pea-soup diet, the first among them showed the symptoms of a strange illness: severe cramps, paralysis of the lower limbs, and a loss of kidney functions.

From Arthur Kessler's account:

> We initially rationalize the first symptoms of the sickness. The boils are caused by dirt and nutritional deficiencies, the feverish intestinal catarrhs were introduced into the camp by one inmate and spread by the flies, bellies are bloated because of the peas in our food. As for the rest, we are all human and subject to influenza or pneumonia and even to TB. Many suffer from bladder problems and run day and night seeking relief. But this is no wonder if one considers how we squat in the open on the ice cold beams of the latrine—squat for hours to rid ourselves of gas. One has only to look at the bare bottom of a neighbor, his skin blue from the cold, to understand the consequences. So many complain about "carcei,"—cramps in their calves, as a colleague explains to me. Others complain about cramps in their arms, in the belly, in the face. They become stiff at night and moan in their sleep. But it's probably nothing special. How many people have muscle pains under normal circumstances, let alone in ours.
>
> Then one day Dr. Moritz comes to me and says: "Listen, I have an old guy among my Ukrainians who walks funny. Come and look at him." Old Moritz and his Ukrainians—he almost loves them! They

Infirmerie, by M. Leibel and Ilie. Kessler archive.

probably remind him of the peasants in his district. We have therefore entrusted him with the medical care of this group of inmates, and he has undertaken this task, like all others, with enthusiasm.

The sick man is one of the sect members and doesn't want to have anything to do with doctors. Only now, when he can no longer fend one off or run away, will he let Moritz and me come close to him. He lies there, on a pile of rags, a dried-up old man with dirty stubble, matted hair, and creased neck, and stares angrily at us through his half-closed lids. With much trouble and some assistance from his family, we manage to open a few buttons and strings and bare part of his body. He is skinny with a sunken belly, gray hair on his chest, and his legs are slightly pulled upward. There are so many lice on his body and in the pile of rags that the mere sight causes us intense itching. "Look quickly for what you need to see and let's get out of here," whispers Moritz urgently, "otherwise we'll be covered with lice ourselves. There's no more room for them to suck on his body." "I'm hurrying, old boy. I just want to check his heart and see why he can't walk." The long rubber tubes of the stethoscope protect me from direct contact. The man's knee and foot reflexes jump when tapped, as do the toes when I stroke the soles of his feet. "That's good enough for now. Listen, Moritz—it's a spastic paralysis of the legs, and given our limited diagnostic possibilities here I would advise you to treat it as though it were syphilis and to start with iodine and bismuth. If he improves we'll have time to think further."

But the man does not recover. Both Moritz and I look at him one more time. He now talks with a strange gurgle and has food coming out of his nose. Then he dies, and follows so many others [in this camp] to the grave.

A few days later, Dr. Moritz once again comes to find me at the infirmary. "Listen, the problem is not that simple," he says. "I now have three men among my Ukrainians who have trouble walking, just like the old man who died."

He is right. Two of the three are prisoners of war who are more than willing to be examined. They walk stiffly, move their legs in awkward circles and tire quickly. The reflexes in their legs have intensified greatly; when I tap their Achilles tendon the whole leg jumps and continues to jerk. And the reflexes of the big toe clearly show damage to the spinal cord. Four patients with spastic paralysis of the legs in such a relatively small group of people at the same time—that is distinctly odd!

Others follow in short intervals, among them some who are quite young. Vasile Bogdanoff is twenty, Grigore Horodnik only seventeen. Soon there are seventeen or eighteen cases of paralysis among the 130 inmates (including some 30 women) in the third building—the one housing the Ukrainians and Russians who arrived at the camp three months before we did. They had come here from different areas—from Leningrad, Siberia, and nearby Ukraine. Some are prisoners of war; others, common criminals. What they have in common is leg cramping, bladder problems, and an uncertain, wobbly gait. And they have all been eating the fodder pea brew—our principal sustenance—since their arrival in July. Our attention and our inquiries within this group thus begin to focus on this diet.

Within a week, hundreds of others in the camp were also paralyzed. By late January 1943, some 1,000 Vapniarka inmates were suffering from this disease in its early and intermediate stages; 120 were totally paralyzed; a number had died.

It was Dr. Kessler who deduced that the epidemic was directly connected to the peas in the soup ration:

> It is clear that we are in the midst of a mysterious epidemic. But it does not spread through contagion. There are sick Ukrainians and Russians who arrived here before us, as well as Jews from our group, but we have not heard of a single case among the guards and the camp command. It must be brought on by our particular living conditions as inmates, since bacteria do not make exceptions. It can't be the water, because everyone drinks it, nor the bread. We have never encountered a deficiency disease like this one. What distinguishes us, the inmates, from the guards and the command is our fodder pea nutrition. The afflicted ones among the Russians and Ukrainians have been eating the peas for the longest period and were the first to get sick. In our group, it is the young ones who are first to succumb to the epidemic—the biggest eaters who have come to Vapniarka starving from other prisons and penal camps, and who devour all leftovers. Among the women there are fewer and less severe cases. Indeed it seems that the longer and the more a person eats, the worse his condition becomes.
>
> So something in the pea fodder ration we receive must be the source. We examine the peas for additives, pollution, a mix with other products, black fungus-riddled grains of ergot, and deliberate or random contamination. We find some dark seed grains, plant fibers, small stones, but nothing suspicious. I dimly remember plant toxins in legumes that cause similar symptoms, and try to destroy these by boiling the peas for an additional three hours. But this seems to make no difference. . . .
>
> That leaves the peas themselves. They are of an unusual kind, larger, irregularly shaped, angular—not like our good vegetable pea, pisum sativum. [It now seems clear that when we ingest them—the principal ingredient in our food]—we are eating poison and will perish from them. Something must immediately be done.

It was subsequently revealed that a steady diet of this particular kind of chickling pea (Lathyrus sativus) was known to have brought on paralysis in animals and humans in many areas of the world—and recognition of its toxic hazards was fairly widespread among rural peoples in the regions in which it grew. As Arthur Kessler later observed:

In Central Europe, reports about stiff legs following the consumption of bread containing flour from the Lathyrus pea, and laws to prohibit such adulteration, date back to the 17th century. In India, North Africa (Algier) and in Southern Russia, larger epidemics of lathyrism have regularly been observed amongst the poor in times of famine.... Malnutrition and low temperatures favored the onset of the disease.[29]

It is significant to note that neither Vapniarka's Romanian camp officers nor its military guards ate the toxic peas—only the inmates. Yet when Dr. Kessler and other leaders among the prisoners appealed to the camp command to change their diet and to be given medical supplies to treat the sick, they were ignored. "Captain Buradescu [the new Commander] listens quietly with a pinched face," writes Arthur Kessler in his account, "and after I am through pleading, curtly limits his reply to these words: 'What makes you think that we are interested in keeping you alive?' That concludes our hearing."

The situation in the Lager continued to deteriorate. It had grown extremely cold during the winter months. In the large hall of the infirmary, those who could still move sat around its small tin stove, holding out their hands to the heat, their legs jerking with unrelenting tremors. They leaned on sticks when they tried to walk, fell, and tried again. Many showed new symptoms: dark blisters on their toes, heels, and the sides of their feet. They developed fevers, extreme pains. Their legs turned pale, cold, losing all feeling. Gangrene set in, and some had to have toes or legs amputated. "It is a hellish, unimaginable scene," writes Arthur Kessler, "hundreds sick and paralyzed, gangrenous legs, loss of urine before they can reach the pails, distorted posture caused by muscle spasms in their arms, back, belly, and legs.... Treating a stinking, gangrenous leg, keeping a cold, bloodless, extremity warm, maintaining a paralytic and keeping his bunk free of excrement are insoluble problems."

And yet, using inmates in the laboring groups that worked outside of the camp, and by means of bribes and the hushed cooperation of guard/soldiers and civilians with whom they had the occasional opportunity to come into contact, the doctors and leaders among the prisoners did manage to send appeals to the outside world—some even reaching Jews in their hometowns, as well as Jewish community officials in Bucharest. Not long after the onset of the mass paralysis and its linkage to the pea-fodder soup, moreover, Vapniarka's inmates embarked on what Dr. Kessler described as "not a hunger strike but the highest degree of abstinence." Having undertaken this course of action, they would no doubt have been forced to make the "choiceless choice" between paralysis, poisoning, or starvation, had the camp not received an inspection in mid-January 1943—routine, it seems—from a government doctor from Odessa checking the region for safeguards against the recurrence of a typhoid outbreak.[30] This visit was followed by one from a neurologist two weeks later, by a medical investigative commission in late February 1943, by clerical visitors, and even by one from Georgiu Alexianu, the governor of Transnistria. Each time, the visiting officials arrogantly dismissed the diagnosis connecting the strange mass paralysis and suffering to the pea-soup diet. Instead, they maintained that it was the result of a viral infection, or that it was a type of inflammation of the bone marrow or spinal column (myelitis) that had spread from person to person, or (in the most bizarre explanation) that it had resulted from the body fluids of inmates who were schizophrenic—it being a "fact of science," they argued, that such fluids were toxic, and thus virulent when transmitted through contact. Overtly, they did not acknowledge the obvious counter-arguments from the inmate physicians: that any virally spread or otherwise contagious disease could not possibly have been contained so thoroughly so that the camp guards, officers, and non-inmate population with whom the Lager population came into everyday contact would not be infected. There was certainly no official recognition—and no acknowledgment and admission—that the pea fodder that was being fed to the inmates had any relevant connection to the epidemic in the camp. But, in fact, while not stopping and withdrawing the pea soup as the daily staple for the prisoners, the Romanian authorities in late January 1943 began to send dried fruit and moldy pig fodder potatoes as a supplement to the peas, and also designated forty old or crippled pack horses for slaughter and consumption within the camp.[31]

It now seems clear that the decision to feed Vapniarka's inmates the toxic pea fodder in the first place was undertaken for both practical and ideological reasons. At a time when large amounts of food supplies were being diverted to the Romanian military for campaigns against the Red Army in the Soviet Union, the ready availability of the chickling-pea fodder for use in the inmates' food would have seemed like a windfall and a logical allocation of resources.

But since it also seems to have been known by some Romanian officials that the pea fodder was toxic for human consumption (hence, their withholding of the pea-soup diet from the camp guards and officers), feeding it to the imprisoned Ukrainian partisans, religious sect members, Jews, Communists, and to other "politicals" did in fact conform to official and unofficial directives from the highest authorities in Bucharest itself. These, in the Romanian version of the Final Solution, had mandated the elimination of such "enemies of the state."[32] The induced lathyrismus epidemic in Vapniarka is yet another manifestation of the exterminationist aspects of the Romanian Holocaust.

Resistance

What, no doubt, contributed immensely to the ability of a significant number of Vapniarka's inmates to resist and to survive the deprivations of the camp and the epidemic that threatened them with paralysis and agonizing death was the effectiveness and power of their internal organization. No kapos or other officially appointed and privileged authority figures from among the inmate population existed in the camps and ghettos of Transnistria: they were all essentially self-administered. In Vapniarka, the recognized "spokespersons" for the "decimal divisions" (the groups of ten inmates), and for the "sections of a hundred" into which the prisoners were arranged by the Romanian camp command, were officially in charge. But an underground political committee, composed of former activists and Communist leaders, in effect "ran" a significant segment of the camp in a sub-rosa manner, instituting measures to distribute food fairly, control against lice and the reappearance of typhus, staff the makeshift infirmary, and repair the broken-down inmate residential buildings. Indeed, largely because so many of the camp's inmates were political prisoners—Communists and others who had once been active in underground activities and who were highly educated, politically and academically—it was perhaps easier for them to organize within the camp, and to maintain discipline among their fellow prisoners. But this was facilitated by the absence of kapos particular to the Romanian administration of Transnistria.

In Vapniarka, thanks to the suggestions of the camp physicians, for example, the underground leadership ensured that each group of ten prisoners selected a "hygiene supervisor" from among themselves to oversee a strict de-lousing inspection shortly after wake-up and before night curfew. Twice daily, every article of clothing, shirt, piece of underwear, as well as every personal crevice and every cranny in the residential buildings, was closely scrutinized by the inmates and by the hygiene supervisor. As difficult as this was to carry out and maintain in all of the three residential pavilions in the camp, lice infestation was virtually wiped out as a problem by early 1943, and the threat of typhus was eliminated.

The illegal underground command also organized a variety of work details within the inmate ranks to thoroughly rebuild the camp—in as much as possible, taking advantage of skills and specializations that prisoners had brought to Vapniarka from their civilian existences. They consequently saved themselves and their fellow inmates from the only option that had been available to them when they first arrived in Vapniarka: to lie in misery on the buildings' cold floors.

Most importantly, the underground leaders (or, as Arthur Kessler referred to them, "the members of the Black Hand") used bribes, payments, promises, perhaps even intimidation, to build up a network of communications and exchanges involving inmates and a few of the (perhaps more corruptible? more sympathetic?) camp guards and officers. They were thus not only able to get the word out about the paralysis that afflicted so many Lager inmates, and about the need for additional food and medications, but also, by early 1943, were themselves able to receive bits of news from the war front and from the world at large.[33] Certainly, when small supplies of additional food did manage to pass into Vapniarka on occasion (other than the supplements and staple changes authorized by the Camp Command), it was the underground leadership that seems to have enabled its entrance and controlled its distribution.[34]

Overall, the internal organization of the Vapniarka camp and its effectiveness attests to the fact that even in a case of extreme physical and mental brutality and danger such as this one, disciplined resistance by inmates could, in some rare instances, break through the walls of despair and depression within which their captors attempted to crush them. But Vapniarka memoirs and testimonies, and some of the art produced there, attest to more than survival: during the period between 1942 until the

Lager's eventual closing in late December 1943, inmates managed to engage in a variety of cultural activities during the evening hours that also no doubt enabled them to survive in spirit and to build solidarity in the midst of suffering. Every evening after darkness began to set in, gendarmes locked the inmates into the three pavilions housing them. Rather than sleeping after long hours of slave labor, however, the inmates often stayed awake and engaged with each other intellectually and artistically. This occurred even during the most miserable months in the camp—during the epidemic, when Murgescu and Buradescu were its commanders—and continued in a much less inhibited fashion during the period in 1943 when the more liberal, and culturally more sensitive, Colonel Hristache Popovici was Vapniarka's commander.

The professional artists, musicians, and theatrical persons who had come to the Lager played a particularly significant role in these after-lock-up doings. On a regular basis, someone in the group would narrate a story—either one recalled from a novel or book of tales, or made up on the basis of lived and imaginary experiences. One inmate, a refugee from Germany, recited fragments of Goethe's *Faust* from memory. Occasionally, such a story would elicit discussion and analysis by listeners, sometimes even lively debates in which differences of opinion emerged. At other times, one of the academically trained inmates—or one who was perhaps more knowledgeable about political history and theory—would present an informal lecture. Andrei Bernath, who had been a member of the Central Committee of the Romanian Communist Party, spoke to the group about the Revolution of 1848 and its history. Marxism, Fascism, and the causes of the war: he and others would lecture about these topics and engage in debates. Judaism and Jewish subjects were by no means concealed or neglected: someone gave a talk about the Maccabee uprising; someone else about Jewish resistance against the Romans; another about early Jewish history. Rabbi Wilner, the only rabbi in the camp, set up a small corner on the second floor of the Second Pavilion for inmates wishing to worship together.

Music was another staple during the evening hours after the lock-ups. Inmates sang, whistled, and hummed songs in groups or for each other. They remembered tunes and lyrics from their homes and taught them to their companions. They composed and made up songs in German or

Romanian, which poignantly included a number about the very place in which they were imprisoned:

Im fernen Wapniarka,
Wo so bitter die Not,
Schmerzt mich Sehnsucht nach Freiheit,
Sehnsucht nach daheim . . .[35]

[In the far-away Vapniarka,
Where such bitter misery is found
I suffer, yearning for my freedom
Yearning for return to home . . .]

The Politics of Survival

Survival was also no doubt due to Romania's shifting political allegiances during the war. By the beginning of spring 1943, with the war in Eastern Europe turning increasingly against Germany, and the Romanian military having suffered massive casualties in the Soviet campaign, Romanian authorities began to reevaluate their support of the Third Reich and to moderate some of their policies against Jews and their political enemies on the left. While, at this point, General Ion Antonescu and his leading advisors still refused to repatriate Jews and others who had been sent to Transnistria, a decision to hedge their bets in the alliance with Germany seems to have been made relatively soon after the devastating losses sustained by the Romanians at Stalingrad during the winter months of 1942–43. As regards Vapniarka and other Transnistria camps and ghettos, this hedging was manifested in the slight relaxation in controls restricting the ability of camp inmates to communicate with outsiders, as well as in the supplementary allocation of dried fruit, pig fodder, and horse meat for inmate consumption.

Eventually, by the end of March 1943, with the lathyrism epidemic brought under some control—or, at least, not claiming additional victims—and a commission in Bucharest finding that some 440 of Vapniarka's inmates had been sent there without "just cause," Romanian authorities decided that Vapniarka would be closed down altogether.[36] Dr. Kessler and other surviving inmates then began to be released from Vapniarka either immediately or in the course of the next few months. But even those who had been officially acknowledged as having been unjustly arrested and imprisoned were not permitted to return home. Instead, they were placed in "ghettos" or in alternate camps in other parts of Transnistria. These shifts in policy in response to the progress of the war are also distinctive aspects of the Romanian Holocaust.

Notes

1. Jean Ancel, *Transnistria, 1941–1942, vol. 1: History and Document Summaries* (Tel Aviv: Goldstein-Goren Diaspora Research Center, 2003), 17–20. For a summary of the terms of the Tighina Agreement, see 1:547; for the full Romanian version of the document, see 2:41–42. The Romanian administration of Transnistria actually began on August 19—eleven days before the signing of the Agreement.

2. www.yadvashem.org/yv/en/about/events/pdf/report/english/1.2_Romanian_German_Relations_before_and_during_the_Holocaust.pdf. "Romanian-German Relations Before and During the Holocaust," 11–13; Ancel, *Transnistria, 1941–1942*, 1:19–20.

3. Which became known as the Reich Commissariat of Ukraine.

4. The provinces, from north to south, were Moghilev, Tulchin, Jugastru (Yampol), Balta, Rybnitsa, Golta, Ananyev, Dubossary, Berezovka, Ochakov, Tiraspol, Odessa, and Ovidopol. See Ancel, *Transnistria, 1941–1942*, 1:21–22;

5. Ancel, *Transnistria, 1941–1942*, 1:17–19; Jean Ancel, "The Romanian Way of Solving the 'Jewish Question' in Bessarabia and Bukovina, June-July 1941," *Yad Vashem Studies* 19 (1988): 187–232; "Romanian-German Relations before and during the Holocaust," 12.

6. In his pretrial interrogation by Israeli police, Adolf Eichmann admitted that "Sonderbehandlung," or "Special Treatment," always meant killing. See "Romanian-German Relations Before and During the Holocaust," 15 and n. 60.

7. Tighina Agreement, Romanian version: Jean Ancel, *Documents concerning the Fate of Romanian Jewry during the Holocaust* 9, no. 83 (New York: Beate Klarsfeld Foundation, 1986), 188–91. For the German version, see Ancel, *Documents*, 5, no. 62: 59–63.

8. The extermination camps Treblinka, Sobibór, and Bełzec, established in the spring of 1942 as part of Aktion Reinhard, were technically not part of the concentration camp system, but they were organized, run, and guarded much like the others. For a brief, excellent, overview of the Nazi concentration camp system see Falk Pingel, "Concentration Camps," in *Encyclopedia of the Holocaust*, ed. Israel Gutman (New York: Macmillan, 1990), 1:308–17.

9. See the discussion, "Ghetto or Camp?," in Rebecca L. Golbert, "Holocaust Sites in Ukraine: Pechora and the Politics of Memorialization," *Holocaust and Genocide Studies* 18, no. 2 (Fall 2004): 218–21.

10. The ubiquity of this identification is notably apparent in Jean Ancel's lengthy introduction to his three-volume compilation of documents on Transnistria in which he invariably precedes any mention of Pechora and Cariera de Piatră with the identifying terms "death camp." This is in spite of the fact that Pechora was originally intended as a labor camp and Cariera de Piatră as a site to concentrate Jewish inmates from the Hospital for the Mentally Ill in Cernăuți. See Ancel, *Transnistria, 1941–1942*, esp. vol. 1; Isak Weissglass, *Steinbruch am Bug: Bericht einer Deportation nach Transnistrien* (Berlin: Literaturhaus, 1995), 36.

11. Ancel, *Transnistria, 1941–1942*, 1:104–5, 114–39.

12. Ibid., 115.

13. Ibid., 100.

14. Ibid., 120.

15. Avigdor Shachan, *Burning Ice: The Ghettos of Transnistria* (Boulder, CO: East European Monographs, 1996), 166–68; Robert Levy, "Review of Jean Ancel, *Transnistria, 1941–1942*," *Jewish Quarterly Review* 98, no. 3 (2008): 427–28; Ancel, *Transnistria, 1941–1942*, 1:120–81.

16. Rebecca L. Golbert, whose work on Pechora is a main source for my understanding and subsequent discussion of this place, noted that "the estate was built by a Polish nobleman in the eighteenth century, when this territory still formed part of the Polish-Lithuanian Commonwealth." See her "Holocaust Sites in Ukraine: Pechora and the Politics of Memorialization," *Holocaust and Genocide Studies* 18, no. 2 (Fall 2004): 224n.5. Also see Faina A. Vinokurova, "The Holocaust in Vinnitsa Oblast," *Jewish Roots in Ukraine and Moldova*, ed. Miriam Weiner (New York: Routes and Roots Foundation, 1999), 332–34.

17. Golbert, "Holocaust Sites in Ukraine: Pechora and the Politics of Memorialization," 215. Estimates about the total number of Jews that were sent to Pechora vary tremendously, ranging from 35,000 at the upper limit to 6,500 at the lower end. Thousands died from starvation. Golbert, "Holocaust

Sites," 230n.70. For Pechora also see Shachan, *Burning Ice*, 198; Matatias Carp, *Holocaust in Rumania: Facts and Documents on the Annihilation of Rumania's Jews—1940–44* (Safety Harbor, FL: Simon Publications, 2000), 218.

18. See Weissglas, *Steinbruch am Bug: Bericht einer Deportation nach Transnistrien*, 31–39; Deborah Schultz and Edward Timms, eds., *Arnold Daghani's Memories of Mikhailowka: The Illustrated Diary of a Slave Labour Camp Survivor* (London: Vallentine Mitchell, 2009), 188, 194; *Klara and Dori L. Holocaust Testimony* (HVT-777) [videorecording], Fortunoff Video Archive for Holocaust Testimonies, Yale University.

19. Weissglas, *Steinbruch am Bug: Bericht einer Deportation nach Transnistrien*, 52–59, 65–74; *Klara and Dori L. Holocaust Testimony* (HVT-777) [videorecording].

20. Nathan Simon, *". . . auf allen Vieren werden ihr hinauskriechen!": Ein Zeugenbericht aus dem KZ Wapniarka* (Berlin: Institut Kirche und Judentum, 1994), 64.

21. Arthur Kessler, "Ein Arzt in Lager: Die Fahrt ins Ungewisse. Tagebuch u. Aufzeichnungen eines Verschickten" (A doctor in the lager: The journey in the unknown. Diary and notes of a deportee), memoir based on notes taken in the camp and written shortly after the end of the war (Kessler Family Archive, n.p.).

22. Matei Gall, *Finsternis: Durch Gefängnisse, KZ Wapniarka, Massaker, und Kommunismus. Ein Lebenslauf in Rumänien, 1920–1990* (Constance: Hartung-Gorre Verlag, 1999), 119–20. According to Simon, *". . . auf allen Vieren werdet ihr hinauskriechen!,"* 64, they were shot by members of a Nazi Einsatzkommando.

23. G. Alexianu, Decree Nr. 0607, February 13, 1942, quoted in Gall, *Finsternis*, 121.

24. Simon puts the number at 1,100, Kessler and Gall at 1,200, and camp survivor Polya Dubbs, whom we interviewed in Rehovot, Israel, in 2000, recalled the number as 1,400.

25. Simon, *". . . auf allen Vieren werdet ihr hinauskriechen!,"* 63–64.

26. Gall, *Finsternis*, 112–14; Simon, *". . . auf allen Vieren werdet ihr hinauskriechen!,"* 65. Kessler and Dubbs also mention this.

27. Simon, *". . . auf allen Vieren werdet ihr hinauskriechen!,"* 66.

28. Ibid., 67.

29. Arthur Kessler, "Lathyrismus," *Psychiatrie und Neurologie* 112, no. 6 (1947): 345–76.

30. The term "choiceless choice" is Lawrence L. Langer's. See his *Holocaust Testimonies: The Ruins of Memory* (New Haven, CT: Yale University Press, 1991).

31. Kessler, Dubbs, Simon, and Gall all present similar versions of this account. Simon was himself struck with lathyrismus.

32. See Gall, *Finsternis*, 127–29; Radu Ioanid, *The Holocaust in Romania: The Destruction of the Jews and Gypsies under the Antonescu Regime, 1940–1944* (Chicago: Ivan Dee, 2008), 110–75; Felicia Steigman Carmelly, ed., *Shattered! 50 Years of Silence: History and Voices of the Tragedy in Romania and Transnistria* (Scarborough, Ont.: Abbeyfield Publishers, 1997), 138.

33. Information about the camp organization and leadership derives from Kessler and Dubbs. Also see Gall, *Finsternis*, 122–23, 126, 129–30; Simon, "... *auf allen Vieren werdet ihr hinauskriechen!*," 66–69.

34. Gall, *Finstneris*, 127, suggests that the inmate leadership had managed to build a radio receiver, or to smuggle one into the camp. But while other testimonies attest to the communications that were established between inmates and persons outside the camp, no one else mentions the radio.

35. Polya Dubbs sang and we recorded the Vapniarka Song when we interviewed her in the year 2000. Also see Gall, *Finsternis*, 151.

36. Gall, *Finsternis*, 153–55; Simon, "... *auf allen Vieren werdet ihr hinauskriechen!*," 90–92.

Bibliography

Ancel, Jean. *Documents Concerning the Fate of Romanian Jewry during the Holocaust*. Vol. 9, no. 83. New York: Beate Klarsfeld Foundation, 1986.

———. "The Romanian Way of Solving the 'Jewish Question' in Bessarabia and Bukovina, June-July 1941." *Yad Vashem Studies* 19 (1998): 187–232.

———. *Transnistria, 1941–1942, vol. 1: History and Document Summaries*. Tel Aviv: Goldstein-Goren Diaspora Research Center, 2003.

Carmelly, Felicia Steigman, ed. *Shattered! 50 Years of Silence: History and Voices of the Tragedy in Romania and Transnistria*. Scarborough, ON: Abbeyfield Publishers, 1997.

Carp, Matatias. *Holocaust in Rumania: Facts and Documents on the Annihilation of Rumania's Jews—1940–44*. Safety Harbor, FL: Simon Publications, 2000.

Gall, Matei. *Finsternis: Durch Gefängnisse, KZ Wapniarka, Massaker, und Kommunismus. Ein Lebenlauf in Rumänien, 1920–1990*. Constance: Hartung-Gorre Verlag, 1999.

Golbert, Rebecca L. "Holocaust Sites in Ukraine: Pechora and the Politics of Memorialization." *Holocaust and Genocide Studies* 18, no. 2 (2004): 205–33.

Hirsch, Marianne, and Leo Spitzer. *Ghosts of Home: The Afterlife of Czernowitz in Jewish Memory*. Berkeley: University of California Press, 2010.

Ioanid, Radu. *The Holocaust in Romania: The Destruction of the Jews and Gypsies under the Antonescu Regime: 1940–1944*. Chicago: Ivan Dee, 2008.

Kessler, Arthur. "Ein Arzt in Lager: Die Fahrt ins Ungewisse. Tagebuch u. Aufzeichnungen eines Verschickten [A Doctor in the lager: The journey in the unknown. Diary and notes of a deportee]. Unpublished manuscript.

———. "Lathyrismus." *Psychiatrie und Neurologie* 112, no. 6 (1947): 345–76.

Klara and Dori L. Holocaust Testimony (HVT-777) [videorecording]. Fortunoff Video Archive for Holocaust Testimonies, Yale University.

Langer, Lawrence. *Holocaust Testimonies: The Ruins of Memory*. New Haven, CT: Yale University Press, 1991.

Levy, Robert. "Review of Jean Ancel, *Transnistria, 1941–1942*." *Jewish Quarterly Review* 98, no. 3 (2008): 427–28.

Pingel, Falk. "Concentration Camps." In *Encyclopedia of the Holocaust*, ed. Israel Gutman, 1:308–17. New York: Macmillan, 1990.

"Romanian-German Relations before and during the Holocaust." www.yadvashem.org/yv/en/about/events/pdf/report/english/1.2_Romanian_German_Relations_before_and_during_the_Holocaust.pdf. Accessed February 21, 2014.

Schultz, Deborah, and Edward Timms, eds. *Arnold Daghani's Memories of Mikhailowka: The Illustrated Diary of a Slave Labour Camp Survivor*. London: Vallentine Mitchell, 2009.

Shachan, Avigdor. *Burning Ice: The Ghettos of Transnistria*. Boulder, CO: East European Monographs, 1996.

Simon, Nathan. "*... auf allen Vieren werden ihr hinauskriechen!*": *Ein Zeugenbericht aus dem KZ Wapniarka*. Berlin: Institut Kirche und Judentum, 1994.

Vinokurova, Faina A. "The Holocaust in Vinnitsa Oblast." In *Jewish Roots in Ukraine and Moldova*, ed. Miriam Weiner. New York: Routes and Roots Foundation, 1999.

Weissglass, Isak. *Steinbruch am Bug: Bericht einer Deportation nach Transnistrien*. Berlin: Literaturhaus, 1995.

6
Interview with Father Patrick Desbois

HENRI LUSTIGER THALER

Father Patrick Desbois is director of the Episcopal Committee for Relations with Judaism. He has been internationally recognized for his extraordinary effort in uncovering the mass graves of Jews in Eastern Europe. He is Secretary of the French Conference of Bishops for Relations with Judaism, advisor to the Cardinal-Archbishop of Paris, and advisor to the Vatican on the Jewish religion. He is the president of Yahad—In Unum, and winner of the B'nai B'rith International Award for Outstanding Contributions to Relations with the Jewish People.

HENRI LUSTIGER THALER: Your relationship to your work has very personal origins. It begins with your grandfather, and what he had witnessed being perpetrated upon Jews during his own internment in Rawa-Ruska. Much has happened since your early exposure to the Holocaust in the East. There has been a growing recognition of your research. Can you speak about the continuing motivation with all the complexities of the work that you're doing?

FATHER PATRICK DESBOIS: First permit me to say that I am not alone in this work. People have a tendency to isolate me. We now have twenty full-time workers in the field. I have five teams. And, each person on those teams has his or her own personal motivation. I would say that at a certain level when you think about what needs to be done, you don't really reflect on the primary motivation anymore. It is the work itself that becomes the object. Having said that, you are right; an original motivation is usually there. I am thinking of a young woman who is working with me. She is Catholic, from Alsace. Alsace was German during the war and she wonders if she was working with us because of that past. She is doing a PhD on the survival of the Jews in Berlin during the Holocaust. Recently, she discovered that, in fact, her family refused to serve in the army and they were sent, the entire family, to the Gross-Rosen concentration camp. She has known this now for two years, and she has been working on Holocaust for many years before that. So I think there is a part of us in this action-based decision that is totally unconscious. There are many entry points into this history and everybody enters through his or her personal story. There is also the perspective of the neighbors, the victims, and the killers. To work on genocide and to think you have no particular personal reason to be doing this kind of work is pure illusion. So I was connected to the story of my grandfather, but now I know many, many, many victims, not only my grandfather.

HENRI LUSTIGER THALER: The Nazis were intent on seeing their crime disappear. We have seen this in the East and we have seen this as well in the West. You are documenting the last living moments of victims but seen through the eyes of villagers, bystanders, the very essence of locality, specificity. Your team and yourself are witnesses to the uncovering of the memories of villagers and the exact locations of the mass graves. Tell me about this interaction, the people, their link to this topography of death and destruction. You are in a sense creating memory by recording "bystander" recollections, in all the complexity of what a bystander actually is, a sort of "dark voyeur."

FATHER PATRICK DESBOIS: So, the first question is, are we witnesses? Or, do we become witnesses because they speak? Most of the people we record never spoke, and normally a witness is somebody who's speaking. So I think these people are transformed with us in what we are doing. We are all in a sense witnessing at different levels.

HENRI LUSTIGER THALER: So they are being transformed as they are re-witnessing with you and your team. And, the resulting memory is consequential in that it becomes part of the recognition of their subjective/historical experience?

Interview with Father Patrick Desbois

FATHER PATRICK DESBOIS: Yes, they are witnesses. They are witness because they speak to us. I would say we succeed in making them witnesses. Let us remember that the memory of the people in the surrounding areas of the mass killing sites are not at all uniform. There are several categories of killings: three cases, at minimum. The first case is very public. It means the entire village could follow the Jews or walk behind, take things as the death procession was in fact occurring, sit down on the grass and watch. The second case of mass killing is semi-public. The Germans didn't want the population to approach too closely. And they constructed a kind of barrier around the Jews to stop people from coming in. However, people hid behind bushes or climbed on the roof of a house, or in a tree. So there were witnesses. The third case is totally secret. The Germans would make a perimeter where no one could approach. We know that in the village *Brani Avari* in Ukraine, the Germans shot 52,000 Jews arriving in a train from Bresse. In everything I have read about it, I gather it was committed in total secrecy. In fact we interviewed the son of the chief of the train station. He saw the shooting and described it to us. He had been taken by force by the Germans, to watch and assist in the shooting. They told him if he didn't stay he would be killed like the Jews.

The villagers themselves are from different categories. For example, some were indifferent neighbors. One woman told me that she will never understand why they shot 1,000 Jews, and chose to do it in front of her window. At the time we interviewed her, she herself was dying in her bed and through her window she still had a full view of the mass grave. Then there are the people who would go out to watch. Others would try to take things, steal something from the victims. Others fell into another category: they were requisitioned by the Germans to aid the killing process in some form or manner. So there are different categories of witnesses. I would say the challenge to people in our team is to be sensitive to these witness categories so that we can rebuild the totality of the murderous crime.

HENRI LUSTIGER THALER: As I am listening, I'm thinking of the organization of the killings in the Holocaust in the East, and the much better known narrative of mass murders in the West. This bystander memory has been sequestered all these years. Nobody came to inquire all this time about what happened to the Jews?

FATHER PATRICK DESBOIS: Firstly, to say that it is "the East" does not capture the whole story. It is Soviet, with Soviet categories of life, structure, family, administration, perceptions, and also individuality. It is very complicated because the memory of the Holocaust has been consciously constructed in the West. These people are witnesses, but they are Soviets. They speak in Soviet categories. So, if you don't know the story of Soviet Union, if you don't understand the administration of the village; if you don't understand what it means to have experienced forced collectivization it is difficult to understand within a Soviet point of view what occurs in a village for example when German troops arrive from one day to the next.

This understanding is really a challenge in our ongoing work. That's why the team is composed of half Western people and individuals who are living in the post-Soviet Union. It is, of course, not only a kind of rote mentality, but also national memory. They think that they delivered Berlin. And when I go to American Holocaust museums, I see American flags. I do not see any Soviet flags. When I am in Moscow, they never mention an American flag. They say that all their lives were spent on the good side of the war. They were fighting Hitler and yet nobody considers their contribution. They find it very difficult to understand that it is the Germans who are now well considered in the United States and not them. Aside from the war, the Soviet memory of the Holocaust was constructed firstly with the shootings, the mass graves, when nobody knew of Auschwitz. It was only after the war that the Soviets as a population discovered Auschwitz.

HENRI LUSTIGER THALER: Very different viewpoints. Just three weeks ago I interviewed a Lubavitcher Hasid, a survivor from Moscow, who was twelve years old during the war. He told me that when the Germans invaded, persecution against religious Jews decreased. The Soviets were busy fighting the Germans.

FATHER PATRICK DESBOIS: Yes, yes, not only for religious Jews, for the villagers too. In some villages when the Germans arrived they immediately reopened a church. It was closed for twenty years. The Germans were religious. Well, it's complicated. But without this specificity, you cannot, you really cannot understand these differing categories of witnesses. And it was the Soviet Army that liberated Auschwitz, and not the American Army. So you have to accept the pride of today's Russian people in relationship to this history. Otherwise, my team cannot do the interview, because you will unconsciously classify them in Western categories, and these categories do not apply.

HENRI LUSTIGER THALER: You have interviewed individuals who were questioned immediately after the war by Soviet investigation teams, "The Soviet Commission" of 1944, and their district attorneys. In many cases, the people you interviewed spoke for the first time since this Commission took their testimonies sixty-seven years earlier. I understand that your testimonies corroborated the initial interviews made in 1944. We can imagine that these first recorded memories were done in an atmosphere of fear that they, the villagers, might be implicated in some way in the detritus of the mass slaughter, for example in terms of what they were requisitioned to do, etc. Yet significant corroboration between the two periods took place. What have you found to be different between these two evidentiary moments, particularly since we can imagine that there may have been varying levels of coercion in these early interviewing processes?

FATHER PATRICK DESBOIS: First, the memory that we are capturing is very late. People are old and they were very young at the time of the mass murders. So it is the memory of children. For example, one girl remembers, that she looked out the window and she saw the arrest of Jews and she then counted on her two hands all the Jewish children in her class. Most of the time they remember people who were the same age as them. One girl told me that she was so small she imagined everybody as giants. Germans were giants. Jews were giants. So, what does it mean to interview people almost seventy years after the event? I spoke with a specialist in Israel. I asked her about it. She told me that it's very well known if a child witnesses a crime of this magnitude, whatever his or her opinion of the victim, i.e., if he or she is an antisemite, philo-Semite, or anticommunist, communist, whatever, it's a trauma to see 2,000 to 3,000 people dying in front of your eyes. It is an inescapable trauma.

The second thing is that in many cases, but not always, at the end of the interview we bring up the information from the Soviet Commission findings. So we ask, "Somebody said this in 1944; do you remember that person's name?" I interviewed a partisan fighting against the Germans. He came to the interview with all his medals on his jacket. He was very proud to be a partisan. This was in Belarus. He witnessed the shooting of the Jews. As the interview was coming to an end, I said, "I have an old paper: oh, do you know this fellow Stephan-something?" And he said, "Stephan—I knew him. He was my boss. He was the chief of the partisans. He was a Jew. He escaped from the shooting and became the head of the partisan group." I was shocked. In the Commission archives, it was not even mentioned that he was a Jew and a partisan. So, in this case we do build intersections directly in front of the camera, what the witness of today states with what the witness of the immediate postwar years testified. This kind of factual confrontation is extremely important when the witness of today sheds light upon the identity of the people who have been interviewed or questioned in 1944.

I'll give you another example. I took testimony in a village that was known to have a chief of police that was especially violent. He was known for kicking the heads of Jews in the ghetto. I will never forget: I had a long interview with a person that had nothing to do with that, and at the end I raised the same question. I asked if he knew that violent policeman. The fellow replied, "Do you want to know the truth?" And I said yes. "He was my grandfather." I couldn't believe it, because we suddenly realized that he knew the chief of police as a person who was totally violent inside the family as well: kicking the children, kicking the horse, and so on. So we are contrasting one form of information and testimony with another, and thereby confronting both. Sometimes they don't know the people, sometimes they say "We don't know this one, we do know this one," but sometimes they say, "Oh, this girl was a sister of the other and the other is still alive." So I would say this active memory reawakened by our team recontextualizes and deepens the witnessing of 1944, because in many cases the testimonies of 1944 are short and likely coercive. And we found out so many things about the fuller identity of the witnesses of today and yesterday.

So, the question you raise is a very important one: how to accept the Soviet Commission archives of 1944 knowing that the testimonies they took in the villages have been given under duress. I would say that part of the work in the team is to identity and to explain why the Soviet archives are so useful, in spite of the coercive context.

Interview with Father Patrick Desbois

HENRI LUSTIGER THALER: You have a situation in the field where newly uncovered memories are in dialogue with earlier traces that took place under completely different circumstances.

FATHER PATRICK DESBOIS: Yes, because for example we interviewed someone who at the end of the interview was informed that his father was the first witness in the Soviet Commission and there was this gap, a contradiction between his and his father's testimonies. So we read what his father said in 1944, and he reacted on camera. Or another case: we said to our interviewee, "Your name is Davidovski, and in 1944 a certain Davidovski gave this testimony and said so and so." Our interviewee states, "Ah it was my uncle. He worked for the Germans. He tried to save his life by giving testimony to the officials. After the war, he was sent to Siberia." So you have also a certain light that is shed upon what happened to people who spoke in the Soviet Commission. We also heard a lot about requisitioning of villagers by the Germans to perform tasks associated with the massacres. There were about fifty different jobs we estimated.

HENRI LUSTIGER THALER: Tell me about the requisitioning process and how it is expressed in the testimonies.

FATHER PATRICK DESBOIS: First, we have ambivalence. Most of the people are ambivalent about this past. One woman told me she was sad in the morning that she had been requisitioned, but happy in the evening because they got clothes. So that was typical of the requisition: sad and happy scenarios, occurring at different times of the day. And they are ambivalent because a lot depends on the type of requisition. Some requisitions are far from the act of the crime, for example a woman is requisitioned in the evening after the executions. All the Jews are dead and she has a requisition with other girls to go and repair the shoes of the Jews to sell them in auction. So overnight, they are repairing the shoes. We found two such witnesses. Another example, a fellow who was requisitioned to guard Jews during the night and the Germans told him if a Jew tried to escape, you have to shoot, otherwise you will be shot. We asked how many Jews tried to escape the first night. He said two. So this young person killed people. Can we say he did this only to save his life? But it is not so clear. Another example was a teenager who was forced to kill the Jews.

He is no longer alive. We have only the testimony of the family, and the family would not totally criticize a member. But on balance, a bit of guilt and a bit of innocence is the way I would characterize the witnesses. They laugh and cry all in the same testimony.

HENRI LUSTIGER THALER: I'd like you to follow this thought a bit further. Two types of memory are threaded throughout your book *Holocaust by Bullets*. One: the conflicted memory of the villager, this ambivalence that you were speaking of, and also the memory of absent Jews. I am thinking of Anna Boulavka who speaks about the murder of a young Jewish girl that her family was hiding. In a context where the punishment for hiding a Jew was met with death, you expose two acts of humanity in Anna Boulavka's testimony: firstly the initial act of hiding a Jewish child and secondly that the brutal murder of the child demands narration. Anna Boulavka's duty is to tell the story. Can you recount for us more such acts wherein the obligation felt by the villagers to bear witness and narrate emerges out of empathy and not necessarily trauma?

FATHER PATRICK DESBOIS: We met both. We met people who hate Jews and who today display extreme antisemitism and were not shedding one tear and not showing the faintest feeling when speaking about the murder of literally half the village. We heard other stories that were really love stories. I remember interviewing a village girl who was in love with a young Jewish boy. She put a star on every day, and entered the designated area where the Jews were kept, to see him and bring food for the family and so on. On the day of the mass shooting, the Jews were lining up to be shot but she doesn't realize it. She puts on her star and she joined the Jewish boy and his family. When her mother suddenly, standing by the window, saw her daughter with a star waiting to be shot, she runs, she tears off the star, hits the girl and she brings her back in the house. This young girl became a coordinator in the local police force with a love story that was crushed by the Holocaust. And I would say we have interviewed more than one hundred love stories like this.

HENRI LUSTIGER THALER: Between the villagers and Jews?

FATHER PATRICK DESBOIS: Yes, yes. The Jews represented a large community. And, as a significant people there were hate stories about them, people would denounce Jews to the local police and those Jews would be killed, [but] some people saved Jews, so love stories are events we don't really speak about. Of course, I know it is not well received in the Jewish community, but it existed. And sometimes it was the key to life or death. I have many, many examples like that. And, people also saved Jews through the war and suddenly because of violence or because a neighbor denounced them, they had to say to the Jews, you have to go now, we cannot keep you anymore. It is too risky. And most of the time, these Jews, now exposed, were captured and killed.

HENRI LUSTIGER THALER: In your discussions with the villagers, could you assess how many of these village-based populations were Orthodox Jewish communities? What's your sense, from speaking with the villagers? Would they be able to distinguish?

FATHER PATRICK DESBOIS: It depends where we were. If it was Soviet, in any case, religion was prohibited. So even in a Hasidic village when I ask where was the rebbe, they look at me and they don't understand my question. So it depends if it was a part of Poland that was Soviet only two years, and other places where people were Soviet over thirty years with many rules against any religious expression. We forget today that the Soviet Union was against all religions. We do, however, speak about the persecution of the Christians, but the Jews were persecuted too. All synagogues were closed; some villagers told us that they were forbidden to eat kosher.

HENRI LUSTIGER THALER: Permit me to move this discussion toward contemporary concerns regarding the memory of the Holocaust. There are many discussions today that the memory of the event is becoming further and further removed from the actual details of the Holocaust. Your work takes us back to the murderous minutiae of the Holocaust in the East, a relatively new area of research. The memory of the Holocaust is moving toward a universalization of the very meaning of the event, by drawing lessons through applications to human rights and issues of tolerance, particularly in the West. As a priest, where do you see the broader implications of your work fitting in?

FATHER PATRICK DESBOIS: I'm not sure that people in Europe, or in America, realize that people in the former Soviet Union, China, the Arab World, Africa, etc., have a remarkable lack of knowledge about the Holocaust. I have spoken in fifteen Chinese schools recently. For many, it was the first time they heard about the Holocaust. So, I think we are actually in a global world where we still have to think about how to transmit this memory of the genocide of the Jews. So I say, if today perhaps this Chinese student is young, tomorrow they will be journalist, perhaps tomorrow a doctor, perhaps tomorrow they will be in the military. Perhaps you will be sent to a country where there is mass crime or genocide. And, if you see that something is happening, like it happened in a village in Ukraine, having been exposed to the history of the Holocaust might make you take out your cell phone, take a picture, and send it quickly to CNN. We cannot wait to stop genocide. First, we have to teach the world that the genocide of Jews was quite unique. Secondly, the way the Jews have worked to save the memory of the victims, to save the memory of what happened is exceptional and very different from the memory of other genocides. This memory can serve humanity. How do we do this? The way forward is to examine what I call micro-histories as a way to give back the responsibility to everyday people. I never forget that the people who saved Jews, the majority of them, were simple people. I interviewed thousands of simple people who were the neighbors during the shootings. I study their reaction. This way you can learn which reaction you would have if something happens around you.

You can study genocide from a satellite and you see the camps. You can study from a plane, and you begin to see the units moving from city to city and then you can study from a farm. My point of view is from the farm. So of course it's not perfect. A farmer sees a killing in his role as a neighbor. My hope is that the next generations will react and say if we are the neighbors, we have to do something. For me, micro-history is also a chance to teach a new generation that they can feel the responsibility for everyday actions and thereby not classify the Holocaust like a tsunami. I'm afraid that some people classify the Holocaust in this way. It was not a tsunami. It was a gradual process.

HENRI LUSTIGER THALER: How do the testimonies that you're gathering in Eastern Europe speak to the concomitant rise of nationalism in that part of the world, and the antisemitism that is occurring and associated with Holocaust revisionism, which appears to be part and parcel of national reconstruction in the East?

FATHER PATRICK DESBOIS: The denier is an antisemite. I never met a denier who loved Jews. So I think deniers represent a network of deniers and are in fact the continuation of Hitler goals. Let us not forget that the first people who denied the genocide were the people who did it, the Germans. The first deniers are always the killers. Holocaust revisionism is a way to continue the job of the killers. Of course, how do we address this current and troubling revisionism? In the Ukraine, we had a very strong collaboration with the Shoah Foundation and it was supported by a gentleman by the name of Victor Pinchuk. We established an educational toolkit mixing the testimonies of survivors and the testimonies of neighbors in all categories. Small notebooks were given to history teachers based in the Ukraine. I never imagined that the academic system in the Ukraine would accept to do this. In collaboration with Victor Pinchuk, a traveling exhibition was created with the Museum of Paris (this has been shown in Paris, Brussels, Stockholm, and the Museum of Jewish Heritage in New York). It was shown in Kiev with full media coverage throughout the Ukraine. There was nobody on the ground, so to speak, able to guide the exhibit. So they trained a team of twenty young students. The guides were between twenty and twenty-five. I stayed in Kiev three days to see who was coming to see this exhibit. I was surprised that many people came. But more surprised that nobody was older than thirty years of age. I am hopeful when I see groups of young Ukrainian students who want to listen and learn from the testimony of the old Babushka who recounts the story of the killings of the Jews. I am not an optimistic person, but I would say in the Ukraine as much as I see the weight of the story, the weight of antisemitism, the weight of xenophobia, I also see a generation ready to learn and study. I am sure that not everybody is happy about this, but it is happening.

HENRI LUSTIGER THALER: Tell me about your work with scholars and educators in Western Europe and the United States.

FATHER PATRICK DESBOIS: I am the founder of Yahad—In Unum. We now have many people working full time with us. We have individuals who translate the archive, especially in Russian, Belarusian, and Ukrainian. Some others are working in German and some people are from other countries of the world—America, for example. So it's an international team with a French organization. We have a strong partnership with the United States Holocaust Memorial Museum in Washington. We have access to their archives and researchers. We are working with a network of historians from the former Soviet Union, Russia, Belarus, the Ukraine, but also with historians from Israel. We try to network with young historians who are ready to work on Soviet archives and survivor testimony. My goal is to reach the last village that was occupied by the Germans, so we are accelerating our investigation. We do about fifteen visits per year with an average of seventeen days each. We are currently looking at the mass graves of Roma. We found forty-eight sites of mass murder of gypsies and now we are confronting the raw memory of the survivors and the memory of the neighbors. It's another genocide. And I'm very moved that we found so much support in the USA. We partner with the Shoah Foundation, with the United States Holocaust Memorial Museum, and the Museum of Jewish Heritage.

HENRI LUSTIGER THALER: One last question, Father Desbois. Can you speak of the transformation that you witnessed, regarding the mass graves from "sites of murder" remembered by the villagers to "sites of memory" and mourning for the families of the victims?

FATHER PATRICK DESBOIS: Well, first we must speak of the site of murder because we discovered in many places where the witnesses say there is one mass grave; in fact there are many mass graves. I will never forget when I interviewed a women who told me her mother was hiding her in the grass because they were afraid the Germans would kill them. They saw the shootings of the Jews. They fled back to their home. When the father came back home later that night he said, "The mass graves are too small, we have to make another one tomorrow." So we first must speak of the site of mass murder because sometimes there is one grave and sometimes there are seventeen mass graves and nobody knows exactly how many graves because they were dug each time the Germans found more Jews.

Sometimes they would bring back people to the ghetto, at the end of the day to dig more mass graves, because there was no more room in the allotted pits.

To the second part of your question, what helps me is when the family of a victim joins us and finally we are able to show them more or less in which mass grave a family member is buried. And with this knowledge they go over to recite the Kaddish. We have tried to help protect the site and it seems to me the best gift I can offer to these families is to say, "Your mother will not disappear, she's buried in this place with many people, but she's buried." And you can now go and pray. I know a family from Washington that recently traveled to the Ukraine to read the Kaddish, and they then contributed to protect the site from the actions of local grave marauders. This is my way to give back to the Jewish people, their grave, and also to acknowledge to humanity the sanctity of the Jewish burial and, by doing so, we bury them for the first time.

So our hope is that the mass graves of the roughly 2 million murdered Jews of the East will be protected and in so doing demonstrate to the world that they will not be forgotten. There is a well-known question at the beginning of the Bible, "Where is your brother?" And Cain said, "Am I the guardian of my brother?" In response to a survivor's question: "Where is my brother?" we can now say, at least in some cases, "We know where they are!"

7

The Flight and Evacuation of Civilian Populations in the USSR

New Sources, New Publications, New Questions

PAUL A. SHAPIRO

An important book by Canadian scholar Rebecca Manley, published in 2009, estimated the number of refugees and evacuees in the USSR who moved or were moved from west to east, from immediate danger to possible survival, in the period from June 1941 to the end of 1942 at some 16.5 million human beings.[1] A more recent article by Sergei Maksudov (Alexander Babyonyshev), a Soviet-educated Research Associate (retired) of Harvard University's Davis Center for Russian and Eurasian Studies and the author of numerous demographic studies focused on the USSR, cites the work of Russian researcher and director of Moscow's Center for Military History G. Kumanev, who placed the number at 17 million.[2] Flight and evacuation took place from eight Soviet republics that were occupied, in whole or in part, and for greater or lesser periods of time, by the military and occupation authorities of Nazi Germany and her allies. Most of those who fled or were evacuated, while perhaps at first believing that safety might be found some hundreds of kilometers from their homes in Chisinau or Leningrad or Kiev or Odessa or Moscow, eventually found themselves thousands of kilometers from home. To the north, they moved across the Urals to Siberia and eastern cities of the Russian Federation such as Sverdlovsk, Omsk, and Novosibirsk. And to the south, where the majority of people who left Kiev, Odessa, Kharkiv, and the rest of Ukraine and southern Russia made their way, they traveled through and to nearly all the Soviet republics whose territories remained partially or fully out of German control—Georgia, Azerbaijan, Kazakhstan, Uzbekistan, Kyrgyzstan, Turkmenistan—and spent months or years in the Caucasus or much further to the east in Samarkand, Tashkent, and even Frunze and Alma-Ata.

It is clear that the mass movement of civilians inside the Soviet Union during World War II was a countrywide phenomenon with tremendous and often long-lasting consequences not only for the refugees and evacuees, but also for the republics from which and to which people moved and for the Soviet state itself, its ability to maintain control in crisis, and its ability to persevere to victory over Germany and her allies. But how has this chapter of history been treated?

Even early studies of the Soviet Union in World War II that were published in the West recognized that massive population transfers had taken place in the USSR during the war. Alexander Werth, for example, in his foundational *Russia at War: 1941–1945* (1964), devoted a short chapter to "The Evacuation of Industry," which he defined as "getting people, plants, and supplies to the same place to produce." But his emphasis was clearly on the Soviet regime's "transplantation of industry," which he characterized as "an altogether unique achievement." Far less attention was devoted to the experiences and tribulations of the people who were moved, beyond the generalization that the government's organization of the evacuations combined "with an almost unparalleled example of mass devotion, for the men and women engaged in restarting the evacuated armaments industry had to work at the height of winter, with worse than adequate food and housing." It was factories and industry rather than the civilians who worked in them or their families, which, perhaps naturally, occupied the attention of an outstanding military historian.[3]

Werth devoted another chapter ("Caucasus Round Trip") to the German invasion of the Caucasus, in which they hoped to reach "the two great oil centres, Grozny and Baku." Here, citing the diary of General Tyulenev, the commander of the Transcaucasian Front, Werth paid attention to the plight of local refugees: "The roads were crowded with thousands of refugees, trying to escape, with their cattle, to the mountains; others stormed trains at every railway station." "Despite intensive German bombing," wrote Tyulenev, "and though having exhausted their meager food supplies, all these people were trying to get away from the

German avalanche." Werth described, in equally dire terms, the influx of refugees—weeping women and children—who crowded into the ports at Makhach-Kala and Baku, desperately hoping to be taken across the Caspian Sea to safety.[4] Werth's pathos, however, applied to civilian refugees running for their lives in the face of rapidly advancing enemy armies, not to the objects of Moscow's formal evacuation plans.

Another theme that appeared early in the literature drew a connection between the evacuation of civilians and the fate of Soviet Jews during the war. The theme was developed, however, from two diametrically opposed perspectives. Seen through the lens of scholars whose work focused on the history of Soviet Jewry, the targeting of all Jews for extermination by the Nazis, their allies, and the Soviet citizens who became Nazi collaborators, as well as establishing the record of the actual mass murder of Jews on Soviet territory, with all its horrifying statistics, took priority. The role of Jews fighting and dying in the Red Army, working in Soviet administration and industry as well as in cultural fields, and the work done by Soviet Jews to gain support abroad for the Soviet war effort also drew attention.[5]

Inside the USSR, predictably, the perspective adopted toward this issue was quite different. Stalin's antipathy toward Jews, which translated directly into official Soviet state-sponsored antisemitism and culminated in 1952–1953 with the show trials, executions, and sentences to the Gulag associated with the so-called Doctor's Plot, prevented recognition of the specificity of the mass murder of Jews that we today call the Holocaust (or Shoah). The accepted formula for reference to German crimes on Soviet territory became the murder of millions of "peace-loving Soviet citizens." This of course reflected one reality, but the fact that in many localities the overwhelming majority of these victims were Jews was passed over in silence. And while the heroism of Red Army soldiers at the front was hailed repeatedly, the fact that among them were hundreds of thousands of Soviet Jews, many of whom sacrificed their lives fighting the invader, was downplayed.[6] Indeed, official Soviet propaganda did little to discourage, and even encouraged, the popular notion that Jews had sought to avoid military service by fleeing east, cowards who found safety either as refugees or as evacuees privileged by the authorities because of their devotion to the (hated) Bolshevik regime or through their close association with the NKVD and other instruments of Stalinist intimidation and terror. Jewish contributions to the wartime economy, to culture, or to support of the Soviet war effort from abroad were eliminated from serious consideration. In this instance, an unusual situation developed. The popular line and the party line were in synch: "The Jews fought the war in Tashkent."

This official Soviet attitude resulted in the Holocaust—that is, the particular targeting of Jews for persecution and complete extermination by the Nazis and their allies—becoming a taboo subject, or at least a subject that had to be submerged in a broader pool of suffering, for most of Soviet postwar history. Nothing exemplifies this attitude more than the story of the "Black Book." Ilya Ehrenburg, arguably the most influential journalist in the Soviet Union during the war, working together with the Jewish Anti-Fascist Committee and a group of writers, journalists, and survivors, with encouragement from Jewish organizations abroad and such prominent individuals as Albert Einstein, planned and collected documents and testimonies intended to provide a comprehensive published account, a "Black Book," of the Nazi persecution and murder of Jews in the USSR during the war. The *Sovinformburo* (Soviet Information Bureau) approved the project in mid-1943. In late July, the Yiddish-language newspaper *Eynikayt* (Unity) printed a public appeal for contributions, and eyewitness testimonies and documentary evidence poured in. In the end, however, not wishing to focus attention on the Jewish tragedy, Soviet authorities prevented publication of the "Black Book" and it was only after the fall of the Soviet regime that a full edition could be published, first in Russia and then in the United States.[7]

If the mass murder of Jews was not an acceptable topic for examination or public awareness and discussion, the fate of Jewish refugees and evacuees during the war was even less likely to receive serious or sympathetic consideration in the postwar USSR. Indeed, the lack of attention paid by scholars and others to refugees and evacuees extended beyond the Jewish story alone, to the millions of non-Jews who fled for their lives or were evacuated eastward by Soviet authorities as well. The factors that explain this lack of attention must therefore extend beyond official Soviet postwar antisemitism. It is not difficult to identify them.

Soviet historiography and propaganda regarding World War II focused on "the front," to the near total exclusion of "the rear," even though without the work done in the rear—east of the Urals, in the Caucasus, in Kazakhstan and Central Asia—in the industries and by the workers that the Soviet regime moved east, as well as in local industry and agriculture, there could have been no "heroic victory" at "the front." Also, of course, flight and evacuation in the face of the enemy were indicators of weakness and of the Soviet failure to prepare adequately for the attack that came in June 1941. Neither of these themes could gain traction while Stalin was alive. Neither of them gained traction after his death, either. To the extent that the issues of flight and evacuation were addressed in Soviet times, historians and writers chronicled the home-front *heroism* of workers in armaments factories or on collective farms, whose mission was to supply the real "front" with weapons, ammunition, and food. No less a figure than military hero General Georgi Zhukov, defender of Moscow, whose statue adorns the entrance to Red Square, echoed the official approach: "The heroic feat of evacuation and restoration of industrial capacities during the war ... meant as much for the country's destiny as the greatest battles of the war."[8] Nothing more needed to be said.

Another recurring theme in Soviet times was the incredible generosity of members of the local population—sometimes Russian, sometimes ethnically "other"—who selflessly, "heroically," shared home and hearth with refugees and evacuees from afar. This, of course, was not the whole story, but it was the part of the story deemed acceptable at the time, that is, the mythology that the Soviet regime wanted to be accepted, for the sake of order and reinforcement of its own authority.[9]

Soviet authorities were keenly aware that refugees and evacuees were not always welcomed by local populations in the regions to which masses of "strangers," often perceived as "privileged strangers," from Moldavia, Russia, Ukraine, and other western republics found their way or were directed. The full story would not necessarily be a positive one if subjected to careful study, and would conflict with the notion of "the brotherhood of Soviet peoples" that remained a central Soviet propaganda line even as tensions between the communist regime and major non-Russian nationalities of the USSR, definitely including the nationalities of the Caucasus and Central Asia, became more evident in the final two decades of Soviet power. Why, therefore, risk delving deeply into the real experiences of the refugees, evacuees, and the local populations in places to which evacuees and refugees were sent? Why risk opening a Pandora's box?

There is even more that explains the lack of attention. There are issues of context that provided powerful incentives to avoid acknowledging the Holocaust and to avoid looking in-depth at the Jewish and non-Jewish refugee/evacuee phenomenon. No country on either side in World War II suffered more civilian casualties than the USSR. The estimate of lives lost ranges as high as 27 million people, among them 20 million civilians, and among these civilians up to 3 million Jews. Thus, nearly half of all the Jews murdered in the Holocaust were Soviet citizens when they were killed—from territory recently acquired from Poland and Romania, from Ukraine, Belarus, Russia, Latvia, Lithuania, Estonia, and other republics. An approximately equal number of Soviet POWs—prisoners of war—were starved or worked to death, or simply executed, after their capture by Axis forces, because Slavs were considered to be an inferior racial group in the eyes of Nazi race theorists and political leaders. Millions of other Soviet citizens were also brutally murdered for various reasons, or for no reason at all. Singling out the story of the Holocaust in this context, even if the fate of the Jews was unique in many respects, would have required a different attitude on the part of the Soviet government, or extraordinary courage on the part of an interested researcher.

Addressing the issue of "evacuation" was equally fraught with risk in a country with an extensive record of state-organized forced movement of populations. Stalin's deportation to special settlements of masses of kulaks, peasants, and others whom he considered potentially hostile to the Soviet system was still a recent memory. Many victims of these earlier mass evacuations had been forcibly resettled in the North Ural regions, Siberia, and Kazakhstan—regions to which World War II evacuees were also directed.[10] The Soviet deportation between 1939 and 1941 of Lithuanians, Latvians, Finns, Poles, Romanians, and Jews from the Baltic republics and Polish and Romanian territories, recently acquired as a result of the secret protocol of the Ribbentrop-Molotov non-aggression pact of August 1939, also produced a high death toll among the victims and bitter memories. Stalin's comprehensive resettlement of various ethnic groups, both before and continuing through (and after) the war, made any systematic exploration of "evacuation" and of related policy or experience a potentially risky undertaking, better avoided by government and researcher alike.[11]

Finally, at least in the early postwar decades, exploration of the experiences of flight and evacuation to the interior of the USSR could easily have stimulated interest in a more thorough exploration of the experience of millions of other Soviet civilians, from virtually all of the Nazi-occupied republics, who were torn from their families and taken away to forced labor inside the Third Reich or on construction projects behind the front that directly supported or facilitated the supply of Axis military operations. Many of these victims perished, never returned home, or never achieved reunification with their families. This was partially the result of Nazi policy and brutality. That aspect of the story might have been safe enough. But in part, the fates of many of these "double victims" resulted from filtration practices of the Soviet government after the war that often labeled returning forced laborers, and even Red Army POWs who had survived Nazi captivity, "unreliable" or "contaminated" by their exposure to the West. Many returnees exited Nazi control only to be sent by Soviet authorities directly to the Gulag for an additional term of forced confinement and labor. Addressing the experiences and concerns of refugees, deportees and evacuees could easily have raised issues that the Soviet state understandably wished to avoid.[12]

It is not surprising, then, that while a heroic version of the evacuation of civilians under Soviet authority, laced with examples of humanitarian, brotherly treatment of the refugees and evacuees by local populations in the destinations to which evacuees were sent, was encouraged, serious research into the full range of issues connected with the mass movement of millions of human beings—perhaps as many as 17 million—was not encouraged. Archives that would permit research into the broader story were inaccessible, and pursuit of a comprehensive picture of the Soviet government's performance and the refugee/evacuee experience during the Great Patriotic War was not possible.

The Collapse of the Soviet Union

The situation changed dramatically with the collapse of the Soviet Union, the establishment of independent states where before there had been Soviet republics, and the drive, in freedom, to explore topics that had long been kept off-limits. Publications relating to the Holocaust began to appear in some of the newly independent states. National and international commissions were established in some of the states where the murder of the Jews had been most extreme or had been carried out with significant participation by local collaborators. A broad array of archives dealing with the wartime period, which had been kept closed by Soviet authorities, slowly but surely were opened for study by academics and other researchers who understood that there was more to learn than Soviet censorship had permitted. As with Holocaust research, this opening of archives has had a dramatic impact on the study of flight and evacuation to the Soviet interior during the war.

Rather than trying to provide a long list of relevant archival and testimony collections, which would be impossible in fifteen or even a hundred pages, it is my intention here to provide a cursory review of some of the enlightening publications on the flight/evacuation phenomenon that have appeared most recently; a sense of the range of issues the authors addressed or identified as still needing to be studied; and a glimpse at the diversity of sources that have been utilized by recent authors and that beg further exploration. If recent publications are indicative, the evacuation center that has drawn the greatest attention of Western scholars thus far is Tashkent. Rebecca Manley's *To the Tashkent Station: Evacuation and Survival in the Soviet Union at War* (2009), which is the only monograph fully devoted to the subject that has appeared thus far, focuses on the flow of refugees and evacuees to Tashkent, the hardship and logistical complications endured along the way, the "standard of living" of various categories of refugees and evacuees in Tashkent, the mechanisms of control exercised by Soviet central and local authorities, relations between evacuees and the local population, both Russians and Uzbeks, and what happened when it became possible for some of the refugees and evacuees to return to their home cities.

Manley's book draws on astonishingly rich documentation from a set of archival repositories in the countries of the former USSR that is as diverse as the topics she seeks to cover, or at least to introduce as requiring additional future research. The list includes the Central State Archive of the Russian Federation and of Uzbekistan; the city and oblast archives of Tashkent, Odessa, Saint Petersburg, Volgograd, and Moscow; the central state film and photo archives of Uzbekistan and Saint Petersburg; literary archives, economic archives, archives of "social-political history," archives of the war, and numerous others, some quite specialized, ranging from national to municipal repositories, to the collections held by museums, libraries, and some private individuals. Through the material she surveyed, Manley is able to tell the story of massive displacement "from the vantage point of those who experienced it as well as those who conceived, organized, and implemented the operation."[13] It is clear from the opening passages of the book that at the human level, the experience was not the heroic tale the Soviets wished to tell, although for many of the citizens removed from home, family, support structures, and familiar surroundings, the actions required to survive physically in evacuation might be considered "heroic." It is also clear that the Soviet authorities' failure to effectively organize or implement key aspects of the evacuation, as well as their disapproval and often dismissive or discriminatory behavior toward refugees and self-evacuees, contributed to many of the hardships that refugees and evacuees experienced and, indeed, were responsible for the deaths of many refugees and evacuees, thus contributing to the tragically high number of civilian deaths the USSR endured during the war.

On this point, shortly after Manley's book was published, a related article by Albert Kaganovitch appeared in *Yad Vashem Studies* that delved even deeper into the impact of Soviet official policy and the attitudes of local authorities on the fate of Jewish refugees.[14] Making extensive use of both primary and secondary sources, both archival and testimonial in nature, Kaganovitch finds the key to understanding Soviet policy and the precarious situation of Jewish refugees and evacuees when he concludes, "Attempts of the Soviet central authorities to aid the evacuees stemmed exclusively from their concern for the functioning of the national economy. Sometimes these efforts not only failed to gain the support of local authorities, but also even met with their covert resistance."[15]

Manley's monograph, of course, is not solely, or even principally, the history of the Soviet government's policy successes and failures. She was motivated initially to undertake her book by letters in the files of the government housing authority, from individuals who had returned from evacuation to Moscow during the final months of the war, only to find that their apartments had been occupied by others. A good deal of her attention focuses on the experiences of normal people caught in an abnormal situation. Her use of memoirs, diaries, letters, and testimonies reveals the human story of flight and evacuation in a way no government file or report could. Her footnotes are full of such sources, too many to list, each signaling an issue requiring further exploration.

While Soviet-era writings on the evacuations, including the massive official history of the Great Patriotic War (1961), nearly always included reference to the priority given to saving the civilian population, in particular children, women with children, organizations dedicated to caring for children, and the elderly, Manley makes it clear that these more vulnerable segments of the civilian population were, in fact, a low priority for evacuation. She provides powerful detail of the struggles of mothers with children to obtain shelter and sufficient food to survive. Medical care, essential for older persons, was also in short supply and reserved for the priority categories of evacuees—skilled workers, engineers, employees of factories and enterprises that had been evacuated from the regions under or at risk of Nazi occupation, young people eligible for military service, party cadres, and select individuals and institutions from the intellectual and cultural spheres. Inclusion in these privileged categories or exclusion from them depended on age, ethnicity, position, skills, and "class" in the Soviet social hierarchy of values. Inclusion or exclusion could determine whether one was evacuated or not, the difficulty of the journey eastward, and the likelihood of survival or death.

Tensions developed quickly between evacuees and local populations, who frequently viewed the evacuees as "foreign," "rich," and "arrogant"; resented having people they did not know assigned housing in their apartments; and viewed the newcomers as competitors for food, shelter, and every other necessity or opportunity. The evacuees who were not among the "privileged," meanwhile, frequently found themselves separated from all family and friends, with none of the connections that were then, and remained, essential to making it in Soviet society. Jews, in particular, found themselves isolated and marginalized, both by the authorities and by local populations.[16] Corruption, favoritism, panic among both officials and civilians every time the front moved eastward, and repeated efforts by Soviet authorities to take control and dictate every detail, including whether one could stay at an evacuation location or had to move on, or perhaps leave the city and work on a collective farm, made many already vulnerable evacuees lose hope entirely.[17] The extreme shortage of virtually everything further exacerbated the situation. Manley captured all of this through the extensive source material she utilized.

In Baku,[18] these tensions and the perception of evacuees as marginal members of society—people without "fixed residence" and not engaged in "socially useful labor," to use Soviet terminology—resulted in the local NKVD, with the approval of the Council of People's Commissars, targeting evacuees as people who were to be removed from the city. The local decision to expel "all citizens who have arrived since the beginning of the war from territory temporarily occupied by the enemy, frontline regions, and regions adjacent to the front lines" was overturned by the Evacuation Council in Moscow, but left little room for doubt about local attitudes toward the evacuees.[19] As the war wore on, the notion that evacuees were not fully engaged in supporting the war effort, akin to "deserters" from the battles at both the "front" and the "rear," became more widespread. Official efforts to restrict evacuees to assigned locations and the establishment of mandatory work assignments from above began to grey the distinction between "evacuee" and "deportee," both of which existed by the millions in the territories still under Soviet control. Government control over who among the evacuees could return home, once that became possible, and when, and to what job or apartment, further blurred the distinction and left a certain stigma on returned evacuees for many years after World War II ended.[20]

In his *Tashkent: Forging a Soviet City, 1930–1966* (2010), Paul Stronski also gives considerable attention to the evacuation phenomenon and its impact. Like Manley, he draws on a rich diversity of source materials and, like Manley, deals in a balanced way with aspects of the mass movement of industry and people that could be considered successes, while also describing the organizational failures and "human costs" that "were tremendous, with large numbers of Soviet citizens left behind or dying of infectious diseases."[21] Stronski provides revealing examples of what he calls the "hierarchies of evacuation," established in accordance with Soviet social, political, and economic norms, and spells out the documentable consequences of being identified as a member of a group that stood higher or lower in these hierarchies. Age, institutional affiliation, job assignment, skills, party activism, the positions held by one's parents or relatives—all such factors determined whether one was evacuated or not; how one was treated if one had fled eastward (self-evacuated) as a refugee outside the parameters of the evacuation organized from above; whether one could take up residence in a city or was assigned to an isolated rural region;

whether one received a work assignment appropriate to one's skills or not; and whether housing or food or medical assistance could be obtained. Indeed, where one stood in the "hierarchies of evacuation" determined one's chances of survival in evacuation.

The "hierarchies of evacuation" also had dramatic consequences for local populations and institutions. Local professionals, individuals, and institutions were displaced or closed down to make way for evacuees and transferred institutions deemed by central authorities and local officials to be of greater significance to the war effort and for the maintenance of regime stability and values. Local cultural institutions were closed down or moved to new locations to make way for research and cultural institutions evacuated from Moscow and elsewhere in Axis-occupied territory or territory at risk of occupation. Local schools were used as housing for newly arrived factory workers or for the education of the children of evacuated elite groups, leaving local children without the opportunity to attend school for months on end. Healthcare facilities were taken over to serve evacuees high on the list of the privileged, or for the needs of wounded soldiers transported from the "real" front to the rear for rehabilitation. Because evacuees resisted work assignments outside urban areas, local people, including the students of universities and advanced training institutes, often were sent in their stead to work on collective farms.[22] All of these practices, combined with the insecurity that came from not knowing whether the USSR and the Soviet regime would survive the Nazi onslaught, only further exacerbated already existing cultural prejudices and stereotypes between evacuees and local populations.

In a convincing manner, Stronski documents that many evacuees, in particular those most committed to the preservation of the Soviet regime, viewed the local populations of Central Asia as "wild and uncivilized Eastern peoples whom Soviet power had not yet 'tamed.'" Many Russian residents of Tashkent, meanwhile, "dehumanized their Uzbek neighbors," viewing them as "primitive or barbaric." However, Stronski continues, both the privileged among the evacuees, as well as Russians long settled in Tashkent and the Uzbeks, "came to agreement in their dislike of a more recent arrival," the Jews. Jews endured ethnic slurs and physical assault. Jewish female evacuees, assigned to rural areas and collective farms without male relatives to protect them, fell victim to rape and other forms of abuse. To the extent that Ashkenazi Jewish refugees were identified as outsiders, of different religion, and were closely identified in the public mind with the Soviet system and the hardships it had inflicted on the regions to which evacuees were moved, their situation was especially disadvantageous. When official circles began to reinforce the notion that Jewish refugees and evacuees were double "deserters," who evaded army service at the front and then shirked labor assignments in the rear, the isolation and despair of the Jews, who were also increasingly aware that their entire families had been wiped out in territories under Axis control, reached new heights.[23]

Censorship (*Gorispolkom*) files found in the Tashkent City Archive, containing excerpts from intercepted letters and telegrams from residents of Tashkent to relatives in the Red Army and unoccupied cities in European Russia, are among Stronksi's most interesting sources. They provide remarkable detail regarding the real situation of evacuees and the many problems outlined above. Deprivation, lack of heat, shelter, food, medical assistance; dismissive treatment by local bureaucrats; the sale of last clothes, blood, anything to buy food; mistreatment by landlords; favoritism; prejudice; orphaned children exposed and unprotected; despair—all are revealed through individual human stories captured by the censors and now a rich source for research.[24]

There can be no question that the evacuation experience encompassed heroic labor and extraordinary generosity and humanity, as Soviet era sources amply chronicled. But it also encompassed enormous official ineptitude, suffering, prejudice, and danger. The sources that have become available since the demise of the USSR now make it possible to learn about both sides of the story.

After reviewing recent publications and some of the sources available regarding one of the major evacuation destinations, it is important to look also at recent scholarship and newly accessible sources that relate to the locations from which evacuees came. Karel Berkhoff's *Motherland in Danger: Soviet Propaganda during World War II* (2012) provides a unique perspective and insightful follow-up to his earlier *Harvest of Despair* (2004), which focused exclusively on Ukraine under Nazi rule. Drawing extensively on World War II–era Soviet print and broadcast media, records of the Soviet Information Bureau and other offices of the Soviet government, as well as a growing array of recent memoir literature, Berkhoff first describes the initial denial in Soviet propaganda that any evacuation at all was underway, denial even as masses of people fled the advance of Axis armies. The government feared that if the evacuation became broadly known, it would be "detrimental to willingness to fight the Germans to the death," which was the overriding thrust of Soviet propaganda in the first months of the war. Until late November 1941, the evacuation of people and factories that had been secretly ordered within days of the Nazis' June 22 attack was an official secret. It was not until November 25, 1941, that the Soviet Information Bureau belatedly announced that the main part of the civilian population had been evacuated east. And it was only much later, in 1942, that the massive evacuation of industry was publicized as a major achievement.

From the start, Soviet propaganda emphasized that evacuees were welcomed in the regions to which they had been sent, and multiple stories were published affirming how well Ukrainian workers and intelligentsia from Ukraine had been integrated into their host communities (their "new paternal home"). The media presented the kinds of problems studied by Manley and Stronski as minor issues. Late in the war, as evacuees started to ask about the possibility of returning home, Soviet propaganda outlets began to indicate that return home might not be permitted, given the interests of the state and the reality that many of the evacuated factories would remain in the east. This development added to the blurring of lines between "evacuee" and "deportee" that the evacuation experience itself had already set in motion.[25]

In addition to his treatment of refugees and evacuees, Berkhoff provides clear proof that by early 1942, with hundreds of thousands of Soviet Jews already murdered, in many cases within plain sight of their non-Jewish neighbors and fellow citizens across the whole expanse of Axis-occupied Soviet territory, official Soviet propaganda had begun to minimize attention paid to the particular fate of the Jews. This policy, begun while the genocide of the Jews was still under way, continued through the remainder of the war and virtually the entire postwar era of Soviet rule. Stalin's personal animosity toward Jews coupled here with concern that many citizens of the USSR would respond positively to Nazi propaganda linking Jews and Bolshevism, resulting in a policy designed to avoid any perception that the war was being fought to save Jews. Ironically, in this regard, Soviet policy mirrored that of the USSR's Western allies, the United States and United Kingdom. The Soviet media blackout on information regarding the mass murder of the Jews was not total. Berkhoff provides examples to illustrate this point, and Ilya Ehrenburg's powerful wartime articles demonstrate the same. But the particular Jewish tragedy was not a focus of attention. Neither was the heroism or ultimate sacrifice of thousands of Jewish soldiers who served in the Red Army. Soviet propaganda shaped the perception of a wartime and several postwar generations of Soviet citizens, who were made to understand that the USSR suffered up to 20 million civilian deaths during the war, but had no idea that no Soviet nationality suffered as many deaths in absolute terms (some 2.6 million), or as a percentage (over 50 percent), as the Jews.[26]

In *Bloodlands: Europe between Hitler and Stalin* (2010), Timothy Snyder also addresses these issues. Snyder provides a rich overview as he creates a picture of the peoples, political and economic forces and interests, and the seemingly centuries-long continuous conflict and suffering that constituted reality in the lands between Germany and Russia. He dedicates an important chapter to Germany's systematic extermination of the Jews, but it is his discussion of the multiple forced migrations of ethnic populations under Stalin that makes the greatest contribution to contextualizing the special nature of the evacuation of civilians and industry toward the Urals, the Caucasus, and Central Asia. Snyder addresses the forced resettlement during the war of ethnic groups that Stalin considered unreliable, and it is the ethnicity-based focus of most of Europe's forced migrations of the twentieth century that is clarified. Snyder's extended treatment of the forced movements of Poles, from west to east, then back to the west, and even further west into former German territories incorporated into Poland after the war, coupled with the forced movement eastward of Ukrainians left inside postwar Poland and the cleansing of Germans from the European territories of the USSR (and to a large extent, from the newly communized states of Soviet-dominated Eastern Europe as well), makes the point very powerfully. The evacuation of civilian populations in the Soviet Union was fundamentally different from other forced migrations directed from above. The topic requires greater attention and, fortunately, has begun to receive it.[27]

While Snyder places the distinct situation of the Jews during the years of Nazi domination of Europe in broad regional and multi-ethnic context, a final set of recent publications focuses attention specifically on the Jews and further clarifies why research on the refugee/evacuee phenomenon is important as part of study of the Holocaust.

Two related articles appeared in the journal *Holocaust and Genocide Studies* in 2012. In the first, Vadim Doubson advocates the creation of a names database of evacuated Soviet Jews and provides extensive references to archival and other sources that would, if thoroughly researched, provide the information needed to make the database nearly comprehensive. The cited sources range from a growing body of statistical, demographic, and historical publications that have appeared in former Soviet republics since they gained their independence, to Western and Israeli scholarship, and finally and most importantly, to archives at both the national and local levels in all of the former republics from which Jewish refugees and evacuees originated and all of the former republics to which they fled or were evacuated. Doubson addresses archival riches that include the massive archives of the Soviet Extraordinary State Commission to Investigate German-Fascist Crimes Committed on Soviet Territory from the USSR, located in the State Archive of the Russian Federation (GARF); records of the Department for the Economic Employment of the Evacuated Population; statistical and census records; records of the Evacuation Council that oversaw the official evacuation on behalf of the Soviet state; central and oblast archives of Uzbekistan, Kazakhstan, and other republics that received large numbers of evacuees or through which evacuees transited; and the records of the Tracing and Information Center of the Russian Red Cross. The potential sources that Doubson suggests are too numerous to name, but the list indicates how massive in scope are the hitherto little used, but now accessible, archival materials relating to the evacuation of Jews and others during World War II. The project that Doubson proposes would have substantial memorial significance, but that is not all. Until it is clearer how many Jews successfully fled eastward as Axis forces advanced through Soviet territory, and until we know how many Jews were evacuated as part of the state-run evacuation, and whether they survived or perished in evacuation, it will remain difficult to gain greater precision than up to now in determining the actual number of Jews murdered by the Nazis and their allies and collaborators on Soviet territory.[28]

In a second article in the same issue of *Holocaust and Genocide Studies*, Sergei Maksudov argues that excessive reliance on official documentation of the sorts enumerated by Doubson might result in a distorted picture. Maksudov makes a convincing case that the systematic use of memoirs and oral histories, in particular of former refugees and evacuees, would ensure authenticity and provide important information that might be lost in official, bureaucratic reporting. Maksudov relates the story of his own extended family during and following evacuation to illustrate this point. One of his relatives was irretrievably lost and never heard from again, as he tried to reach Baku, where a part of his family was already living.[29]

The validity of Maksudov's point was reinforced two years later in an innovative article by Anna Shternshis that explores why some Soviet Jews chose to flee their homes following the Axis attack on the USSR in June 1941, while others decided that staying put was the better course. Based principally on memoir literature and on hundreds of interviews "with Jewish men ... and women ... who spent at least a portion of the war years as evacuees or refugees in Central Asia or the Urals," 198 of which Shternshis conducted personally, the article identifies a multiplicity of factors that impacted the decision-making process, including a fear of violence at the hands of one's neighbors that rivaled fear of the invader. While Shternshis concludes that oral testimony "can be both extremely useful and misleading at the same time," she is effective in applying the kind of rigorous scrutiny to this relatively underutilized research resource that has long been applied to archival documentation, for example, and leaves no doubt about the contribution that the use of written and oral testimony can make to our understanding of complex historical events.[30]

One final contribution bears mention in this review of recent scholarly literature. In 2007 Kiril Feferman authored an important short study of the experience of Jewish refugees and evacuees in the North Caucasus, providing an early indication of the important research he had undertaken for the doctoral dissertation he completed that same year at the Hebrew University of Jerusalem.[31] Feferman's revised and updated dissertation, published as *The Holocaust in the Crimea and the North Caucasus* (2016), places the fate of Jewish refugees and evacuees in the context of a study focused on the fate of all Jews in a geographic region that was home to significant communities of local Jews and to and through which huge numbers of refugees and evacuees passed, seeking safety in the Soviet interior.[32] Feferman draws on published, archival, and testimonial sources to present a nuanced picture of the vulnerability of the hundreds of thousands of Jews who either passed through the North Caucasus or tried to settle there as they fled or were evacuated in advance of the Nazi drive toward Moscow, Stalingrad, and Baku. The range of testimonies consulted by Feferman is particularly impressive, including substantial numbers of both affidavits gathered in 1943–1944 by the Soviet Extraordinary State Commission and postwar testimonies of evacuation survivors and their families recorded from the 1960s to the 1990s. On the basis of the sources he consulted, Feferman is able to provide information on the number of Jews who settled in various localities in the North Caucasus, describe their interactions with local populations, and provide a detailed micro-history of the Jewish evacuees who had reached Krasnodar Krai as of October 1, 1941. On that date, there were 218,000 evacuees in the district, 73 percent of whom were Jews, in the main from Bukovina, Ukraine, and Soviet Moldavia (Bessarabia). Feferman's analysis of evacuee/refugee registration documents provides a statistical breakdown of the evacuees by gender and age, and reveals a disproportionate number of children among the displaced, the result of the organized evacuation of 24 children's homes from localities threatened by the Nazi advance.

As elsewhere, considerable prejudice was directed toward the Jews by segments of the local population, and as Nazi forces came closer, animosity toward the Jews increased and sympathy decreased. The Nazi occupation of the region from August to December 1942 constituted a death sentence for the Jewish evacuees who did not manage to flee further eastward. German propaganda exploited a variety of antisemitic themes, from the identification of Jews with Bolshevism to the charge that Jewish influence was responsible for the Red Army's massive losses of soldiers killed and captured. These losses, so the argument went, were the result of a Jewish-dictated government policy that prioritized the evacuation of Jews to presumed safety in the east, at the expense of the Soviet war effort. Understandably, this propaganda line had an impact on local families from which fathers and sons had been sent to the front or had fallen in battle. Having effectively diminished the likelihood that Jews would find local protectors or assistance in their efforts to move on, German forces gathered the Jews settled in the towns and villages of the North Caucasus region and executed them.

Conclusion

All of these recent publications—and it is important to remember that I have presented only works by Western authors—illustrate the wealth of sources that can be tapped to better understand the refugee/evacuee experience in the Soviet Union during World War II. Published works, memoirs, archives, and testimonies all offer new insights, both as to what happened and as to the issues requiring further exploration even today, some seven decades after the event. I have suggested some of these issues in the paragraphs above. They are issues that go to the very heart of how the refugee/evacuation phenomenon will be remembered, what we can learn from it, and what our obligation is to teach future generations about one of the most massive movements of population that took place in a century characterized by the mass movement—most often the forced mass movement—of civilians.

There can be no question that for Jews evacuation meant possible survival, while falling under German control meant near-certain death. But for others, did evacuation represent salvation or punishment? How clear was the distinction between evacuation and deportation or exile? Was evacuation intended to be temporary or permanent, that is, more akin to other forced migrations under Soviet rule? Did the evacuation phenomenon attenuate or exacerbate tensions among Soviet nationalities, and how significant an impact did this have on developments in the USSR after the war was over? How were evacuees treated after the war? Veteran fighters at the front were heroes. Were veterans of what Zhukov labeled "heroic evacuation" also treated as heroes, or did they carry a permanent stigma for having survived "in the rear"? For Jews, Soviet postwar antisemitism made these questions easy to answer: Jewish military heroes were no heroes, and Jewish refugees and evacuees lived out their lives with "The Jews fought the war in Tashkent!" ringing in their ears. After the war, some Jewish evacuees chose to remain in the republics to which they had fled or been evacuated.[33] Why they did so and the consequences of their choice, if it was a choice, remain topics to be explored. In an era of open access to research resources and free expression of ideas, it is time to look at all of these issues with sensitivity and openness to what new research findings will reveal.

Notes

1. Rebecca Manley, *To the Tashkent Station: Evacuation and Survival in the Soviet Union at War* (Ithaca, NY: Cornell University Press, 2009), 1.

2. Sergei Maksudov, "Evacuation Documentation and Testimonies as Sources for the Study of Soviet Jewish Population Losses during World War II," *Holocaust and Genocide Studies* 26, no. 1 (Spring 2012): 125.

3. See "The Evacuation of Industry" in Alexander Werth, *Russia at War: 1941–1945* (New York: E. P. Duttan, 1964), 213–14.

4. Ibid., 565, with quotations from I. V. Tyulenev, *Cherez Tri Voiny* (Through Three Wars) (Moscow, 1960), 176.

5. See, for example, Lionel Kochan, ed., *The Jews in Soviet Russia since 1917* (London: Oxford University Press, 1970),140–43, on Jews killed; 114–15, on the trip by leaders of the Jewish Anti-Fascist Committee to the United States and England in 1943; and 198–202 and 262–63 on Jewish writers. For a more complete history of the Jewish Anti-Fascist Committee, its indictment and trial, and the execution of its leadership, see Joshua Rubenstein and Vladimir P. Naumov, *Stalin's Secret Pogrom: The Postwar Inquisition of the Jewish Anti-Fascist Committee* (New Haven, CT: Yale University Press, in association with the United States Holocaust Memorial Museum, 2001).

6. On Jews in the Soviet military, see, for example, Oleg Budnitsky, "The 'Jewish Battalions' in the Red Army," in *Revolution, Repression, and Revival: The Soviet Jewish Experience*, ed. Zvi Gitelman and Yaacov Ro'i (Lanham, MD: Rowman & Littlefield, 2007), 15–36; and the recorded testimonies of Jewish Red Army veterans in the Blavatnik Family Foundation Oral History Archives (New York).

7. On the "Black Book," see Rubenstein and Naumov, *Stalin's Secret Pogrom*, 17–18; and Joshua Rubenstein and Ilya Altman, eds., *The Unknown Black Book: The Holocaust in the German-Occupied Soviet Territories* (Bloomington: Indiana University Press, in association with the United States Holocaust Memorial Museum, 2008).

8. As quoted in Manley, *To the Tashkent Station*, 3.

9. On themes during the Soviet era, see Paul Stronski, *Tashkent: Forging a Soviet City, 1930–1966* (Pittsburgh: University of Pittsburgh Press, 2010), 142.

10. See Lynn Viola, *The Unknown Gulag: The Lost World of Stalin's Special Settlements* (New York: Oxford University Press, 2007).

11. On the deportation of Poles to the Soviet interior in 1939–1941 and the forced movement of ethnic minorities during the war, including

minorities from the Caucasus, Germans, Karachais, Kalmyks, Chechens, Ingushi, Balkars, Crimean Tatars, Meshketian Turks, and others, see Timothy Snyder, *Bloodlands: Europe between Hitler and Stalin* (New York: Basic Books, 2010), 126–28 and 329–33; Karel C. Berkhoff, *Motherland in Danger: Soviet Propaganda during World War II* (Cambridge, MA: Harvard University Press, 2012), 216–22; and Yitzchak Arad, *The Holocaust in the Soviet Union* (Lincoln: University of Nebraska Press and Yad Vashem, Jerusalem, 2009), 49–50.

12. On forced labor for the Nazis, see "Deportations and Forced Migrations" in Karel C. Berkhoff, *Harvest of Despair: Life and Death in Ukraine under Nazi Rule* (Cambridge, MA: Belknap Press of Harvard University Press, 2004), 253–74. There are hundreds of thousands of documents relating to Soviet forced laborers in Nazi Germany in the archives of the International Tracing Service in Bad Arolsen, Germany, and also in the archives of organizations such as *Memorial* in Moscow which, following the collapse of communism, assisted former Soviet forced laborers to apply for modest compensation payments made available by the Federal Republic of Germany under a series of forced labor settlement agreements concluded in the 1990s and the first years of the following decade. Soviet authorities had not permitted individual citizens of the USSR to make application to earlier compensation programs of this kind. Copies of the International Tracing Service records are available at the United States Holocaust Memorial Museum. For an early treatment of the return of Soviet forced laborers and POWs to the Soviet Union, including both Allied and Soviet policies on the matter, see Nikolai Tolstoy, *The Secret Betrayal, 1944–1947* (New York: Charles Scribner's Sons, 1977).

13. Manley, *To the Tashkent Station*, 2.

14. Albert Kaganovitch, "Jewish Refugees and Soviet Authorities during World War II," *Yad Vashem Studies* 38, no. 2 (2010): 85–121. Kaganovitch has continued to make substantive specialized contributions to our understanding of this topic. See, for example, his "Stalin's Great Power Politics, the Return of Jewish Refugees to Poland, and Continued Migration to Palestine, 1944–1946," *Holocaust and Genocide Studies* 26, no.1 (Spring 2012): 59–94, and also his "Estimating the Number of Jewish Refugees, Deportees, and Draftees from Bessarabia and Northern Bukovina in the Non-Occupied Soviet Territories," *Holocaust and Genocide Studies* 27, no. 3 (Winter 2013): 464–82.

15. Kaganovitch, "Jewish Refugees," 120.

16. On the particular animosity directed at Jewish refugees and evacuees, see Manley, *To the Tashkent Station*, 229–36.

17. The vulnerability of Jewish deportees to repeated forced relocation during the war and facing restrictions on their ability to return home once the war ended is convincingly presented in a recent special-case study of Lithuanian Jewish deportees; see Eliyana R. Adler, "Exile and Survival: Lithuanian Jewish Deportees in the Soviet Union," in *Ha-Kayitz ha-norah ha-hu: 70 shana le-hashmadat ha-kehilot ha-yehudiot be-'are ha-sadeh be-Lita*, ed. Michal Ben Ya'akov, Gershon Greenberg, and Sigalit Rosmarin (Jerusalem: Efrata College, 2013), xxvii–xlix.

18. An early draft of this chapter was presented at the symposium "Caucasus, Azerbaijan, and World War II" held in Baku on October 17–19, 2012.

19. See Manley, *To the Tashkent Station*, 153, citing documentation in the State Archives of the Russian Federation (GARF).

20. On Baku and the imposition of greater control over evacuee freedom of movement and employment, see Manley, *To the Tashkent Station*, 153–59.

21. Stronski, *Tashkent*, xx.

22. See ibid., chaps. 4 ("War and Evacuation") and 5 ("Central Asian Lives at War"), 72–144, for Stronski's examination and analysis of these issues.

23. See ibid., 121–24. In addition to this particular animosity toward Jewish newcomers (though apparently not toward Mountain, Bukharin, and other local Jewish communities), local populations also resented the fact that large ethnic groups suspected of being enemies of the state (e.g., Volga Germans, Crimean Tatars, etc.) were being resettled in their midst; see ibid., 132–33. On the concerns of Soviet authorities regarding the loyalty of Caucasus and Central Asian nationalities, and in particular the Muslim nationalities, see Werth, *Russia at War*, 574–76.

24. Stronski, *Tashkent*, 134–42.

25. Berkhoff, *Motherland in Danger*, 107–10.

26. Berkhoff's treatment of this subject is in chap. 6 ("A Bestial Plan for Physical Extermination") in ibid., 134–66 and 218–22. Earlier he dedicated chap. 3 ("The Holocaust of the Jews and Roma") in *Harvest of Despair*, 59–88, to the topic.

27. See Snyder, *Bloodlands*, chap. 6 ("Final Solution"), 186–223; and 128–30 and 326–35, regarding ethnic cleansings of Poles, Ukrainians, and Germans.

28. Vadim Doubson, "Toward a Central Database of Evacuated Soviet Jews' Names, for the Study of the Holocaust in the Occupied Soviet Territories," *Holocaust and Genocide Studies* 26, no. 1 (Spring 2012): 95–119.

29. Maksudov, "Evacuation Documentation and Testimonies," 120–30.

30. Anna Shternshis, "Between Life and Death: Why Some Soviet Jews Decided to Leave and Others to Stay in 1941," *Kritika: Explorations in Russian and Eurasian History* 15, no. 3, n.s. (2014): 477–504.

31. Kiril Feferman, "Jewish Refugees and Evacuees under Soviet Rule and German Occupation: The North Caucasus," in Gitelman and Ro'i, *Revolution, Repression, and Revival*, 155–78.

32. Kiril Feferman, *The Holocaust in the Crimea and the North Caucasus* (Jerusalem: Yad Vashem, 2016).

33. See Kochan, *The Jews in Soviet Russia since 1917*, 142.

Bibliography

Adler, Eliyana R. "Exile and Survival: Lithuanian Jewish Deportees in the Soviet Union." In *Ha-Kayitz ha-norah ha-hu: 70 shana le-hashmadat ha-kehilot ha-yehudiot be-'are ha-sadeh be-Lita*, ed. Michal Ben Ya'akov, Gershon Greenberg, and Sigalit Rosmarin, xxvii–xlix. Jerusalem: Efrata College, 2013.

Arad, Yitzchak. *The Holocaust in the Soviet Union*. Lincoln: University of Nebraska Press and Yad Vashem, Jerusalem, 2009.

Berkhoff, Karel C. *Harvest of Despair: Life and Death in Ukraine under Nazi Rule*. Cambridge, MA: Belknap Press of Harvard University Press, 2004.

———. *Motherland in Danger: Soviet Propaganda during World War II*. Cambridge, MA: Harvard University Press, 2012.

Budnitsky, Oleg. "The 'Jewish Battalions' in the Red Army." In *Revolution, Repression, and Revival: The Soviet Jewish Experience*, ed. Zvi Gitelman and Yaacov Ro'i, 15–36. Lanham, MD: Rowman & Littlefield, 2007.

Doubson, Vadim. "Toward a Central Database of Evacuated Soviet Jews' Names, for the Study of the Holocaust in the Occupied Soviet Territories." *Holocaust and Genocide Studies* 26, no. 1 (Spring 2012): 95–119.

Feferman, Kiril. *The Holocaust in the Crimea and the North Caucasus*. Jerusalem: Yad Vashem, 2016.

———. "Jewish Refugees and Evacuees under Soviet Rule and German Occupation: The North Caucasus." In *Revolution, Repression, and Revival: The Soviet Jewish Experience*, ed. Zvi Gitelman and Yaacov Ro'i, 155–78. Lanham, MD: Rowman & Littlefield, 2007.

Kaganovitch, Albert. "Estimating the Number of Jewish Refugees, Deportees, and Draftees from Bessarabia and Northern Bukovina in the Non-Occupied Soviet Territories." *Holocaust and Genocide Studies* 27, no. 3 (Winter 2013): 464–82.

———. "Jewish Refugees and Soviet Authorities during World War II." *Yad Vashem Studies* 38, no. 2 (2010): 85–121.

———. "Stalin's Great Power Politics, the Return of Jewish Refugees to Poland, and Continued Migration to Palestine, 1944–1946." *Holocaust and Genocide Studies* 26, no.1 (Spring 2012): 59–94.

Kochan, Lionel, ed. *The Jews in Soviet Russia since 1917*. London: Oxford University Press, 1970.

Maksudov, Sergei. "Evacuation Documentation and Testimonies as Sources for the Study of Soviet Jewish Population Losses during World War II." *Holocaust and Genocide Studies* 26, no. 1 (Spring 2012): 120–30.

Manley, Rebecca. *To the Tashkent Station: Evacuation and Survival in the Soviet Union at War*. Ithaca, NY: Cornell University Press, 2009.

Rubenstein, Joshua, and Ilya Altman, eds. *The Unknown Black Book: The Holocaust in the German-Occupied Soviet Territories*. Bloomington: Indiana University Press, in association with the United States Holocaust Memorial Museum, 2008.

Rubenstein, Joshua, and Vladimir P. Naumov. *Stalin's Secret Pogrom: The Postwar Inquisition of the Jewish Anti-Fascist Committee*. New Haven, CT: Yale University Press, in association with the United States Holocaust Memorial Museum, 2001.

Shternshis, Anna. "Between Life and Death: Why Some Soviet Jews Decided to Leave and Others to Stay in 1941." *Kritika: Explorations in Russian and Eurasian History* 15, no. 3, n.s. (Summer 2014): 477–504.

Snyder, Timothy. *Bloodlands: Europe between Hitler and Stalin*. New York: Basic Books, 2010.

Stronski, Paul. *Tashkent: Forging a Soviet City, 1930–1966*. Pittsburgh: University of Pittsburgh Press, 2010.

Tolstoy, Nikolai. *The Secret Betrayal, 1944–1947*. New York: Charles Scribner's Sons, 1977.

Tyulenev, General I.V. *Cherez Tri Voiny* (Through Three Wars). Moscow, 1960.

Viola, Lynn. *The Unknown Gulag: The Lost World of Stalin's Special Settlements*. New York: Oxford University Press, 2007.

Werth, Alexander. *Russia at War, 1941–1945*. New York: E. P. Dutton, 1964.

8

Ravensbrück Women's Concentration Camp

Memories in Situ

INSA ESCHEBACH

Memorials are "stages for socially recognized and official commemorative practices." They "do not merely represent the mainstream of memorial culture," but also sanction and canonize certain interpretations of history.[1] Memorials are therefore also agents of memorialization processes. However, there are differences between the various national spaces of memory. In France, for example, public memory of the German camps has a very different emphasis than in the countries of the former Soviet Union.

Ravensbrück, located in the Brandenburg Lake district about 100 kilometers north of Berlin, was the largest women's concentration camp within the German Reich. Around 139,000 women and children and 20,000 men from more than thirty countries were deported to the camp. Apart from the women's camp, the Ravensbrück complex comprised a smaller men's camp, the Siemens camp, the Uckermark or "juvenile protective custody camp," as well as around forty satellite camps. Roughly 28,000 Ravensbrück prisoners lost their lives in these camps. On April 30, 1945, the Red Army liberated the camp, subsequently occupied the entire grounds, and continued to use the former camp for military purposes until 1994.

From 1948, a small piece of land outside the camp's wall was used for commemorative purposes. Until then, this area by the banks of Lake

Ravensbrück Women's Concentration Camp

Ravensbrück Women's Concentration Camp shortly after liberation, June 1945.
Photo: Lysenko, Gosudarstvennyj archiv Rossijskoi federacii (GARF), 9526/4/46/31.

Schwedt had been used both by the local population and the Red Army as a source of building materials and was otherwise completely neglected. Ashes and human remains had been carelessly left lying around the crematorium. Members of the Association of Victims of Nazi Persecution started with renovation work in 1948 and initiated the first commemoration ceremonies with the help of an improvised wooden monument. In the 1950s, East Germany's Ministry of Cultural Affairs commissioned a group of architects known as the Buchenwald Collective to draw up a concept for the design of a Ravensbrück Memorial. The crematorium's annex was demolished and new, larger doors were put in to "enable the demonstrations to pass through the crematorium more rapidly."[2] These alterations were carried out to adapt the crematorium to the requirements of public commemorative celebrations—a process that occurred often during the design of concentration camp memorials after 1945 and which Volkhard Knigge has aptly described as the minimization of the relics in favor of a maximization of meaning.[3]

INSA ESCHEBACH

The Site

In that comparatively small area, the Ravensbrück Memorial Museum was inaugurated in 1959 as one of the three major concentration camp memorials of the German Democratic Republic (GDR), the other two being Buchenwald and Sachsenhausen. The design of the Ravensbrück Memorial includes three historical monuments: the crematorium, the camp prison, and the camp wall with a mass grave, where the ashes that were found at and around the crematorium, along with 283 bodies found in the area of the camp, had been buried.[4] On the banks of Lake Schwedt, a sculpture titled *Burdened Woman* was erected on a pedestal projecting into the lake: a female bronze figure carrying another slumped woman stands on a plinth around twenty-five feet high. Many survivors who visit the Ravensbrück Memorial for the first time do not recognize the grounds. The majority of the prisoners knew the camp only from the inside and had never had access to the area outside the camp wall on the banks of Lake Schwedt. Survivors find it difficult to reconcile their memories of the prisoners' compound made up of wooden huts with the memorial site on the banks of Lake Schwedt. As mentioned, the site of the former camp was used by the Soviet Army: the grounds served as a fuel depot and were not publicly accessible. Not a single wooden hut was left standing after the CIS troops withdrew in 1994.

What role did the survivors' memories play in the development of the Ravensbrück Memorial? I would like to suggest that individual memories were not the decisive factor. Rather, the memorial manifested the GDR's policies to honor the dead and to ensure that they were remembered as heroes. Another important goal was to create a site where large groups of people could gather for commemorative ceremonies.

Early forms of commemoration and designs of monuments were often modeled on conventions and traditional views of history, not only in Ravensbrück, but in other places as well. Immediately after 1945, the aim of commemorative practices was not to show the unprecedented nature of the Nazis' crimes or to make clear how much of a breach of civilization they had been. Rather, in their design and wording, the new memorial sites, monuments, and plaques followed national and religious traditions of honoring the dead. One example is the provisional pedestal and cauldron of flames from 1954. For the official opening of the Ravensbrück

Ravensbrück Women's Concentration Camp

Ravensbrück Memorial Site on the banks of Lake Schwedt with the crematorium and a bronze cauldron, 1984. Photo: Diwischek, Mahn- und Gedenkstätte Ravensbrück, photo no. 2358.

Memorial in 1959, a bronze cauldron was erected. Compared to the cauldrons at the Buchenwald Memorial, which feature very prominently at the site, the Ravensbrück cauldron seems rather small and modest. However, we need to keep in mind that only a few years previously, cauldrons of flame formed almost indispensable elements of Nazi public ritual culture; the flames belong to a long national tradition of honoring the dead. This analogy between death in a concentration camp and the patriotic motif of a soldier's ultimate sacrifice takes the Nazi genocide out of its historical context. At the same time, this interpretation also allowed people to assign meaning to the violent deaths of concentration camp prisoners by placing them in the tradition of sacrifices made in doing a patriotic duty. For decades, this interpretation was a formative element of the public memory of the concentration camps in the GDR (but also, to a certain extent, in West Germany). Many groups of prisoners such as Jews, Sinti, Roma, and Jehovah's Witnesses, or the so-called anti-social elements, did not fit into this national model of interpretation and were therefore not commemorated at Ravensbrück for a long time.

Burdened Woman, by Willi Lammert, 1959. Photo: Ernst Schäfer, Mahn- und Gedenkstätte Ravensbrück, photo no. 2321.

However, practical considerations also played an important role in the transformation of part of the former concentration camp into a place for honoring the dead. For example, after the liberation of Ravensbrück, several cemeteries were established in the vicinity of the camp. These cemeteries held the corpses of prisoners found at the camp during the liberation, as well as the bodies of those who died after the liberation from the effects of their imprisonment. In 1952, the two cemeteries were dissolved, and the remains of 283 adults and children were reburied. The newly created mass grave was located at the foot of the camp wall. As already mentioned, large amounts of human ashes and bones found at the crematorium had been buried here in 1948. In 1959, roses were planted on this new grave. A total of three cemeteries located in the immediate vicinity of the former prisoners' compound were leveled at the time, an act which effectively centralized the commemoration of the dead in the area along the banks of Lake Schwedt. This concentration, however, also served to consign to oblivion the vast size of the Ravensbrück camp complex and the actual circumstances under which its prisoners had died.

I do not think that this centralization rested on a conscious decision by identifiable individuals, made as part of an explicit commemorative policy. Rather, it was based on pragmatic considerations: records from the late 1940s show that commemorative ceremonies were held, during which attendees would visit the various cemeteries. This made bus transfers to and from the various sites necessary, which suggests that centralizing the commemoration at one particular site (in this case, on the banks of Lake Schwedt) was simply more pragmatic.

The Iconography

The statue known as *Burdened Woman* by sculptor Will Lammert served as a topographical point of reference for the site. This sculpture is frequently referred to as the "Ravensbrück Pieta." Unlike traditional Pieta representations, however, the foot of *Burdened Woman* appears to be stepping over the edge of the pedestal, giving the impression that she is striding across the lake. The statue thus points to new beginnings and the defeat of death. According to contemporary sources, *Burdened Woman* was intended to be viewed as a "symbol of freedom" and thereby represents the end of the story, providing a sense of closure. Her gesture evokes thoughts of overcoming death, of a new beginning—something the GDR claimed to have achieved. The lamentation of Mary is transformed into an act of compassionate solidarity.[5]

How does this sculpture reflect the memories of former prisoners? We do have numerous accounts of acts of solidarity among Ravensbrück prisoners, and many of them mention individual women—often from the same national group—forming so-called camp families, groups based on mutual support, to increase their chances of survival. However, there are also many statements from survivors that contradict this image of a harmonious prisoner society based on mutual solidarity. Margarete Buber-Neumann, for example, writes:

> Christianity claims that man is spiritually purged and ennobled through suffering. Life in the concentration camp has proven the opposite to be true. I believe there is nothing more dangerous than misery and excessive suffering.... The women tried to make up for what was being done to them.... One would look at another with great envy and resentment. A dry piece of bread or a slightly larger bit of margarine or sausage was enough to provoke outbreaks of hatred and oaths of revenge.[6]

I propose to consider whether the idea of a "counter-memory" might not be more useful for interpreting *Burdened Woman* than the term "memory." Geoffrey H. Hartman defines "counter-memories" as follows: "Forgetting on a collective scale can itself assume the guise of a memory," he writes. "That which appears in the guise of memory is a 'counter-memory,'" a "highly selective story, focused on what is basic for the community and turning away from everything else."[7]

The idea of solidarity among the female prisoners has been crucial for the public memory of Ravensbrück. In this context, *Burdened Woman* represents something that is "basic for the community." Irrespective of the large number of former prisoners who recall very different forms of behavior in the camp, *Burdened Woman* represents an attitude that offers comfort through the memory of maternalism in the face of the camp's horrors.

Sara Horowitz has pointed out that maternalism has played a preeminent role in literary Holocaust representations. Maternalism is the very essence of goodness and altruism. Maternalism unites the extraordinary with the ordinary, and, according to Horowitz, "tames the Holocaust."[8] Could we say that maternalism, as represented at Ravensbrück, "tames the Holocaust?" Does *Burdened Woman* really refer to the Shoah? Can this sculpture be seen as a Holocaust monument at all?

The intentions behind both the memorial site and the monument at the time it was erected may be discerned from a book, 10,000 copies of which were published in four languages shortly after the Memorial Museum was opened.[9] It was presented to groups of visitors and school groups right up to the end of the GDR in 1989. This book can be described as an important manifestation of the influence of communist memorial culture on Ravensbrück.

The first sentence of this book, defining Ravensbrück in Christian terms as "Golgotha" ("Calvary"), is followed by the memorial's dedication:

> It is a memorial to the women of strong will, to the women with knowledge, who stood firmly together and who supported and sustained their weaker comrades, the defenseless victims; it is a monument, built here to the everlasting glory of our heroines, who fought here to the very last breath.

It becomes evident that the memorial is dedicated to the "heroines who fought." The "defenseless victims" are mentioned only because they were supported and sustained. The heroines, the book suggests, were the "antifascist prisoners of all nations," among whom German inmates are given a special role: "The great ideal of solidarity... came to Ravensbrück with the first German antifascists."[10] Acts of solidarity and compassion are presented as a particular characteristic of German antifascists. The genocide of the Jewish people is not mentioned once; Jewish prisoners, in general, figure only marginally into this narrative, and if they do they serve as a dark background against which the actions of the political prisoners appear all the more heroic.

Interventions

At first glance, it might look as if the memorial's design and the commemorative ceremonies in the following decades took their course in harmony and without any conflict. However, there are indications that survivors did take a critical view of the memorial's iconography. In a letter to the GDR's prime minister in 1957, the East German Committee of Former Ravensbrück Prisoners complained that the design of the central monument "exclusively expresses the idea of solidarity and not the struggle against fascism, which the women also fought in the camp."[11] Apparently, the former political prisoners who were organized in the committee did not want to find themselves represented only through a charitable act traditionally associated with female gender roles, but also as fighters, as "heroines who fought." However, their intervention did not yield any results. The second monument erected at Ravensbrück in 1965, the group of sculptures titled *Ravensbrück Group of Mothers* by Fritz Cremer, does not depict female fighters, but instead shows three women with children, one of which is dead and lying on a stretcher, while the other child seems to be trying to hold onto and hide in the first woman's skirt. Iconographically defining the role of women through the reproductive tasks of childcare and mourning the dead again emphasized maternalism as the central point of the memorial's narrative.[12]

The commemorative ceremonies also became the objects of criticism from former prisoners. At the annual ceremonies, members of the Soviet Army figured prominently. As in Buchenwald and Sachsenhausen, the Ravensbrück ceremonies also started at the Soviet monument in order to stress the important role of the Red Army in the liberation of Germany.

In reference to Émile Durkheim, Don Handelman described public events as constructs that create a certain social order. As a small, cohesive world of its own, the public event resembles a mirror "held up to reflect versions of the organization of society."[13] The Ravensbrück commemoration ceremonies did manifest an order, namely, the one the GDR leadership considered the correct, ideal social order. Government representatives, the group of former prisoners who had been invited, the Soviet and GDR "brother armies," the local population, and a group of children always represented a happily united community.

In 1975, members of the Dutch Comité Vrouwen van Ravensbrück took part in the ceremony celebrating the thirtieth anniversary of the camp's liberation. Afterward, Liesbeth Snam wrote a letter in which she argued that the address by government representative Paul Verner had

Ravensbrück Group of Mothers, by Fritz Cremer, 1984. Photo: Diwischek, Mahn- und Gedenkstätte Ravensbrück, photo no. 2458.

been "a political propaganda speech. The Swedish Red Cross, who evacuated thousands of women, was not mentioned once. They only thanked the Soviet Army, even though the camp was already more than half empty when they arrived." And she went on: "Ravensbrück belongs to all of us, and there are others who also want to commemorate their dead comrades there."

Emmy Handke, then Secretary General of the International Ravensbrück Committee, wrote a note in which she tersely stated, "The letter will not be answered because of its provocative and slanderous content."[14] In the context of communist memorial culture, critical remarks about the Soviet Army constituted an outrage. For the same reason, the rapes of former prisoners committed by members of the Red Army during the liberation of the camp were never mentioned at Ravensbrück or in the GDR. Memories of these rapes were only voiced at the Ravensbrück Memorial after the withdrawal of the CIS troops in 1994.[15]

The Significance of Memories

Primo Levi once described a dream that he said almost all concentration camp prisoners dreamt at some point during their imprisonment: the nightmare of coming back from the camp with nobody willing to believe or even listen to their experiences.[16] This fear might be one of the reasons why some of the survivors wrote memoirs of their imprisonment immediately after their return. In the case of Ravensbrück, at least, the number of personal accounts written and published in 1946 was not reached again until the 1990s.[17]

There are indications that survivors began to write and collect accounts in the camp itself, in the context of the liberation. In Ravensbrück, these survivors included Erika Buchmann, who was imprisoned on political grounds and gave—or was forced to give—her first completed reports to a Soviet investigative committee assigned to the camp;[18] the Soviet prisoner doctor Antonia Nikiforowa apparently experienced a similar situation.[19] These losses did not prevent the two women from continuing to collect accounts in the following years and decades, however. Their two collections now make up a significant portion of the Ravensbrück Memorial archive.[20]

If the witness statements from survivors in early investigations and trials are taken into account as well, it is apparent that an extensive body of knowledge relating to the history of the women's concentration camp was accumulated even in the first postwar years. Some of the survivors went on to become historians and wrote about the camps in which they were imprisoned; for example, Hermann Langbein wrote about Auschwitz,

Eugen Kogon about Buchenwald, Hans Marsalek about Mauthausen, and Germaine Tillion and Wanda Kiedrzynska about Ravensbrück.

Historical works based on accounts of former prisoners were written in the first years after the war. One of these works is *Buchenwald—Mahnung und Verpflichtung* (*Buchenwald—An Admonition and an Obligation*), published in 1960. Philipp Neumann recently published a remarkable study about the genesis of the book. He points out that the vast majority of the 200 accounts the volume contains were written by communist former prisoners, and that even these texts were heavily edited before publication. The editors of this widely circulated book expressed their hope that "our documentary account will help us to ... arrive at an official version to make sure that the same events are not constantly described in different variations."[21]

Describing the same events "in different variations" is something that hinders the establishment of a canonized version. The "living, human, insubordinate details"[22] that make personal recollections so exciting need to be left out if a master narrative is to be constructed. Maybe this is one of the reasons why an anthology, like the one on Buchenwald, was never published on Ravensbrück in the GDR.[23] As mentioned, the Ravensbrück Memorial Museum does hold an extensive collection of personal memoirs compiled by the former political prisoner Erika Buchmann,[24] but they were never published in an anthology, probably because of the heterogeneous nature of these texts. For a long time, the volume *Die Frauen von Ravensbrück* (The Women of Ravensbrück), first published in 1959, was considered the pivotal book on the history of the camp in the GDR. As is to be expected, this book, too, documents the communist claim to an exclusive interpretation of history. With this book, the GDR had found its "official version" of the Ravensbrück camp's history and held onto it for a long time.

In the 1980s, inspired by the British history workshop movement, people in Germany started recording audio and video interviews with eyewitnesses according to the methods of oral history. The development was an expression of the general interest in micro- and local history that had begun to manifest itself in West Germany in the late 1970s. Correspondingly, when the so-called memorial movement began to develop in the early 1980s, not many professional historians were involved. The first memorial initiatives and associations were made up of people and groups interested in their local history.²⁵ They were part of a generation that "in the wake ... of the students' movement" had become outraged about "their mothers' and fathers' refusal to face up to history" and therefore wanted to secure evidence and to uncover hidden facts.²⁶ Aleida Assmann remarked that during those years, a "social atmosphere of compassion" was slowly beginning to build, which finally allowed the survivors to make their voices heard.²⁷

Initially, interest focused on resistance against the Nazi regime. In 1980, filmmaker Loretta Walz from West Berlin started to conduct interviews with former Ravensbrück prisoners. Her archive, which today contains around 200 interviews, has become a document of contemporary history in itself.²⁸ At first, Walz mostly interviewed former prisoners living in West Germany or Western Europe. After the fall of the Berlin Wall and through her contact with the Ravensbrück Memorial Museum, she also had the opportunity to record interviews in the former GDR. At the same time, Walz began to shift her focus from concentrating on former political prisoners to also include groups of prisoners that had been previously ignored.

> For me, the talks with Jehovah's Witnesses, Jews, Sinti, Roma or prisoners classified as "anti-social elements" opened up a new phase for my interview collection. In this new phase, the hierarchy among the prisoners started to play an important role in the interviews, and we began to be confronted with very different memories. The history of the Ravensbrück camp became more nuanced, less uniform. Conflicting statements and experiences were presented on equal footing.²⁹

In the 1990s, interviews with women from Eastern Europe became possible for the first time, which further added to the heterogeneity of voices. These were women who had never visited the Ravensbrück Memorial Museum before and who often had not dealt with their memories of the camp since 1945. Accordingly, their accounts were often "unaffected by any books or films" and evoked images of the camp "that we sometimes found disconcerting."³⁰

The vast differences in the individual recollections of the Ravensbrück women's concentration camp firstly result from the great differences in living conditions between the various groups of prisoners at the

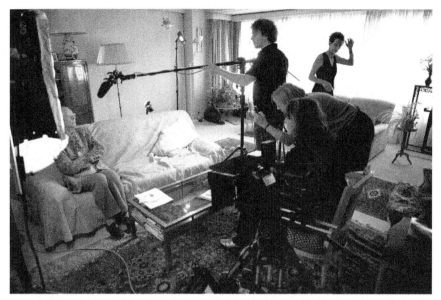

Loretta Walz interviewing Christiane Rème, survivor of the Ravensbrück concentration camp, Paris, 2008. Photo: Ulrich Rydzewski, Mahn- und Gedenkstätte Ravensbrück.

camp. But they are also an expression of the changes that the camp itself underwent during the six years of its existence. This means that memories of the camp's early days greatly differ from accounts of the final phase. And finally, these divergences also result from the differences between the various work details. Life was much harder for prisoners having to perform hard physical labor outdoors than for those who were assigned to a detail working in a heated indoor space.

So, on the one hand, the differences in personal memories of the camp are based on the different historical circumstances, that is, on the changing history of the Ravensbrück camp. However, memories always depend on their historical context and are therefore themselves subject to change. Memories are constantly reformed and rephrased in accordance with the current commemorative discourse. To give an example: the personal recollections of a former Jewish prisoner of Ravensbrück were recorded twice, once in the GDR and again after the fall of the Berlin Wall. In retrospect, we can see that the survivor presented different versions of her recollections at different times. It was not until the 1990s that she talked of herself as a Holocaust survivor. The differences between the two interviews are symptomatic for the differences between the GDR's memorial culture and that of the reunited Germany.[31]

In the course of German reunification, the Ravensbrück Memorial Museum became part of the Brandenburg Memorials Foundation, which was established on January 1, 1993. This step went hand-in-hand with the development of a new profile for the exhibition concept: the Museum of Anti-Fascist Resistance, which had opened during the East German era and explained a great deal about resistance, but very little about the Ravensbrück women's concentration camp, was closed and quickly replaced by two new permanent exhibitions. These exhibitions focused on the topography and history of the women's concentration camp (1993) and on the biographies of twenty-seven former prisoners (1994). The Memorial Museum's work in the 1990s also revolved primarily around biographical and topographical aspects: once the bipolar view of history had been eliminated, the focus of interest turned away from broad historical narratives to the life stories of individual women and the history of the site.

This heralded a development in memorial work that intensified in the following decade. The interest of subsequent generations in the experiences of former prisoners shifted from forms of politically motivated resistance against the Nazi regime to the working and living conditions in the concentration camps. Attention increasingly turned to the variety of different prisoner groups, the prisoners' relationships with one another and with the SS, and, finally, the camp's topography; Gabriele Hammermann confirms that the same development took place at the Dachau concentration camp memorial.[32]

In 2013, the Ravensbrück Memorial Museum replaced the two exhibitions which had been created in the early 1990s with one large new exhibition. Even its title—"The Ravensbrück Women's Concentration Camp: History and Memory"—indicates that the history of the remembrance of Ravensbrück is a constitutive part of the exhibition. Although the exhibition includes 159 profiles of former prisoners and some of the SS staff, its purpose is not just to realize a biographical concept, but also to present the heterogeneous memories of the women's concentration camp.

When drawing up the new exhibition, presenting the history of Ravensbrück from multiple perspectives meant two things: on the one hand, there were vast differences between the different groups of

Ravensbrück Women's Concentration Camp

Margrit Rustow, survivor of the Ravensbrück concentration camp, in front of her profile at the new permanent exhibition of the Ravensbrück Memorial Museum, April 2013. Photo: Oz-Salzberger, Mahn- und Gedenkstätte Ravensbrück.

prisoners and between citizens of different countries that were at war with each other. The prisoners came from a range of national, social, and political contexts and their chances of surviving the camp differed greatly. On the other hand—as mentioned—the widely varying memories are also the result of the many changes the Ravensbrück camp itself underwent over time, so recollections of its early period diverge from depictions of its final phase. And finally, the differences between the individual accounts from survivors also highlight the significance of the different forms of prisoner labor. In short, the exhibition tries to bring together contrasting memories wherever possible, in order to give an impression of how diverse the conditions of imprisonment and the experiences of individual prisoners were.

One example of this is a collage of quotes from former prisoners concerning labor in the Siemens plant, which individual survivors indeed remember very differently. For some, working in the heated factory halls meant warmth and a clean environment, while others remember having to work there as a genuine form of slave labor. The second example is another collage of quotes, this time concerning the liberation of the camp. Many survivors remember this moment as an altogether exhilarating experience, like Zdena Nedvědová-Nejedlá, who had to work in the camp's infirmary as a prisoner doctor: "The camp gate was wide open! I went to the head nurse's office, the one who had humiliated me the most, sat at her desk, and only then really realized that I was a free woman." For Irma Trksak, on the other hand, a different event was more important: "And then this Russian came towards us, a liberator. And he looked at us, [pointed] his gun at me and told me to lie down. For four years I'd looked forward to freedom. Should I lie down or let myself be shot? Well, that's what happened. It was horrible." The multiplicity of individual experiences is also evident in the prisoners' artistic outputs, which are collectively presented as their own genre in the exhibition. The scenarios depicted in prisoner drawings relating to food in the camp, for example, vary widely. On the one hand, there is a drawing of a scene in which women are eating together at long tables; on the other, there is one of prisoners lying on the floor and licking up soup from a toppled pail. The same holds true for drawings in which the privileged prisoner functionaries are depicted: in one drawing, an oversized human figure hands out soup, while in another, a female member of the camp police beats a prisoner to the ground, and in yet another one, a privileged prisoner is shown having her nails manicured and her hair done.

My team and I chose this multi-perspective approach for our exhibition not only because we wanted to represent the actual multiplicity of perceptions and memories. The history of the Ravensbrück camp cannot be told as a unified master narrative that presents this history "the way it really was." It is not just the combination of differing memories that makes this impossible, but also the discrepancies found in the other sources. Files, memos, construction plans, photographs, trial minutes, accounts from memory—to name just a few of the types of documents used in the exhibition—all have their own parameters according to which they yield information. The exhibition offers the opportunity to combine the different narratives and visual strategies across genres and types of documents.

The new permanent exhibition of the Ravensbrück Memorial Museum, first room, April 2013. Photo: Britta Pawelke, Mahn- und Gedenkstätte Ravensbrück

To sum up, how can we describe the relationship between survivors' personal recollections and the history of public memory of the Ravensbrück concentration camp? I have tried to show that personal memories did not play any major role in the establishment of the communist narrative on Ravensbrück. This narrative, which became manifest in the memorial's iconography and in the commemoration ceremonies held there, did not allow for any interventions or corrections from individuals. For a long time, the Ravensbrück Memorial Museum served as an instrument of the state's official historical policy. Personal recollections, which are also always potential objections to official historical interpretations, were not welcome.

After the downfall of the GDR, the memorials in East Germany increasingly began to focus on the heterogeneity of the prisoner societies, and this brought the biographies of very different prisoners into the picture. The topography of the camp became a matter of interest as well. When the CIS troops withdrew in the early 1990s, the grounds of the former concentration camp—covering nearly one hundred hectares, with an infrastructure that is almost entirely intact—became publicly accessible for the first time. This infrastructure includes a water works, a sewage works, the camp's own transformer station, production sites, the so-called loot huts, the former SS housing estate, two nurseries, the SS experimental farm, the grounds of the former Uckermark or "juvenile protective custody camp" mentioned above, the remains of the camp wall, and much more. Survivors have provided a wealth of information to us about the historical function of these relics.

In addition to the historical topography, as well as the biographies of the prisoners and their living and working conditions, it is the heterogeneous voices of memory that particularly concern the Memorial Museum today. To borrow an expression from John R. Gillis: this is a process of the democratization of memory.[33] Concentration camp memorial museums, which had previously been responsible for propagating a single interpretation of the past, are now needed as civic sites in which individuals and groups with differing memories of the same events can communicate with one another. Today, concentration camp memorials are no longer just cemeteries and sites of commemoration, but also places of education, research, and lively debate. The personal recollections of former prisoners form an integral part of the memorial museums' work. In light of the impending loss of the last witnesses to the Nazi era, preserving the voices of these former prisoners and making them publicly accessible through different media is one of the most important and challenging tasks of a memorial museum.

Notes

1. Matthias Pfüller, "Leuchttürme, leere Orte und Netze. Neue Möglichkeiten der Erinnerung im Übergang vom kommunikativen zum kulturellen Gedächtnis der Gesellschaft," in *Arbeit an Bildern der Erinnerung: Ästhetische Praxis, außerschulische Jugendbildung und Gedenkstättenpädagogik*, ed. Birgit Dorner and Kerstin Engelhardt (Stuttgart: Lucius und Lucius, 2006), 31.

2. Letter from the Institute for the Preservation of Historical Monuments to the Ministry for Cultural Affairs dated February 27, 1957, DR 1/7525, Federal Archives Berlin.

3. Volkhard Knigge, "Buchenwald," in *Das Gedächtnis der Dinge: KZ-Relikte und KZ-Denkmäler 1945–1995*, ed. Detlef Hoffmann (Frankfurt am Main: Campus Verlag, 1998), 119.

4. For more details, see Insa Eschebach, "Zur Formensprache der Totenehrung: Ravensbrück in der frühen Nachkriegszeit," in *Die Sprache des Gedenkens: Zur Geschichte der Gedenkstätte Ravensbrück 1945–1995*, ed. Insa Eschebach et al. (Berlin: Hentrich, 1999), 13–48.

5. Cf. Susanne Lanwerd, "Die Bildformel Pietà: Religiös tradierte Geschlechterbilder in Symbolisierungen des Nationalsozialismus," in *Gedächtnis und Geschlecht: Deutungsmuster in Darstellungen des nationalsozialistischen Genozids*, ed. Insa Eschebach et al. (Frankfurt am Main: Campus Verlag, 2002), 163–80.

6. Margarete Buber-Neumann, *Under Two Dictators: Prisoner of Stalin and Hitler* (London: Pimlico, 2008).

7. Geoffrey H. Hartman, "Introduction: Darkness Visible," in *Holocaust Remembrance: The Shapes of Memory*, ed. G. H. Hartman (Oxford: Blackwell, 1994), 15.

8. Sara R. Horowitz, "Geschlechtsspezifische Erinnerungen an den Holocaust," in *Forschungsschwerpunkt Ravensbrück: Beiträge zur Geschichte des Frauen-Konzentrationslagers*, ed. Sigrid Jacobeit and Grit Philipp (Berlin: Hentrich, 1997), 131–35.

9. Komitee der Antifaschistischen Widerstandskämpfer in der deutschen Demokratischen Republik, ed., *Ravensbrück* (Berlin: Kongress Verlag, 1960).

10. Ibid., 11, 48.

11. Letter dated November 30, 1957, from Marga Jung, Committee of Former Ravensbrück Prisoners, to Prime Minister Otto Grotewohl; MGR/SBG, RA I/4–3, Ordner 11.

12. Cf. Kathrin Hoffmann-Curtius, "Caritas und Kampf: Die Mahnmale in Ravensbrück," in Eschebach et al., *Die Sprache des Gedenkens*, 55–68.

13. Don Handelman, *Models and Mirrors: Towards an Anthropology of Public Events* (Cambridge: Cambridge University Press, 1990), 8.

14. Copy of a letter from the Comité Vrouwen van Ravensbrück to Frau Handke, Berlin, May 28, 1975; StGB/MGR RA I/3–5 XXX V 82f. The file contains the translation of an article published in *Het Parool* on June 3, 1975, titled "Former Prisoners Return Shattered after Communist Commemoration Ceremony at Ravensbrück Camp."

15. In *Under Two Dictators: Prisoner of Stalin and Hitler*, Margarete Buber-Neumann does mention the rapes. However, for a variety of reasons, the book could never be published in the GDR. Regarding the debate about the rapes within and around the Dutch Ravensbrück committee, cf. Jolande Withuis, "Die verlorene Unschuld des Gedächtnisses. Soziale Amnesie in Holland und sexuelle Gewalt im zweiten Weltkrieg," in Eschebach et al., *Gedächtnis und Geschlecht*, esp. 80ff.

16. Primo Levi, *La tregua* (Turin: Einaudi, 1963); in English, *The Truce*, trans. Stuart Woolf (London: Penguin, 1979); Primo Levi, *I sommersi e i salvati* (Turin: Einaudi, 1986); published in English as *The Drowned and the Saved*, trans. Raymond Rosenthal (London: Joseph, 1988).

17. Cf. Susan Hogervorst, "Erinnerungskulturen und Geschichtsschreibung. Das Beispiel Ravensbrück," in *Opfer als Akteure: Interventionen ehemaliger NS-Verfolgter in der Nachkriegszeit (Jahrbuch 2008 zur Geschichte und Wirkung des Holocaust)*, ed. Fritz Bauer Institut (Frankfurt am Main Campus Verlag, 2008), 205.

18. Cf. Grit Philipp, *Erika Buchmann (1902–1971): Kommunistin, Politikerin, KZ-Überlebende* (Berlin: Metropol Verlag, 2013), 141. Philipp points out that the first records served not only to document Nazi crimes, but also to provide information about the behavior of individual comrades in the camp.

19. Ramona Saavedra Santis, *Im Auftrag der Erinnerung: Der Nachlass von Antonia Nikiforowa: Ein Beitrag zum Ravensbrück-Gedächtnis in der Sowjetunion und in Russland* (Berlin, Metropol, 2013).

20. In other countries, too, survivors began collecting personal accounts early on; cf. Amicale de Ravensbrück, ed., *Les Francaises à Ravensbrück* (Paris: Gallimard, 1965).

21. Quoted from Philipp Neumann, "'... eine Sprachregelung zu finden'. Zur Kanonisierung des kommunistischen Buchenwald-Gedächtnisses in der Dokumentation 'Mahnung und Verpflichtung,'" in *Opfer als Akteure. Interventionen ehemaliger NS-Verfolgter in der Nachkriegszeit (Jahrbuch 2008 zur Geschichte und Wirkung des Holocaust)*, ed. Fritz Bauer Institut (Frankfurt am Main: Campus Verlag, 2008), 151.

22. Hartman, "Introduction: Darkness Visible," 26.

23. Accounts of Ravensbrück explicitly based on recollections of former prisoners or containing them were published in Vienna in 1945 and elsewhere.

24. The origins of the texts in this collection still require some research. An initial overview can be found in Grit Philipp, "Erlebnisberichte als Quellen historischer Forschung," in *Das Frauenkonzentrationslager Ravensbrück: Quellenlage und Quellenkritik: Eine Tagungsdokumentation*, ed. Insa Eschebach and Johanna Kootz (Freie Universität Berlin, 1997), 123–28.

25. At the time, many members of local history projects carried out their work in the framework of government job creation schemes.

26. Detlef Garbe, "Von den 'vergessenen KZs' zu den 'staatstragenden Gedenkstätten?,'" in *Gedenkstätten-Rundbrief* 100/2001, 78.

27. Aleida Assmann, "Vier Grundtypen der Zeitzeugenschaft," in *Zeugenschaft des Holocaust: Zwischen Trauma, Tradierung und Ermittlung.*

Jahrbuch 2007 zur Geschichte und Wirkung des Holocaust, ed. Fritz-Bauer- Institut (Frankfurt am Main: Campus Verlag, 2007), 43.

28. Cf. Loretta Walz, "Im Strom der vielfältigen Erinnerung," in *Der Nationalsozialismus im Spiegel des öffentlichen Gedächtnisses: Formen der Aufarbeitung und des Gedenkens: Für Sigrid Jacobeit*, ed. Petra Fank and Stefan Hördler (Berlin: Metropol, 2005), 237–46.

29. Ibid., 239.

30. Ibid., 242.

31. Cf. Friedhelm Boll's study on Irmgard Konrad's recollections in Friedhelm Boll, *Sprechen als Last und Befreiung: Holocaust-Überlebende und politisch Verfolgte zweier Diktaturen* (Bonn: Dietz, 2003), 111–30.

32. Gabriele Hammermann, "Zeitzeugeninterviews und Zeitzeugengespräche in der KZ-Gedenkstätte Dachau. Veranstaltungen—Bestände—Perspektiven," in *Freilegungen. Überlebende—Erinnerungen—Transformationen. Jahrbuch des International Tracing Service*, vol. 2, ed. Rebecca Boehling et al. (Göttingen: Wallstein Verlag, 2013), 309–16.

33. John R. Gillis, "Memory and Identity: The History of a Relationship," in *Commemorations: The Politics of National Identity*, ed. John R. Gillis (Princeton, NJ: Princeton University Press, 1996), 3–24.

Bibliography

Amicale de Ravensbrück, ed. *Les Francaises à Ravensbrück*. Paris: Gallimard, 1965.

Assmann, Aleida. "Vier Grundtypen der Zeitzeugenschaft." In *Zeugenschaft des Holocaust: Zwischen Trauma, Tradierung und Ermittlung. Jahrbuch 2007 zur Geschichte und Wirkung des Holocaust*, ed. Fritz-Bauer-Institut, 33–51. Frankfurt am Main: Campus Verlag, 2007.

Boll, Friedhelm. *Sprechen als Last und Befreiung: Holocaust-Überlebende und politisch Verfolgte zweier Diktaturen*. Bonn: Dietz, 2003.

Buber-Neumann, Margarete. *Under Two Dictators: Prisoner of Stalin and Hitler*. London: Pimlico, 2008.

Eschebach, Insa. "Zur Formensprache der Totenehrung: Ravensbrück in der frühen Nachkriegszeit." In *Die Sprache des Gedenkens: Zur Geschichte der Gedenkstätte Ravensbrück 1945–1995*, ed. Insa Eschebach et al., 13–48. Berlin: Hentrich, 1999.

Garbe, Detlef. "Von den 'vergessenen KZs' zu den 'staatstragenden Gedenkstätten?'" In *Gedenkstätten-Rundbrief* 100/2001, 75–82.

Gillis, John R. "Memory and Identity: The History of a Relationship." In *Commemorations: The Politics of National Identity*, ed. John R. Gillis, 3–24. Princeton, NJ: Princeton University Press, 1996.

Hammermann, Gabriele. "Zeitzeugeninterviews und Zeitzeugengespräche in der KZ-Gedenkstätte Dachau. Veranstaltungen—Bestände—Perspektiven." In *Freilegungen. Überlebende—Erinnerungen—Transformationen. Jahrbuch des International Tracing Service*, vol. 2, ed. Rebecca Boehling et al., 309–16. Göttingen: Wallstein Verlag, 2013.

Handelman, Don. *Models and Mirrors: Towards an Anthropology of Public Events*. Cambridge: Cambridge University Press, 1990.

Hartman, Geoffrey H. "Introduction: Darkness Visible." In *Holocaust Remembrance: The Shapes of Memory*, ed. G. H. Hartman. Oxford: Blackwell, 1994.

Hoffmann-Curtius, Kathrin. "Caritas und Kampf: Die Mahnmale in Ravensbrück." In *Die Sprache des Gedenkens: Zur Geschichte der Gedenkstätte Ravensbrück 1945–1995*, ed. Insa Eschebach et al., 55–68. Berlin: Hentrich, 1999.

Hogervorst, Susan. "Erinnerungskulturen und Geschichtsschreibung: Das Beispiel Ravensbrück." In *Opfer als Akteure. Interventionen ehemaliger NS-Verfolgter in der Nachkriegszeit (Jahrbuch 2008 zur Geschichte und Wirkung des Holocaust)*, ed. Fritz Bauer Institut, 197–215. Frankfurt am Main: Campus Verlag, 2008.

Horowitz, Sara R. "Geschlechtsspezifische Erinnerungen an den Holocaust." In *Forschungsschwerpunkt Ravensbrück: Beiträge zur Geschichte des Frauen-Konzentrationslagers*, ed. Sigrid Jacobeit and Grit Philipp, 131–35. Berlin: Hentrich, 1997.

Knigge, Volkhard. "Buchenwald." In *Das Gedächtnis der Dinge: KZ-Relikte und KZ-Denkmäler 1945–1995*, ed. Detlef Hoffmann, 92–173. Frankfurt am Main: Campus Verlag, 1998.

Komitee der Antifaschistischen Widerstandskämpfer in der deutschen Demokratischen Republik, ed. *Ravensbrück*. Berlin: Kongress Verlag, 1960.

Lanwerd, Susanne. "Die Bildformel Pietà: Religiös tradierte Geschlechterbilder in Symbolisierungen des Nationalsozialismus." In *Gedächtnis und Geschlecht: Deutungsmuster in Darstellungen des nationalsozialistischen Genozids*, ed. Insa Eschebach et al., 163–80. Frankfurt am Main: Campus Verlag, 2003.

Levi, Primo. *The Drowned and the Saved*. Trans. Raymond Rosenthal. London: Joseph, 1988. Originally published as *I sommersi e i salvati*. Torino: Einaudi, 1986.

———. *The Truce*. Trans. Stuart Woolf. London: Penguin, 1979. Originally published as *La tregua*. Turin: Einaudi, 1963.

Neumann, Philipp. "'... eine Sprachregelung zu finden'. Zur Kanonisierung des kommunistischen Buchenwald-Gedächtnisses in der Dokumentation 'Mahnung und Verpflichtung.'" In *Opfer als Akteure. Interventionen ehemaliger NS-Verfolgter in der Nachkriegszeit (Jahrbuch 2008 zur Geschichte und Wirkung des Holocaust)*, ed. Fritz Bauer Institut, 151–73. Frankfurt am Main: Campus Verlag, 2008.

Pfüller, Matthias. "Leuchttürme, leere Orte und Netze. Neue Möglichkeiten der Erinnerung im Übergang vom kommunikativen zum kulturellen Gedächtnis der Gesellschaft." In *Arbeit an Bildern der Erinnerung: Ästhetische Praxis, außerschulische Jugendbildung und Gedenkstättenpädagogik*, ed. Birgit Dorner and Kerstin Engelhardt, 27–52. Stuttgart: Lucius und Lucius, 2006.

Philipp, Grit. *Erika Buchmann (1902–1971): Kommunistin, Politikerin, KZ-Überlebende*. Berlin: Metropol, 2013.

———. "Erlebnisberichte als Quellen historischer Forschung." In *Das Frauenkonzentrationslager Ravensbrück: Quellenlage und Quellenkritik: Eine Tagungsdokumentation*, ed. Insa Eschebach and Johanna Kootz, 123–28. Berlin: Freie Universität Berlin, 1997.

Santis, Ramona Saavedra. *Im Auftrag der Erinnerung: Der Nachlass von Antonia Nikiforowa: Ein Beitrag zum Ravensbrück-Gedächtnis in der Sowjetunion und in Russland*. Berlin: Metropol, 2013.

Walz, Loretta. "Im Strom der vielfältigen Erinnerung." In *Der Nationalsozialismus im Spiegel des öffentlichen Gedächtnisses: Formen der Aufarbeitung und des Gedenkens: Für Sigrid Jacobeit*, ed. Petra Fank and Stefan Hördler, 237–46. Berlin: Metropol, 2005.

Withuis, Jolande. "Die verlorene Unschuld des Gedächtnisses: Soziale Amnesie in Holland und sexuelle Gewalt im zweiten Weltkrieg." In *Gedächtnis und Geschlecht: Deutungsmuster in Darstellungen des nationalsozialistischen Genozids*, ed. Insa Eschebach et al., 80–87. Frankfurt am Main: Campus Verlag, 2002.

9

The Belzec Memorial and Museum

Personal Reflections

MICHAEL BERENBAUM

Kenneth Keniston, the author of *Young Radicals* and *The Uncommitted*, once noted that pure objectivity does not exist in the social sciences. The most we can hope for is for writers to admit to their subjective biases and for the reader to compensate accordingly. I admit that I can fall victim to subjective bias—and the reader is hereby warned.

For more than two decades, I was deeply involved in the creation of the Memorial and Museum at the site of Belzec, the Nazi death camp in German-occupied Poland. This involvement began during my service at the United States Holocaust Memorial Museum (USHMM), and continued during my time at the Survivors of the Shoah Visual History Foundation. I subsequently served on the committee as one of four curators who oversaw the international design competition for the Belzec Memorial, working with Jacek Nowakowski of the United States Holocaust Memorial Museum; Jerzy Halbersztadt, then representative of the USHMM in Poland; and the late Robert Kuwalek, a historian on the staff of the Majdanek Museum who became the Belzec Memorial's first director.

Origins

It is said that failure is an orphan and success has many fathers. This project was initiated by one man, the late Miles Lerman, who in the late 1980s served in two positions as chairman of the International Relations

Committee and as Chairman of the Campaign to Remember, the fundraising arm of the US Holocaust Memorial Museum, still unbuilt at the time. We first visited the site of Belzec in the 1980s when it was neglected and being used as a garbage dump and a shortcut to get into town. The original memorial, a Communist-era monument, made no mention of the Jews and was—to put it most charitably—unimpressive.

Once he visited the site, Lerman was determined to change the facts on the ground because of its deep personal significance to him. His mother and his sister were killed there and the camp overlooks the site of the Lerman family flour mill in nearby Tomaszow, their hometown. As his mother was marched to the gas chambers of Belzec, she was able to see the life she was leaving forever.

At that time, the USHMM was actively involved in obtaining artifacts from Poland to help shape the museum's exhibitions. The commitment to presenting an evidentiary-based exhibition was deep and the museum designers and curators were fortunate to work in a climate that inspired Polish cooperation with the proposed museum. Communism was on the wane and many Poles—political and cultural officials—were interested in cooperating with the United States. Many of them understood that unless relationships between Poland and the American Jewish community were improved, American Jews would very likely create formidable obstacles to prevent acceptance of Poland in the West. It was imperative to them that the breach between Poles and Jews be narrowed.

As a Polish native, Lerman understood Polish culture, and because of his political skills, he understood the practicalities of bridging the Polish–Jewish divide. The compelling nature of the proposed exhibition, its location in Washington, DC, and its formal sponsorship by the US government led political and cultural officials to welcome cooperation. Agreements were forged between the USHMM and the Main Commission for the Investigation of Nazi War Crimes, which later became the Polish Institute of National Remembrance. Contracts were signed with the museums at Auschwitz and Majdanek that provided the USHMM with artifacts for its permanent exhibition: shoes and uniforms from Majdanek, a barracks and bunk suitcases, eyeglasses, bowls from Auschwitz II (Birkenau). It also included the railroad car that anchors the exhibition on deportation and serves as the segue to the museum's depiction of the German death camps.

Lerman did not operate alone. Martin Smith, then USHMM's Director of Exhibitions, Ralph Appelbaum, the museum designer, and this author, then Project Director, worked closely with him during the initial negotiations. While Lerman worked the political level, the professional team worked closely with our counterparts, a group that was unusually cooperative because they were intrigued by the pioneering and compelling design for the museum and by how the artifacts and materials would be used in the museum's exhibitions.

Jacek Nowakowski proved enormously valuable as the museum's "ambassador" to Poland. A native of Poland and former director of the Polish Museum in Chicago, Nowakowski was comfortable in both cultures, sanguine in his advice, skilled in his political outreach, and well able to follow up with every detail. Without him, the project could not have succeeded. Ralph Grunewald, Director of External Affairs for the museum, was the consigliere who skillfully followed through on negotiations with the museum's general counsel. Gerard Leval of Arendt Fox gave generously of his time and wisdom, and Rabbi Andrew Baker of the American Jewish Committee proved indispensable when the American sponsorship shifted from the USHMM to the American Jewish Committee (AJComm).

An overture on Belzec had to wait until the museum project was further along, but Lerman was tenacious. Almost a decade later, after the museum was successfully opened and its reputation solidified, Lerman made his move. Then as chairman of the United States Holocaust Memorial Council, he used the power of his office, the prestige of the museum, and the good will he earned in repairing relations between Poland and the American Jewish community to press toward an agreement to build a new memorial at Belzec.

In March 1994, Lerman and Jeshajahu [Shaike] Weinberg, then director of the USHMM, met with the Polish Minister of Culture to discuss possible cooperation with the Polish authorities toward that end. During a joint visit to the site, they reached the decision to clean it up, improve the existing memorial, and fence the entire site. Costs were shared between the Polish government and American philanthropists.

The Secretary General of the Council for Protection of Monuments in Poland—the Polish government organization responsible for all of the Holocaust related sites—represented the Polish government on the

Belzec project. By early 1995, they offered several architectural proposals to improve the existing Belzec memorial. In the judgment of the American team that viewed these proposals, they simply were awful.

It was then decided to create a new memorial and, in order to keep it simple, have a closed architectural design competition involving only a select group of Polish artists. Given the monumental creations at Treblinka and Majdanek, there was a high measure of trust in the sensitivities and talents of Polish artists. There was also an internal debate as to what kind of monument to build.

It was clear that the site required a memorial but more than that as well.

Treblinka Offered a Model

The memorial at the death camp of Treblinka offered an impressive model. Belzec and Treblinka were two of the three Aktion Reinhard camps developed exclusively for the implementation of the "Final Solution to the Jewish Problem," the German name for the mass murder of the Jews. In 1943, the Germans plowed both sites under when the camps were closed and both offered the opportunity to create memorials that outlined the contours of the camp. Sobibor, the third Aktion Reinhard camp, has not been completely plowed under. A remnant remained.

The design for a memorial at Treblinka II was chosen by the Warsaw Regional Council in February 1960. Selected were two Poles, sculptor Franciszek Duszenko and architect Adam Haupt. Their design focused on the experience of the victims and the loss of the Jews who were murdered at Treblinka. They created a field of 17,000 jagged stones, each stone a different shape. Seven hundred of them had the names of the towns, villages, and hamlets that had stood by as their now anonymous Jews were deported to their deaths.

Only one individual was mentioned by name. That was Janusz Korczak, the famed Polish pediatrician, writer, and radio personality who might be considered a combination of the Mr. Rogers and Dr. Benjamin Spock of his time. Korczak, loved by Poland's children, ran an orphanage in the Warsaw Ghetto. Offered the opportunity to escape to the Aryan side, Korczak valiantly attempted to save his children. When he could not, he marched with them out of the ghetto and died with them in Treblinka.

Courage knew many forms in the Holocaust, and Korczak's principled decision not to abandon his children is the stuff of legend, a majestic example of moral courage. A teacher does not flee from his students; a father does not abandon his children.

The stones of Treblinka outline the contours of the camp. At the entrance, concrete blocks give an impression of railroad ties that abruptly veer to the left. They move up to an area that conveys the sense of being a ramp. It leads to a path running straight to the monument—built on the ruins of the gas chambers.

The Germans had a macabre sense of humor and called this path the *Himmelstrasse*, the path to heaven. Beyond the monument is a pit on the site of one of the burning fields where they disposed of the corpses. Historians know that Jews were first buried in mass graves at Treblinka. When it appeared that the Soviet Union might win the war and discover evidence of the crime, the corpses were exhumed by prisoners and burned on pyres to disappear the evidence. No bodies, no evidence, no crime.

In the opinion of this author and of many who visit the haunting and haunted site, the memorial is brilliantly effective. It evokes the presence of absence and seemingly offers visitors to Treblinka a sense that the victims, whose graves were in the sky, now have an earthly burial ground, where Jewish visitors can leave small stones on some of the jagged stones in the manner in which Jews mark visits to a grave or light memorial candles. Kaddish and *El Moleh Rachamim* (the Jewish memorial prayer) are recited by Jewish visitors. Treblinka is, as the architects and sculptor intended it to be, a Jewish cemetery.

Few words are used: the crime is reiterated. The countries from which Jews were shipped to the camps are named. Even though it was created in Communist times, the word "Jew" is mentioned and there is no possibility of misimpression: the iconography on the central monument is replete with Jewish symbols, and the language of the victims, Yiddish, is used. The people murdered in Treblinka were Jews. Visitors to the site whisper, unmistakably aware they are on sacred ground.

Yet visitors to Treblinka do not learn the story of what happened there in detail. They visit a memorial that conveys the feeling and magnitude of the loss, but nothing about the nature of the crime.

The History of Belzec

Understanding what was to be built on the site required understanding what happened at the site. On November 1, 1941, construction began at Belzec. By the end of February 1942, about 120 Jews from Lubycza Krolewska became its first gas chamber victims. Between March 17, 1942, and April 14, 1942, "the great action" of killing Jews began as some 70,000–75,000 Jews, most of them from Lublin and Lvov, were murdered.[1]

The three gas chambers were in a small barrack, approximately eight meters by four meters. The walls and floors were covered with tin and the door was made of hard wood to prevent it from being broken open from the inside.

Too many Jews had to be killed too quickly, so on April 17 the gassing ceased, resuming only in the middle of May 1942 when transports from the Krakow district started arriving again to the functioning camp. Once again the speed of deportation outpaced the camp's facilities. So deportations were halted again and murder by gassing ceased in mid-June to permit the old gas chambers to be torn down and replaced with much larger and more efficient ones.

They were made of brick and concrete with one door for entering the gas chambers and another for clearing out the bodies. The size of each gas chamber was approximately four meters by less than five meters. At the entrance to the building was a sign: "Shower and Disinfection Room." The capacity was 1,000–1,200 bodies at a time, approximately ten freight cars of arriving prisoners.

By the second week of July 1942, deportations and gassing resumed, continuing uninterrupted until December when the gassing operations were halted for good. Work detachments of Jewish forced laborers excavated mass graves and burned the bodies to remove evidence of the crime. When the work was completed, the Germans murdered virtually all surviving forced laborers (see below).

From spring 1943 to summer 1944, German officials and Trawniki-trained auxiliaries plowed under the site of the Belzec camp, planted trees, and built a manor house nearby in order to conceal any traces of the killing center. At the end of July 1944, the Soviet Army overran Belzec. There were between fourteen and thirty SS officials running Belzec, many of them veterans of the murder of mentally retarded, physically infirm, and emotionally disturbed Germans in the pioneering Nazi program of murder by gassing. Some 90 to 120 Trawniki-trained Ukrainian guards joined them in their dirty work.

Until recently, historians cited 600,000 as the number of Jews killed at Belzec. First established in 1946, the figure was based on the prewar population of Jewish communities presumably deported to Belzec. Because this estimate does not account for Jews murdered in the ghetto deportation operations, or shot in other locations, it is probably too high but not by much. At least 500,000 Jews were killed in Belzec; there were only two known survivors.

The Memorial at Belzec

The visitors to Treblinka still do not learn what happened there, but they do experience the magnitude of the loss, a majestic experience. For the memorial at Belzec the design team felt that it could do no less.

A decision was made that the memorial had to outline the camp's footprint; it had to have the power commensurate with the unspeakable crimes committed on the site. Because a generation had passed and only a few of the visitors would know what happened at Belzec, the curators decided to create a memorial and museum, a memorial to shape the nature of the camp and a museum to tell the story of the crime, the perpetrators, and their victims. A national competition was organized in 1997. Nine different Polish artists submitted proposals, and an international committee was established to choose among them. Representing the Americans were David Mickenberg, then director of the Block Museum of Art at Northwestern University; James Ingo Freed of Pei, Cobb and Freed, the architect of the United States Holocaust Memorial Museum; and this author, previously the Project Director of the USHMM overseeing its creation and at the time serving as president and CEO of the Survivors of the Shoah Visual History Foundation. At the last moment, Freed could not go to Poland; joining the committee in his place was Jozef Szajna, a Polish scenery designer, stage director, playwright, painter, and graphic artist who had been a prisoner in Auschwitz and Buchenwald. Representing the Poles on the committee were three prominent artists and architects.

The design from Polish artists and architects Andrzej Solyga, Zdzislaw Pidek, and Marcin Roszczyk won unanimous approval. The model we viewed was so powerful that choosing the artists proved to be the easiest part of the project. As the design was implemented, it exceeded even the committee's most exalted hopes.

With the funds raised and the designer in place, one might have expected smooth sailing, but that was not to be the case.

When the old monument was dismantled, workers discovered human remains on the site. This did not initially hamper the Polish archeological team from the University of Torun that was dismantling the site, but given the attention that site was receiving, the Poles were persuaded that direct consultation with rabbinic authorities was a political as well as a religious necessity.

The Poles conducted four separate archeological surveys at the Belzec site. (Over the past several years additional archeological explorations have been made—and filmed—at Sobibor and Treblinka, but these have been conducted with ground-imaging radar, which indicates to the archeologist what is under the ground.)

In the fall of 1997 a two-week survey was conducted that revealed the approximate location of the mass graves and the location of the remnants of the buildings that had been destroyed.[2]

According to a USHMM document:

> In the spring of 1998 a two-month survey mapped the entire memorial site marking the mass graves, building structures as well as other remnants of the Death Camp. The area was divided into 5x5 m squares and a very narrow but deep (up to 6m deep) borehole was placed at every corner of every square. During the survey there were 2001 boreholes made, and in 225 of them traces of the mass graves were found. That allowed archeologists to draw a map containing 33 mass graves—most of them 4–5 m deep. In addition, they have found traces of the rail spur and a platform, along with three buildings and external fence. As a result of the survey it was determined that the actual boundary of the camp extended beyond the limits of the current memorial site in the northwest and south directions. Archeologists also have found about 140 different objects-remnants of the Killing Center—mainly victim belongings. Most of these items were preserved and will be exhibited in the future

museum to be located at the site. The then Polish Prime Minister Jerzy Buzek presented two spoons for the collection of the United States Holocaust Memorial Museum during his visit to the Museum in July 1998.[3]

Later that year, from October 25 to November 14, 1998, the third survey was conducted to mark the boundaries of the camp. Among its discoveries were remnants of a large building located by the rail ramp and a significant collection of victim belongings.

In October 1999, the last archeological survey was conducted to find the remnants of the gas chamber. A large building was discovered.

When the design, which included a long trench, was first proposed, this author had religious reservations about the plan and contacted two prominent rabbis, each representing a different strand of Orthodox Judaism: Rabbi Chaskel Besser, an ultra-Orthodox Polish-born American rabbi who was then a senior advisor of the Ronald S. Lauder Foundation, which was active in rebuilding the Jewish community of Warsaw, and Rabbi Irving Greenberg, a liberal modern Orthodox rabbi who has written brilliantly on the Holocaust and was most sensitive to ensuring that its memorialization be according to Jewish law. This author had worked with both—with Rabbi Besser on the board of the Ronald S. Lauder Foundation and with Rabbi Greenberg on the National Jewish Conference Center (later CLAL) and on the President's Commission on the Holocaust. They agreed with the all-important proviso that the excavation for the project must not touch human remains. Their reservation was to prove crucial as the project developed, more crucial than one could have imagined when the design was chosen.

The USHMM, which was mindful of its status as a federal institution—and hence of the requirements of church-state separation—advised the Poles to turn to Rabbi Michael Schudrich, the charismatic, American-born chief rabbi of Poland, for guidance. Schudrich immediately contacted Rabbi Elyakim Schlesinger, the head of the rabbinical board of the London-based Committee for the Preservation of the Jewish Cemeteries in Europe (CPJCE), and asked for guidelines as to how the project could be undertaken. Pointedly, dare one say wisely, Schudrich asked how it should be done, not whether.

Proceeding with caution, care, and sensitivity, Rabbi Schudrich invited Rabbi Schlesinger to visit the site, and he was clearly distressed by what he saw. In a letter answering Rabbi Schudrich's question, he wrote: "I am still under the distressing impression left on me by our visit to the site of the death camp at Belzec and the shocking state in which the mass graves of hundreds of thousands of our brothers and sisters have been left since their cruel martyrdom.... It is essential that something be done." He was never to waver from that commitment.

Rabbi Schlesinger set some basic ground rules:[4]

- The entire area of the Death Camp must be fenced in.
- The entire area of the mass graves must be covered with a thick layer of concrete ... covered in such a way as to make it impossible for people to walk on it.
- No work at the ground level may be carried out without the presence of an authorized supervisor approved by Chief Rabbi Schudrich and the CPJCE.
- No earth is to be moved about the site in order to level the area of the mass grave. The earth covering a grave has a level of sanctity and may not be moved for any purpose at all.
- A footpath across may be laid along the section where there appear to be no mass graves.

Once Rabbi Schlesinger had issued his decision, Rabbi Yisroel Meir Lau, then the Ashkenazic chief rabbi of Israel, approved the guidelines set by Rabbi Schlesinger; the letter endorsing the decision written on the chief rabbi's stationery was signed by an associate, which kept Rabbi Lau at arm's length from the project.[5] Rabbi Schudrich put this decision into practice and issued his own specific guidelines:

- All work must be done in the presence of rabbinic supervision.
- In the areas of a trench, the top 30 cm shall be removed manually and not by heavy equipment.
- After the removal of the 30 cm the archaeologists may drill in the area of the trench at the distance of every two meters.
- If any bones are found, the Rabbinic supervisor must be informed and work stopped until permission is given by the Rabbinic supervisor to continue.

- A halakhically trained Israeli civil engineer is to be brought in to suggest the use of geo fabric and sand to protect the sacred ground.
- As a Rabbinic supervisor is to be present at all times, no work is to be done on the Sabbath or Jewish holidays.[6]

There were also internal disputes within Poland that delayed the project.

An internal US Holocaust Memorial Museum report traces what happened and did not happen between 1997 and 2001:

> Between the selection of the Belzec monument design and November of 2001 there was no real progress with the design process and the preparations for construction. Misunderstandings between the designers and our Polish counterpart as well as conflicts among the artists made any advancement impossible. We were desperate to save the project by applying constant pressure on different levels of Polish bureaucracy. As result of that pressure there were numerous assurances that the project has the backing of Polish political leadership and that the Polish state will cover half of the monument's cost. Four consecutive Prime Ministers of Poland had made that pledge—two of them repeated it publicly during their visits to the USHMM.... Prime Minister Leszek Miller, who in the previous years was actively supporting the project, confirmed ... government financial backing of the project during Museum's leadership recent visit to Poland.[7]

With such high-level commitments, the stakes were raised and there was no question as to the urgency of proceeding. And then in 2002, a third internal controversy threatened to derail the project.

The former director of the United States Holocaust Memorial Museum, Dr. Walter Reich, had been forced to resign in the aftermath of a controversy over a proposed visit by PLO president Yasir Arafat to the USHMM. Avi Weiss, a prominent rabbi and communal activist from Riverdale, New York, and also Reich's brother-in-law, came out in public opposition to the memorial at Belzec and held a protest at the annual Holocaust Commemoration in New York. He also raised religious objections because of the archaeological digs on the site and sued the museum in federal court.

Belzec Memorial and Museum

Rabbi Weiss and his associate, Rabbi Shmuel Herzfeld, visited the Belzec site in 2003 and wrote that human remains were strewn about. He demonstrated in front of the office of the Polish president and called for a halt to the project.[8]

Since Rabbi Weiss had previously demonstrated at the convent at Auschwitz, his demonstration in Warsaw was widely covered in the Polish press, but his impact there was slight. In the United States, by contrast, Jewish newspapers covered his activities extensively. A *New York Post* photographer accompanied him to Poland, so there was some coverage in the secular press as well.

Two lawsuits were filed in federal court. One was on behalf of the Israeli Center for Holocaust Survivors and the Second Generation, calling for an injunction against construction on the site; and the other was brought by Norman Salsitz, which was withdrawn soon after he met with Rabbi Schudrich, who reassured him that the project complied with Jewish law. Salsitz's wife was ill at the time and he said that he did not have the strength to carry on with the lawsuit. He later cooperated in the construction of the museum at Belzec and donated his important collection of artifacts. Another suit was filed at the New York State Supreme Court calling for damages for the intentional infliction of emotional distress. Rabbi Weiss's co-plaintiff was a Scottish woman whose brother had been killed in the camp.

By the time the matter was adjudicated, the trench was finished and the court denied the petition aimed at halting the construction. The other lawsuit for the damages was remanded to state court and has not proceeded to this date.

As the rabbinic controversy heated up, Rabbi Lau ran for cover. According to a letter from his brother, the former Israeli Consul-General in New York, Naftalie Lau-Lavie, Rabbi Lau had no knowledge of the specifics of the matter and his letter of support was not based on an extensive review. On the other hand, Rabbi Schlesinger doubled down. He wrote, "This holy work should continue without any delay." In what the press interpreted as a direct swipe at Rabbi Weiss, Rabbi Schlesinger wrote: "It is shocking that individuals with no connection to the rescuing of Jewish cemeteries are creating unjust obstacles."[9]

Yet another controversy, internal to the American supporters of the Belzec Memorial, threatened the project. Lerman resigned as chairman of the United States Holocaust Memorial Museum in 2000, when he turned eighty, and President Bill Clinton named Irving Greenberg as his replacement. Greenberg remained committed to the Belzec project. When his term expired, President George W. Bush replaced him with Fred Zeidman. Zeidman and museum director Sara J. Bloomfield came under considerable pressure from many on the museum's executive committee—on which this author served—who had not voiced their opposition when Lerman was chairman. They wanted an end to the internal controversy. Zeidman, however, preferred to concentrate on the museum's federal role at home and to constrain what he regarded as extraneous commitments overseas. That was his prerogative as chairman. Zeidman and especially Bloomfield were tired of the fight; they preferred that the museum steer clear of controversy and concentrate on its own role.

To her enormous credit, Bloomfield did not kill the project but looked to hand it off to another organization that would be the American partner to the Poles. She graciously allowed the museum's talented staff to support the project with intellectual resources, material, and time. Peter Black, the museum's chief historian, and Steven Luckert, its curator, gave their input, while Edward "Ted" Phillips and Laura Surwit Magnus served as editor and exhibition coordinator, respectively. Their service, both individually and collectively, was invaluable; it is to Bloomfield's credit that she made this happen.

Though officially retired, Lerman was still determined to complete the project, and he turned to the American Jewish Committee, which viewed the creation of the Belzec Memorial as an opportunity to enhance its presence in Poland. Lerman had funding commitments from American donors and also a commitment from Poles to match the American contributions so that the memorial would not financially burden either the museum or the American Jewish Committee. The donors were willing to go along with the switch of sponsorship. For some, Belzec was the place where their parents and loved ones had been murdered, and their primary concern was that the site itself be suitably memorialized.

David Harris, AJComm's executive director, turned the project over to Rabbi Andrew Baker, Director of International Jewish Affairs for the AJComm, who ably handled the relationship with Polish authorities, increasing his own portfolio and presence. Professional leadership continued with the Polish artistic team, and the creation of the museum was undertaken by the team of Nowakowski, Kuwalek, Halbersztadt, and this author. The museum graciously allowed Nowakowski to continue his involvement in the project. Kuwalek was assigned from the staff of Majdanek and Halbersztadt (then the Warsaw representative of the USHMM as well as director of the emerging Museum of the History of Polish Jews from the staff of the Museum of Polish Jewish History). This author participated on a pro-bono basis. The team turned to the firm of Patrick Gallagher and Associates of Bethesda, Maryland, for design development and in turn enlisted Miroslaw Nizio as their Polish counterpart.

The Belzec Memorial Design

As in Treblinka, the design for Belzec used the entire camp.

A fence and walled-in area marked the outlines of the camp. The memorial consisted of a long path—a trench that evoked the tube prisoners ran through from the ramp to the gas chamber. The walls on both sides grow ever higher, leading to the Memorial Wall with its appropriate inscription from Job: "Earth, do not cover my blood; let there be no resting place for my outcry."

The Vietnam Veterans Memorial in Washington, DC, immediately comes to mind as a precedent, but the iconic wall of that memorial grows higher only on one side. The second side is open and provides a sense of safety, of escape from the pressure of the wall. At Belzec, there is no

The Belzec Memorial encompasses the entire death camp. The fields to the right and left of the path cannot be walked upon. They are the sites of mass graves, ringed by a path with the names of the town and the months of each of the deportations from the ghettos of Galicia to Belzec. Photo: Edward Serotta, Centropa, Vienna.

Belzec Memorial wall. Photo: Edward Serotta, Centropa, Vienna.

escape. A biblically sensitive visitor might be reminded of the words from the Song of the Sea in Exodus 15: "And the waters are for them a wall to the right and to the left." The walls there held back the deluge, creating a path of safety between them for the Israelites. In contrast, at Belzec the path between the walls led to death.

As one walks more deeply down the path, the walls tower thirty feet above. As the visitor reaches the Memorial Wall, the inscription's letters in Hebrew, English, and Polish blend into its contours like tears.

On the back of the memorial are two areas for inscriptions; one wall contains the first names of victims—not the last names. That is because for every Moshe, there were hundreds, for every Sarah, there were thousands—all killed in Belzec. On the other wall are inscribed the cities and towns, villages and hamlets, from which Jews were deported to the camp.

At each end of the Memorial Wall, there are staircases ascending from the depths; visitors emerge to see the entire landscape of the camp spread out before them. The main area of the camp is filled with industrial sludge—giving an impression of what our planet might look like after a nuclear catastrophe.

No visitor can walk on the field. It is forbidden territory. The late Stephen Feinstein described it as a "volcanic lava field." And the areas of the camp that were the site of mass graves are darkened so that as one views the entire site, the locations of mass graves are apparent. From the top of

The path cuts through the entire memorial leading to the Memorial Wall. Photo: Edward Serotta, Centropa, Vienna.

the Memorial Wall, the visitor walks around one half of the camp and each concrete landing is marked by the name of the towns from which the Jews were deported; town by town, month by month, for each of the ten months that Belzec was operational. Some 50,000 Jews were murdered each month, with half a million people gassed in less than ten months of killing.

The Polish and Yiddish names of the town are inscribed in steel letters. Over time they began to rust. To a few visitors, the rust gives the impression of neglect; to most, the significance is apparent: the letters are bleeding for the Jewish inhabitants of those cities and towns.

As one enters the camp, to the left is a memorial to the trains (the Deportation Memorial) and to the right is the entrance to the Museum and Visitors' Center, housing an information desk that doubles as a small bookstore as well as restrooms.

During construction two changes were made to introduce character to the overall nature of the memorial. Steel rods, rebar, were used to hold the walls in place before the concrete was poured. As the walls reached for new heights, observers on the ground noticed that the rebar sticking out of the wall looked more powerful than the effect of a solid wall ascending to thirty feet. So the rods were left in place and the walls were left shorter to create an evocative image.

The second change, a memorial to deportation, was a gift of the architects who were engaged with the project and also with the Holocaust. Railroad ties and tracks were piled high to form the monument. And on the wall behind it, a famous poem by the Romanian-born Israeli poet Dan Pagis was inscribed in three languages—Polish, Hebrew, and English:

> Written in a Pencil in a Sealed Railway Car
> here in this carload
> I am eve
> with abel my son
> if you see my other son
> cain son of man
> tell him that I
>
> Dan Pagis

This extraordinary poem is somewhat problematic: most visitors are likely to believe that the poem is a historical document rather than a work of art. We risked using it, however, because of its power. Sometimes things that happen are not "true" and that which never happened is deeply true.

Why a monument to the deportations? Railroads were essential to the killing process. Railroads made the Jews mobile and each of the six killing centers was situated on a rail line appropriate to the accomplishment of its regional or transnational task. At first, the Nazis tried killing the Jews by sending mobile killing units—Einsatzgruppen—to stationary victims. When this proved difficult for the killers, who began to suffer from what today would be called post-traumatic stress disorder, they reversed the process. The victims were made mobile and sent to stationary killing centers where they could be processed in an orderly and deadly assembly line.

The Belzec Museum

The Belzec Museum is the place where the visitor has the opportunity to learn the history of Belzec. Unlike some other death camps, the Nazis situated Belzec in a relatively populated area, close to the heavily traveled railway line. Poles and Ukrainians in the area witnessed the systematic murder of Jews; they saw ghetto liquidations and trains arriving at the killing center.

The creation of the museum followed a basic pattern based on a philosophical premise.

A museum must primarily be a storytelling institution. Unlike most artifact-centered historical museums, which tell the stories of the artifacts they possess, the museum at Belzec—in design and exhibition—was driven by the story of the camp. On the basis of that story, artifacts were collected and exhibited, photographs were gathered and chosen, and diverse media—film, video, narrative tale, text, design, and atmosphere—were selected.

The visit to the Belzec Museum is a prelude to visiting the memorial. No genuine "ending" to the exhibition was necessary. For those who visit the museum after the exhibition, even a glimpse at the scope and scale of the memorial provides ample conclusion to their experience.

Our goal was to layer the information and create an exhibition that is intellectually informative and emotionally compelling. Museums are not encyclopedias on the wall, and few people take the time to read in depth while walking through them. A museum must provide information on multiple levels. The result must be an experience that engages the casual visitor and more deeply informs the already engaged visitors and even the specialized visitor.

The story told in the Belzec Museum was basic. Given the location of the exhibition, we believed that simplicity and clarity would prove most effective. We provided just a glimpse of the world of Polish Jewry before the war, presuming that the most sensitive of the visitors to the Belzec Memorial and Museum would confront Jewish life elsewhere in Poland, even in its absence. We provided no sense of the rise of Nazism within Germany, which is a German story, but rather began with the German invasion of Poland and the division of Poland between German-annexed, German-occupied, and Soviet-occupied territories. We then told the story of the ghettoization of Polish Jewry and the evolution of the killing process from the Einsatzgruppen to the Wannsee Conference.

Christopher Browning's book *Ordinary Men: Auxiliary Police Battalion 101 and the Final Solution in Poland* provided an important quote: "In mid-March 1942 [two months after the Wannsee Conference] some 75 to 80 percent of all victims of the Holocaust were still alive, while 20 to 25 percent had perished. A mere eleven months later, in mid-February 1943, the percentages were exactly the reverse."[10]

The curators then described life and death inside the ghetto which culminated in the deportation of Jews as the "Final Solution" evolved. Then we entered the world of the death camps, most specially the Aktion Reinhard camps, of which Belzec was the first and prime example. After presenting the entire Aktion Reinhard program, we focused on Belzec and included a list of the perpetrators: Odilo Globocnik, who received the order to establish the death camps in November 1941; Christian Wirth, the Commandant; and Gottlieb Hering, who succeeded him. Lorenz Hackenholt was instrumental in designing its gas chambers.

Claude Lanzmann graciously offered the use of testimony from his classic documentary *Shoah*.

The testimony chosen was of Franz Suchomel and Joseph Oberhauser and, later in the exhibition, of Jan Karski, who believed he had visited Belzec, but in actuality was taken to see Izbicia, a transit camp nearby. The exhibition presented those who told of the efforts of some people to get the word out, specifically Kurt Gerstein, who visited Belzec as an SS member. After he saw the gas chambers and the murder program he revealed them to the Vatican and neutral ambassadors, to little avail.

Since the memorial itself focused on the crime, we wanted to balance that by describing its victims and the communities they came from, including Lvov in occupied Poland, Wurtzberg in Germany, and the Hasidic community of Bobov. Material was given to the USHMM by Norman Salsitz, born Naftali Saleschütz, who is mentioned above. During the war, he photographed everyday life in the Kolbuszowa and Rzeszów ghettos with a camera he received in 1933 as a bar mitzvah gift from his American brother. Just before the dismantling of the labor detachment in Kolbuszowa, Saleschütz hid his photographs in different locations around the city and then escaped to the forest. He recovered them all after the liberation, and today they serve as the only wartime record of the Kolbuszowa Jewish community. Artifacts were integrated throughout the exhibit. In the section about the killers, a plaque was displayed that once hung at the Belzec camp. It bears instructions for the arriving victims. Jan Glab, a local resident, discovered it right after the war.

Attention!

Undress completely!

You will leave all the items brought with you in the designated area, with the exception of currency, valuables, documents, and shoes. You ought to keep currency, valuables, and documents with you until their collection at the designated window; do not let them out of your hands. Shoes should be tied in pairs and deposited in the designated area. You will approach bathing and inhalation completely undressed.

Among the more evocative objects are the keys collected in the archeological dig. Keys are deeply personal artifacts, which tell the visitor something of the mindset and the expectations of the victims. We all carry keys with the expectation that the home we left this morning will be safe on our return, and we fully expect to return to that home. That the victims carried keys in their pockets touches visitors and gives them a glimpse of what the victims expected—but they never did go back home.

Among the most difficult objects to view is a diesel muffler from the gas chamber—a remnant of the machinery used to murder Jews, a potent witness as to how the Germans perpetrated their crime.

The centerpiece of the exhibition on Belzec is the testimony of the lone survivor to offer witness: Rudolph Reder, who escaped in November 1942. As the visitor sees a model of the gas chamber at Belzec, Reder's words, recorded by Theodore Bikel in English, Hebrew, and Yiddish and by a distinguished Polish actor in Polish, can be heard in the audio recording visitors carry with them.

The haunting character of Reder's testimony is striking both for its completeness and the clarity of his presentation.[11]

And finally the exhibition concludes with a brief history of the postwar life of Belzec.

- 1944/1945: The area of the camp has been abandoned and was vandalized by demoralized people.
- 1945–1946: District Commission on the Investigation of Nazi Crimes in Poland in Lublin investigates the crimes committed in Belzec.
- 1946: The eyewitness account of Rudolf Reder published by the District Jewish Historical Commission of Cracow.

- 1959: State Prosecutor in Munich investigates the SS men from the Belzec crew.
- 1963: Monument unveiled at the Belzec site, the first commemoration of Belzec's victims.
- 1965: Trial of the former SS man of the Belzec crew Josef Oberhauser. He was the only SS guard convicted for the crimes committed in Belzec. His sentence was 4.5 years in prison. The other seven SS men tried together with Oberhauser were acquitted by the Munich court. The Main Commission for the Investigation of Nazi Crimes in Poland conducted the second investigation of the Belzec crimes but didn't find any new information evidences about the camp.
- 1995: United States Holocaust Memorial Museum enters an agreement with the Council for Protection of Monument of Combat and Martyrdom in Poland to erect a new monument at the Belzec site.
- 1997: Design by Andrzej Solyga and his team is selected by an international jury.
- 1997–1999: Archeological survey is conducted at the Belzec site marking down thirty-three graves as well as remnants of the building structures.
- 2002–2004: A new monument is constructed as a joint effort by the Polish Government and the American Jewish Committee. Archeological research is continued.
- January 1, 2004: Belzec memorial becomes a division of the State Museum of Majdanek in Lublin.
- June 2004: Unveiling of the new monument at Belzec.

Before the creation of the memorial and museum, few people visited Belzec, only those who, like Miles Lerman and several of the donors, had lost loved ones at Belzec. Despite its out-of-the-way location, however, thousands of visitors now come annually, including many Jewish groups from Israel and the United States, and the responses have been overwhelmingly positive. Visitorship is likely to increase as a better road, erected for the soccer championship, connects Krakow and Lviv in the Ukraine and shortens the travel time between those cities considerably.

What remains to be done is to create a parallel museum at Treblinka, where the memorial is majestic but the visitor needs be informed about the death camp and the Jews who were murdered there, and then to tackle the problem of the memorialization of Sobibor.

Notes

1. For an excellent treatment of Belzec, see Yitzhak Arad, *Belzec, Sobibor, Treblinka: The Operation Reinhard Death Camps* (Bloomington: Indiana University Press, 1987).

2. Robin O'Neil and Michael Tregenza, "Holocaust Education and Archive Research Team: Belzec. Archaeological Investigations: A Review by Historians," www.holocaustresearchproject.org/ar/modern/archreview.html.

3. "The Current Status of the Belzec Project," internal report of the United States Holocaust Memorial Museum, n.d.

4. Committee for the Preservation of Jewish Cemeteries in Europe. Consent document. 11 Iyar 5763 (May 13, 2003).

5. Rabbi Raphael Frank, "Mass Grave Belzec," letter to Rabbi Michael Schudrich (on Chief Rabbi Israel Meir Lau's stationery), 9 Shevat 5763 (January 12, 2003).

6. Rabbi Michael Schudrich, "Rabbinic Guidelines for Work to Be Performed in the Death Camp of Belzec."

7. "The Current Status of the Belzec Project," internal report of the United States Holocaust Memorial Museum, n.d.

8. Amcha Footprints [Rabbi Avi Weiss], "A Monumental Failure at Belzec Part II: Rabbis Visit Holocaust Death Camp, Temporarily Halt Desecrations: Camp Archaeologist Admits Bones Are Everywhere," July 30, 2003, www.qwebdevelopers.com/hir.org/amcha/belzec_july_2003.html.

9. Irving Greenberg, "Belzec's Victims Have Waited Long Enough," *The Forward*, August 22, 2003.

10. Christopher R. Browning, *Ordinary Men: Reserve Police Battalion 101 and the Final Solution in Poland* (New York: HarperPereennial, 1992), xv.

11. On August 10th at dawn all the exits of the Jewish quarter were surrounded by guards. Gestapo SS men, and Sonderdiensts in groups of five or six covered the street. They were helped by Ukrainian police....

I was in my shop working but I did not have a stamp for work permit. I locked myself in and did not answer when they beat on the door. The Gestapo broke down the door, beat me up with a whip, and dragged me out. We were all loaded on streetcars so tight that we could not move, and we were taken to camp Janowski.

By then it was evening. We were herded in a circle on a large meadow. There were six thousand of us. We were ordered to sit without moving, without even stretching a hand or a leg. We were surrounded by armed bandits; we sat squashed together, all together—young and old, women and children of all ages. . . .

We spent the night this way in silence. No one made a sound.

At six in the morning we were ordered to get up, line up in fours, and march to the Kleparowski train station. We were completely surrounded by Gestapo and Ukrainians. No one could escape. They herded us onto the loading ramp where [a] long cattle train, consisting of fifty wagons, was waiting. The loading process began. The sliding doors were open, two Gestapo stood on each side with whips with which they hit the faces and heads of those entering the wagon. Everybody had lash marks on their faces and lumps on their heads. The women sobbed. Children huddled to their mothers, crying. There were mothers with nursing babies. Everybody was prodded by the Gestapo who beat them without pity. Everybody was pushing everybody. The entrance was high up. One had to climb high to enter. It was hard, people were pushing each other down, but we were trying to climb up in a hurry. We wanted to get it behind us—over. A Gestapo man with a machine gun was sitting on the roof of each wagon.

The Gestapo men were beating us and counting about one hundred per wagon. Everything happened very fast. In less than an hour the loading of several thousand people was finished. . . .

Finally the wagons were lead-sealed. Squashed into one shaking mass of humanity, we stood pressed together almost on top of each other. Not a drop of water, stifling hot, we were almost crazed. At eight AM the train started moving.

No one was talking to anyone; no one was consoling lamenting women, no one was stopping sobbing children. We all knew: we were going to certain and horrible death.

About noon the train arrived in Belzec. It was a very small station surrounded by small houses. . . . At the Belzec station the train moving from the main line and onto a siding about one kilometer long led straight into the gate of the death camp. . . .

The area between Belzec and the camp was surrounded by SS men. No one was allowed in. Civilian people were shot at if they happened to wander in. . . .

A moment later "the receiving of the train" began. Dozens of SS men would open the wagons yelling "Los!" [get out]. With whips and their rifle butts they pushed people out. The doors of the wagon were a meter or more above the ground. Driven out by whips the people had to jump down: everybody, old and young; many broke their arms and legs falling down. They had to jump down to the ground. The children were mangled in the bedlam. Everybody pouring out—dirty, exhausted, terrified. . . .

The sick, the old, and the tiny children—those who could not walk on their own—were put on stretchers and dumped at the edge of huge dug out pits—their graves. There the Gestapo man Irrman shot them and pushed their bodies into the graves with his rifle butt.

Tall, handsome, dark-haired, looking like any normal man, he lived in Belzec in a small house next to the station alone—like the others, without a family and without women.

Immediately after the victims were unloaded they were gathered in the courtyard surrounded by armed askars for Irrman to give a speech. The silence was deadly. He stood close to the crowd. Everyone wanted to hear. Suddenly there was hope. "If they talk to us . . . maybe they want us to live . . . maybe there will be work . . . maybe?"

Irrman talked loud and clear: "You are going now to bathe. Later you will be sent to work. That's all."

Everybody was glad, happy that, after all, they will be working. They even applauded.

The men went straight ahead to a building with a sign "Bade und Inhaletionsräun" [bath and inhalation rooms]. The women proceeded 20 meters more to a large barrack about 30 x 15 m to have their heads shaved. They entered quietly not knowing what to expect. Silence was everywhere.

Later I learned that after a few minutes they were made to line up and made to sit on wooden stools, eight at a time. When eight Jewish barbers entered and silently like automated figures started to shave off hair completely to the skin with shaving machines, that's when they realized the truth. They had no doubts then.

Everybody—young and old, children and women—everybody went to certain death. Little girls with long hair were herded into the shaving barracks. Those with short hairs went to the barracks with the men.

Suddenly, without even a transition from hope to despair—came the realization that there was no hope. People began to scream—women became hysterical, crazed. . . .

I was chosen to be one of the workers. I would stand on the side of the courtyard with my group of gravediggers and looked at my brothers, sister, friends, and acquaintances herded toward death.

While the women were rounded up naked and shaved, whipped like cattle into a slaughterhouse, the men were already dying in the gas chambers. It took two hours to shave the women and two hours to murder them. Many SS men using whips and sharp bayonets pushed the women toward the building with the chambers.

Then the *askars* counted out 750 persons per chamber. . . .

I heard the noise of sliding doors, moaning and screaming, desperate calls in Polish, Yiddish—bloodcurdling screams. All that lasted fifteen minutes.

Screams of children, women, and finally one common continuous horrible scream. All that lasted fifteen minutes.

The machine ran for twenty minutes and after twenty minutes there was silence.

The *askars* pulled open the doors on the opposite sides of the chambers, which led to the outdoors.

We began our assigned task.

We dragged bodies of people who minutes ago were alive. We dragged them—using leather straps to huge prepared mass graves. And the orchestra played—played from morning till night.

The Jews were arriving from everywhere and only Jews.

With each transport it was the same as with the one that I arrived on. People were told to undress, leave their things in the courtyard. Irrman always gave the same speech—everything the same. People always showed a spark of hope in their eyes that they are going to work. But seconds later babies were torn away from their mothers, the old and the sick were thrown on stretchers, and the men, little boys, and girls were pushed with rifle butts further and further down the path.

The storeroom for hair, underwear, and clothing of the victims of the gas chamber was located in a separate rather small barracks. Hair was collected for ten days.

Baskets filled with gold teeth.

"How did it feel to work in this atmosphere?" Reder was asked.

When the barracks were locked for the night and the lights were out one could hear a whisper of prayers for the dead. The Kaddish, and then there was silence. We did not complain; we were completely resigned.

We moved like automated figures, just one large mass of them. We just mechanically worked through our horrible existence.

Every day we died a little bit together with the transports of people, who for a small moment lived and suffered with delusions.

Only when I heard children calling: "Mommy. Haven't I been good?"

Bibliography

Amcha Footprints [Rabbi Avi Weiss]. "A Monumental Failure at Belzec Part II: Rabbis Visit Holocaust Death Camp, Temporarily Halt Desecrations: Camp Archaeologist Admits Bones Are Everywhere." www.qwebdevelopers.com/hir.org/amcha/belzec_july_2003.html.

Arad, Yitzhak. *Belzec, Sobibor, Treblinka: The Operation Reinhard Death Camps*. Bloomington: Indiana University Press, 1987.

Committee for the Preservation of Jewish Cemeteries in Europe. Consent document. 11 Iyar 5763 (May 13, 2003).

"The Current Status of the Belzec Project." Internal report of the United States Holocaust Memorial Museum. N.d.

Frank, Rabbi Raphael. "Mass Grave Belzec." Letter to Rabbi Michel Schudrich (on Chief Rabbi Israel Meir Lau's stationary). 9 Shevat 5763 (January 12, 2003).

Greenberg, Irving. "Belzec's Victims Have Waited Long Enough." *The Forward*, August 22, 2003.

O'Neil, Robin, and Michael Tregenza. "Holocaust Education and Archive Research Team: Belzec. Archaeological Investigations: A Review by Historians." www.holocaustresearchproject.org/ar/modern/archreview.html.

Schudrich, Rabbi Michael. "Rabbinic Guidelines for Work to Be Performed in the Death Camp of Belzec." Office files of the Chief Rabbi of Poland, 2003.

10

Locating Loss

The Physical Contexts of Genocide Memorials

PAUL WILLIAMS

The Siting of Memory

This essay concentrates on what I consider a particularly productive context for analyzing the role and significance of memorial museums: their geography and sense of place.[1] The site-specific nature of most memorial museums—standing on ground where an atrocity took place—makes an appreciation of their larger geographic location vital. Factors such as the physical size and grandeur of the institution, the prominence and accessibility of its location, and the proximity of other city features determine the "geographic reach" of the event, and in turn its infiltration of public consciousness. The visibility of memorial museums (alongside historical statues, plaques, street signs, and honored buildings and parks) affects the "scaling of public memory"—the way an incident's recollection is prompted as people physically move through cities, regions, and nations.[2] The site is not only a backdrop or sightline for interpretation, but constitutes meaning through complex forms of signification. This includes not just architectural and landscaping design and symbolism, but the more ineffable qualities of the site—the quality of its air or its light, the feeling of the earth underfoot, the emotions surrounding the initial glimpse of a building. All this interacts with the expectations of the coming experience ("What will it be like?") and the media-influenced "imagined memory" of the event ("Will it look like the photos or films I've seen?") with which the visitor arrives, forming powerful initial impressions.

While "imagined memory" may strike some as a problematic phrase (to the extent that all memory is creatively reconstructed), the concept allows us to distinguish memories grounded in lived experience from those produced by media fragments and creatively conjured in different ways by each of us.[3] The site itself is the visual symbol that stands between the viewer and the event commemorated, and sets in motion powerful connotations of meaning. Next, I move through three physical-architectural themes—site-specific authenticity, reorganized landscapes, and aesthetic minimalism—to explore aspects of the physical construction of meaning across different genocide memorials.

Unearthing Authenticity

As different communities attempt to cope with the continued unease and loss associated with mass violence, the damaged landscapes associated with such destructive events are increasingly claimed as hallowed ground. Yet the relationship between the location of the catastrophe and the site of a memorial can be unreliable or insecure. To be sure, in many cases the site may be uncontested where locals and survivors vouch for its historical accuracy: *this* building was used for *this* purpose; *these* people were killed *here*. Historic locations may have existed without much attention for years before political and economic conditions—and the will of an individual, group, or government—made it possible to be framed as "rediscovered" or "unearthed."

A primary case for consideration occurred along Berlin's Niederkirchnerstrasse in the early 1980s when, after decades of purposeful silence, historians, researchers, and locals made an effort to memorialize the area where the Gestapo and SS headquarters had once stood. Engraved metal plates were initially planned for the site. It gained greater dramatic potential in 1986, when attention turned to an archaeological strategy that would unearth cellars of the buildings used for torture. The Topography of Terror gains much of its power from not just its open-air, minimally fabricated, in-situ mode of interpretation—it allows it to act as a ground-level "map of the past" via an open wound that interrupts the urban fabric of everyday Berlin. The "museumification" of the site that accompanied the opening of its Documentation Center in 2010 was a pitch-perfect addition. It did not obstruct or clutter the footprint of the historic site, and, in its use of photographs, documents, and supporting text, retained the larger emphasis on the visitor's contemplation of evidence.

A lesser-known case where an authentic site is used to illuminate a buried past can be found at the Unit 731 Memorial Museum, located in Harbin, northeast China—a region that was part of the puppet state of Manchukuo during the Imperial Japanese occupation. The museum commemorated around 10,000 prisoners directly killed by Japanese wartime medical experiments, and another 300,000 who were harmed through resulting germ warfare. Unit 731 was the world's largest germ warfare complex, boasting 150 buildings, a railway stop, and a staff of 10,000. It now consists of the remains of structures such as rat-breeding facilities and laboratories for the production of anthrax, cholera, and the bubonic plague. Although the Japanese destroyed much material evidence from the site as the war ended, around 1,200 items were dug up prior to opening in 2001.[4] Locals from Harbin set up an Exhibition Hall that displays surgical knives and saws, pieces of incinerators and incubators, and germ-loaded shells. In rooms off long grey narrow corridors with high ceilings,

The former Unit 731 Museum in Harbin, set in a wing of the chemical warfare research base.

life-size plaster cast models are shown on tables after being injected or cut open without anesthetics by military doctors. Photographs and newspaper stories also provide evidence, while a short film features select interviews with Japanese soldiers confessing to certain deeds.

Receiving 30,000 visitors upon opening in 1998, the museum averaged about 150,000 per year. This number, it can be surmised, did not come for the relatively crude exhibits, or because it is a tourist draw card. Instead, the availability of an authentic *place to go* that could serve as a physical focus point for Chinese anger about so far little-acknowledged wartime atrocities made it vital. Although it lay dormant in plain sight for decades, it was "rediscovered" for the public by being opened, signposted, and arranged. Its very physical existence is itself powerful. Notably, the half-century of silence before opening has contributed toward a view, popular among some Japanese, that it has been recently "invented" to suit Chinese political ends. This shows that, while sites are not often entirely forgotten by those in the locality of a heinous act, the motivation to exhume them by certain people denotes a political intervention as much as an archaeological unveiling.

In 2015 the museum received a major revitalization. Renamed the Museum of Evidence of War Crimes, it reopened to the public in August 2015—timed to coincide with the seventieth anniversary of Japan's surrender in World War II. A large-scale new architectural intervention has enlarged the scale and visibility of the museum, and its new permanent exhibition represents a more professional approach to its original makeshift exhibition. Where originally exhibits were housed in remnant buildings, they now sit within a complex that has a more sophisticated allegorical treatment:

> The vision for the museum comes from the metaphor of a black box of a plane crash. The point is to say that the site of Unit 731 is the black box that recorded one of the darkest periods of human history. In showing the contents of the black box, we find out what happened and remember the lessons learned from the disaster. The area round the museum was made to look as if the ground split open to reveal the black box.[5]

There is understandably a desire, borne from the will of the stakeholders, political interests, and tourism industry, for a site of atrocity to

The new Museum of War Crime Evidence by Japanese Army Unit 731, on the grounds of the former chemical warfare research base.

achieve the status of an architecturally designed and professionally curated memorial museum. Yet it potentially changes the dynamic, as institutions associated with grassroots victims and families see their deeply personal stories become part of an aesthetic visitor experience that carries politically symbolic overtones.

The perceived authenticity of a historic site is greatly enhanced when it contains tangible proof of the event *in place*. Given their sacred qualities and the sense of finality they provide an event, graves form a forceful basis for a memorial museum's location. For instance, the Nanjing Massacre Memorial Museum was built in the west of the city over a shallow pond that once formed a mass grave for hundreds. Photographs of this grave appear in the museum and some of the skeletal remains are displayed within a glass chamber in an exhibit hall. The display of these remains as evidence, lying in the dumped heap where they were discovered, reflects a felt need to establish the veracity of the event—even if such a truth claim is compromised by nearby curatorial tactics like a concrete wall with artificial bullet holes, and mannequins arranged in realistic slaughter scenes. While all memorials are self-referencing—that is, their artifice is intended to act as an enduring reminder of why they were built—those like the Nanjing Memorial that showcase skeletal remains make this relation especially blunt.

In situations like the Argentinean and Chilean "dirty wars" or the Srebrenica massacre where death was concealed, graves stand as visual evidence of the scale of killing. Since their discovery across scattered sites has made a centralized memorial location more complicated, the question of where to rebury is loaded with importance. The mutilated and tortured remains of those executed by Pinochet's military government after the 1973 coup were taken to Chile's National Cemetery "Patio 29" and buried in graves marked with small metal crosses with "NN" (*no nombre*) painted on them. In 1982, in a new attempt to conceal some of their most egregious excesses, the military government disinterred hundreds of bodies and disposed of them in unknown locales and ground the bones into chicken feed. After the return of civilian government a decade later, the remains of those that had not disappeared were found in this plot, identified with forensics, and relocated to the crypts in the memorial wall at the opposite end of the cemetery.[6] An awareness of how the bodies came to rest is an imperative (and often overlooked) element of interpretation. Although they moved a short distance, the act of exercising control over their physical location was vital for families. Consider also the families of 9/11 victims, who have sought the retrieval and re-interment of human remains discovered at Fresh Kills Landfill to a private viewing chamber at the National September 11 Memorial & Museum. These cases suggest that memorial complexes can provide the valuable function of providing a meaningful burial site in situations where few suitable options otherwise exist. Their reburial in a public memorial space reflects a desire that the unnatural and historically significant nature of their deaths be socially recognized. Properly conceived, sites can use their authentic geographical essence to stake twin claims: that *this* event has permanently marked this place, and that *this* memorial experience will stay with you. Both of these effects, as I suggested above, typically occur in that first dramatic physical encounter.

Reorganized Landscapes

Locations themselves are not stable, inasmuch as they shift as a result of wrenching political changes. Nowhere in this better recognized than in Germany. Buchenwald is a case in point. In April 1945, within eight days of liberation, survivors raised a wooden obelisk made from camp barracks, later replaced by stone. When it was dedicated in 1958 as an East German national memorial site, a memorial plaque stated that it would "bear witness to the indefatigable strength of the anti-fascist resistance fighter." Along with the remains of the concentration camp, a museum of anti-fascist resistance was a focal point, which juxtaposed Nazi barbarism and Soviet martyrdom, and Fritz Cremer's monument. After reunification, the historical geography of Nazi concentration camp emphasized the victim/perpetrator dichotomy.[7] Not only did distinctions between victims become a notable theme for the first time, but in 1993 new routes were marked and guidebooks issued that drew attention to the mass graves from the Soviet "special camp number two" where German prisoners were detained and 7,000 were allowed to die from malnutrition and disease. As we see, the political reorganization of territory also involves the physical reorganization of highly potent historical symbols.

We can see a related process in the emergence of the Holodomor in the Ukrainian landscape. As of March 2008, the parliament of Ukraine voted to recognize the actions of the Soviet government as an act of genocide. In November 2008, a design competition was announced for a national Holodomor museum and documentation center in Kiev, Ukraine, on this site where Soviet disinformation campaigns were carried out for fifty years, well into the 1980s, until Soviet authorities broached the subject in the spirit of *glasnost*. Since independence, the Ukrainian government has remade the landscape by devoting public space to the topic, such as the new memorial park recently opened in Kiev. Hence, we see how political self-determination provides the opportunity to remake the physical terrain, which in turn is a key tactic in raising public consciousness and rescaling collective memory.

If parks were designed as a refuge from the perils of base humanity—its conflict, squalor, and politics—it is a curious historical reversal that sees two Eastern European cities creating parks as political graveyards. Budapest's Szoborpark ("Statue Park") opened in 1993 in a field near a highway in the southern part of the city. In 1991 the Cultural Committee of the Budapest Assembly had invited a tender around the question "What is to be done with the statues?" The winner, architect Ákos Eleod, devised a scheme to be experienced as follows:

The park is arranged in the form of a straight path, from which "figure-of-eight" walkways lead off (so that the wandering visitor will always return to the true path!), around which statues and monuments are displayed. In the centre of the park is a flowerbed in the form of a Soviet Star. Eventually, the path ends abruptly in a brick wall, representing the "dead end" which state socialism represented for Hungary: visitors have no choice but to walk back the way they have previously come.[8]

At Statue Park the sculptures are clustered close together to achieve a superfluity of ideological symbolism. Lithuania's "Grūtas Parkas" (also known as "Stalin World") is a similar sculpture garden that opened in 2001 in a wooded park beyond Vilnius. The tender put forth by the Lithuanian Ministry of Culture in 1998, for the establishment of an exposition of dismantled Soviet sculpture, was won by Viliumas Malinauskas. The local millionaire (who made his fortune canning mushrooms) designed and financed the park. A cattle-car marks the gateway to the numerous statues of Lenin and Stalin, which are surrounded by barbed wired and interspersed with guard towers. Lithuanian figures also appear, such as Kapsukas, a founder of the Lithuanian Communist Party. The relocation

Statue of Lenin at Grūtas Park, Lithuania.

Kapsukas and Lenin, Grūtas Park, Lithuania.

of city sculptures to a Budapest suburban field or a Lithuanian forest park has several effects. It banishes them from their "natural" habitat where they exerted significant ideological power. In doing so, it denies obvious rallying points for leftist political groups. At its time of opening—on April Fool's Day—Grutas Parkas spurred a fierce debate between its supporters and those who saw it as sacrilegious.[9] The almost comical repetition and proximity of figures within a landscape where they have little function (and risk being grown over) is an uncommonly effective distancing mechanism. Nonetheless, in the future it could also be perceived as a blatant form of reverse propaganda. For these nations seeking to rebuild affiliations with central and Western Europe, the parks serve as an expression of a very different brand of civility than that imagined by Victorian social reformers: as political artifacts are insolently intermingled with nature, visitors' sense of sophistication involves appreciating the irony associated with putting the past "out to pasture." Purpose-built political parks have, in these novel examples, become the way that inner cities can again be politically redeemed.

Minimalist Aesthetics

In the past two decades or so, there has emerged in the West a distrust of majestic state monuments. In reaction to both right- and left-wing monumental statist aesthetics, a more skeptical visual language of size, scale, line, color, and weight has come to dominate new artist-competition style memorial projects. Modern artists and monument designers alike wanted works "that would not be *about* things in the world but would themselves *be* things in the world."[10] The current ideal is that subjects will physically engage with the form in order to arouse some sensory mode, rather than standing back to contemplate a semi-realistic representation.

The seminal example of this minimalist genre is probably Maya Lin's Vietnam Veterans Memorial. The design is based around two long reflective black granite walls sunk into the ground, the tops of which are flush with the earth behind them. The names of the 58,249 American casualties are inscribed in chronological order according to the year of their death. While it was derided by some as being explicitly ideological, by associating the efforts of servicemen with a "black ditch" or "gash of shame," most would agree that its success lies in the way it does not move the visitor in any particular direction—whether comfort, anger, or sadness. Given the distressing events they aim to evoke, the slash and void have perhaps unsurprisingly emerged as key symbolic forms in minimalist design. Daniel Libeskind is the architect most closely associated with this brand of minimalism. Voids and shards feature most notably in the Jewish Museum, Berlin (2001), the Imperial War Museum North, Manchester (2002), and in plans for New York's 9/11 Memorial.[11] In this last case, Libeskind proposes sections of the building that would leave parts of the pit exposed, to complement Michael Arad and Peter Walker's "Reflecting Absence" memorial. This memorial, based around two nine-meter deep pools where the towers once stood, into which water would cascade from the edges, received a behind-the-scenes push from Maya Lin herself, who had designed a civil rights memorial with cascading water and names for the Southern Poverty Law Center. Her design also appears to have been influential in the design of Buenos Aires' *Parque de la Memoria* (2001). Its main feature, the forthcoming "Monument to the Victims of State Terror," is a sinuous fissure cut into and crisscrossing the fourteen-acre park that aims to express the "open wound" permeating Argentinean society.

Some standardization in the symbolization of atrocity has emerged. Those memorials geared toward softer themes of healing and forgiveness tend to use emblems associated with the elements, suggesting a source of redemption greater than the mortals who perpetuated or suffered the act. Pools of water, beams or shafts of light, stone plinths, and an eternal flame are common, sharing stylistic elements with conventional world war memorials. Newer spaces are typically designed in ways that encourage more idiosyncratic metaphorical readings. The Oklahoma City Memorial features an empty chair for each person killed. Evenly spaced, they each face a reflecting pool. This design borrows from the convention of leaving seats empty at social gatherings to honor those absent, and from riderless horses at state funeral parades. More generally, it expresses themes of unfulfilled lives, people denied their place in the world, and, given that victims included children at a daycare center in the building, classroom chairs. A similar memorial at the 9/11 Pentagon Memorial Park opened in 2008. Its 184 cantilevered outdoor benches, each one inscribed with the name of a victim, will be lit from underneath to create a field of glowing light pools.

Although minimalism is traditionally associated with the avant-garde, it can also be seen, at least in the memorial field, as signaling a refuge from overtly political ideas about responsibility and blame. We can observe this in plans for the imminent $30 million Flight 93 Memorial to be constructed at the 9/11 crash site 130 kilometers from Pittsburgh. The winner of the design competition, Paul Murdoch, has divided the 890-hectare site, to be run by the National Park Service, into three sections. The "Tower of Voices," ninety-three feet high (matching the flight number), will aid the visibility of the site from the road, and is to be filled with wind chimes. A semi-circular arrangement of maple trees ("Crescent of Embrace") will blaze red each fall. (Some commentators expressed uproar at this design due to the symbolism of the Red Crescent—used on the national flags of Muslim nations like Turkey, Algeria, Pakistan, and Uzbekistan—forcing Murdoch to offer to make alterations. It is likely that critics sought a more triumphant memorial, given that Flight 93 was the only instance resembling "victory" on that morning.)[12] On the south end of that arc, a series of low black slate walls will shield the crash site ("Sacred Ground") from the public. The total design represents, according to Christopher Hawthorne, "Hallmark-card minimalism" for the way it attaches reassuring interpretation (such as the "Voices / Embrace / Sacred" themes) to design that carries few concrete referents.[13] Predictably, perhaps, the tenor of the names of the three sections of the memorial strongly suggests the site will delimit the possible interpretations of the event, instead upholding a message that is affirming and nationalist in orientation.

Other sites use representative spatial analogies to represent the social and cultural ruin wrought. The theme of loss—spanning possessions, culture, and people—is found in Berlin's cobblestone stretch called the Bebelplatz, where Nazi book burning took place in May 1933. On that site in 1995, Micha Ullman, an Israeli-born artist, created a small ground-level window that looks into a subterranean white room lined with empty bookshelves. The 2,711 slabs that form Berlin's Monument to the Murdered Jews of Europe aim to express, in a more abstract manner, similar themes. Yet in this case it is not clear for whom a feeling of being trapped or uncomfortable, brought about by oppressive surfaces and unevenness in scale, is directed. Does it matter that the physical encounter produces a somewhat common experience among all who visit, despite critical differences in visitors' subjective relation to the event? Stephen Greenblatt wrote about the entries for the competition for the memorial in the following way:

> It has become increasingly apparent that no design for a Berlin memorial to remember the millions of Jews killed by Nazis in the Holocaust will ever prove adequate to the immense symbolic weight it must carry, as numerous designs have been considered and discarded. Perhaps the best course at this point would be to leave the site of the proposed memorial at the heart of Berlin and of Germany empty, to abandon it to weeds and, in Hamlet's words, to let things rank and gross in nature possess it merely.[14]

Wariness about the way that memorial projects might reify or enshrine the memory of an event has turned some artists and critics in another direction: toward deliberately *not* building, or even destroying. At least one commentator expressed the view that leaving the World Trade Center's seven-story pit of debris would best memorialize 9/11. A submission for the memorial competition by artist Horst Hoheisel proposed to blow up the Brandenburg Gate, grind its stone into dust, sprinkle the remains over the proposed site, and then cover the entire area with granite plates.[15] Hoheisel has a clear mistrust of the way that commemorative forms promise an assured, knowable position toward historical calamity. If, for Hoheisel, the event seizes him as dreadful, then his creative response will also reflect some similar negativity. While his proposal is unlikely to be taken seriously by those seeking some broadly accepted symbol of reconciliation, it is worth noting for the way it brings attention to the potential folly of assuming that a properly designed memorial can help us unlock and understand the past.

Conclusion: Signifying Topographies

As the cases touched on here suggest, the way that sites are used to frame historical events is vital in the production of meaning. While interior exhibitions "explain" the site, the site enhances the arguments put forward by the exhibition and adds credibility to its version of history. More than this, the physical existence of memorial museums is a claim to conscience not easily effaced. As Deyan Sudjic has written, "Architecture matters because it lasts, of course. It matters because it is big, and it shapes the landscape of our everyday lives. But beyond that, it also matters because, more than any other cultural form, it is a means of setting the historical record straight."[16]

Coming to this site at Bergen-Belsen, we might worry that events represented by memorial museums situated in more remote or obscure places are more likely to be overlooked. Yet, as the tradition of the pilgrimage suggests, the commitment involved in traveling to more obscure sites may heighten the significance of the visit, and that a remote location that expresses the concealed nature of a crime can heighten a museum's interpretive drama. The meaning of a site is formed in the way that we imagine the terrible drama of an event playing out within an enclosed spatial framework. Along with certain monuments, historic houses, squares, parks, bridges, cemeteries, and street names, museums are markers that remind us of a range of questions about our personal relationship with the past: Do we seek them out to aid remembering, or bypass them to enable forgetting? Do we embrace them as cornerstones of community, or isolate them as sections of tourist routes? Such questions suggest that the significance of memorial museums cannot be established a priori, but is decided through social attitudes toward them and the quality of the practices with which they are popularly associated.

Memorial museums operate against the conventional premise that we preserve markers of that which is glorious, and destroy evidence of what is reviled. There is now a widespread sensibility that if events are to be remembered, they require a concrete locus for public attention. "Memory attaches itself to sites, whereas history attaches itself to events," wrote Pierre Nora.[17] We exist in a time when there is great confidence in the idea of physical locations as appropriate repositories for genuine local memory, and as loci that will help others gain a tangible sense of an event. For those with firsthand knowledge of what transpired, this remembrance works on a sensory level: the reinstatement of a location can trigger memories not likely to emerge elsewhere. As Maurice Halbwachs wrote:

> Every collective memory unfolds within a spatial framework. Now space is a reality that endures: Since our impressions rush by . . . we can understand how we recapture the past only by understanding how it is, in effect, preserved by our physical surroundings. It is to space—the space we occupy, traverse, have continual access to, or can at any time reconstruct in thought and imagination—that we must turn our attention.[18]

Location affords not only the ability to picture the traumatic episode, but also to reawaken the feeling of an event triggered by ambient textures of sound, light, and smell. It is, arguably, a sense of place—rather than objects or images—that gives form to our memories, and provides the coordinates for the construction of the "imagined memories" of those who visit memorial sites but never knew the event firsthand.

Notes

1. For more on this topic, see Paul Williams, *Memorial Museums: The Global Rush to Commemorate Atrocities* (Oxford: Berg, 2007), 77–104.

2. I borrow the term "the scaling of memory" from Derek. H Alderman, "Street Names and the Scaling of Memory: The Politics of Commemorating Martin Luther King, Jr. within the African American Community," *Area* 35, no. 2 (2002): 163–73.

3. Andreas Huyssen, "Present Pasts: Media, Politics, Amnesia," *Public Culture* 12, no. 1 (2000): 27.

4. See Xiaolong Zhao, "The Landscape Planning and Design of Japanese Imperial Army Unit 731 Site Park," *Electrical and Control Engineering* (ICECE), Conference proceedings, 2011.

5. Didi Kirsten Tatlow, "Gao Yubao on Documenting Unit 731's Brutal Human Experiments," *New York Times*, October 21, 2015, http://sinosphere.blogs.nytimes.com/2015/10/21/china-unit-731-japan-war-crimes/?_r=0, accessed March 28, 2016.

6. Teresa Meade, "Holding the Junta Accountable: Chile's 'Sitios de Memoria' and the History of Torture, Disappearance, and Death," *Radical History Review* 79 (2001): 133–34.

7. Maoz Azaryahu, "RePlacing Memory: The Reorientation of Buchenwald," *Cultural Geographies* 10 (2003): 10–11.

8. Duncan Light, "Gazing on Communism: Heritage Tourism and Post-Communist Identities in Germany, Hungary, and Rumania," *Tourism Geographies* 2, no. 2 (2000): 168.

9. There was resistance. See Gediminas Lankauskas, "Sensuous (Re)collections: The Sight and Taste of Socialism at Grūtas Statue Park, Lithuania," *Senses & Society* 1, no. 1 (2006): 29.

10. William Hubbard, "A Meaning for Monuments," in *The Public Face of Architecture: Civic Culture and Public Space*, ed. Nathan Glazer and Mark Lilla (New York: Free Press, 1987), 133.

11. See James E. Young, "Daniel Libeskind's Jewish Museum in Berlin: The Uncanny Arts of Memorial Architecture," *Jewish Social Studies* 6, no. 2 (2000): 1–23.

12. Patricia Lowry, "Flight 93 Memorial Emphasizes Contemplation," *Pittsburgh Post-Gazette*, September 13 2005.

13. Christopher Hawthorne, "Reading Symbolism in the Sept. 11 Era," *Los Angeles Times*, October 5, 2005.

14. Stephen J. Greenblatt, "Ghosts of Berlin," *New York Times*, April 28, 1999.

15. James E. Young, "The Counter-Monument: Memory against Itself in Germany Today," *Critical Inquiry* 18, no. 2 (1992): 267–96.

16. Deyan Sudjic, "Engineering Conflict," *New York Times Magazine*, May 21, 2006.

17. Cited in Isabelle Engelhardt, "A Topography of Memory: Representations of the Holocaust at Dachau and Buchenwald in Comparison with Auschwitz, Yad Vashem and Washington, DC," *Series Multiple Europes* 16 (Brussels: Peter Lang, 2002), 44.

18. Maurice Halbwachs, *On Collective Memory* (Chicago: University of Chicago Press, 1992), 146.

Bibliography

Alderman, Derek H. "Street Names and the Scaling of Memory: The Politics of Commemorating Martin Luther King, Jr. within the African American Community." *Area* 35, no. 2 (2002): 163–73.

Azaryahu, Maoz. "RePlacing Memory: The Reorientation of Buchenwald." *Cultural Geographies* 10 (2003): 1–20.

Engelhardt, Isabelle. "A Topography of Memory: Representations of the Holocaust at Dachau and Buchenwald in Comparison with Auschwitz, Yad Vashem and Washington, DC." *Series Multiple Europes* 16. Brussels: Peter Lang, 2002.

Greenblatt, Stephen J. "Ghosts of Berlin." *New York Times*, April 28, 1999.

Halbwachs, Maurice. *On Collective Memory*. Chicago: University of Chicago Press, 1992.

Hawthorne, Christopher. "Reading Symbolism in the Sept. 11 Era." *Los Angeles Times*, October 5, 2005.

Hubbard, William. "A Meaning for Monuments." In *The Public Face of Architecture: Civic Culture and Public Space*, ed. Nathan Glazer and Mark Lilla, 124–41. New York: Free Press, 1987.

Huyssen, Andreas. "Present Pasts: Media, Politics, Amnesia." *Public Culture* 12, no. 1 (2000): 21–38.

Lankauskas, Gediminas. "Sensuous (Re)collections: The Sight and Taste of Socialism at Grūtas Statue Park, Lithuania." *Senses & Society* 1, no. 1 (2006): 27–52.

Light, Duncan. "Gazing on Communism: Heritage Tourism and Post-Communist Identities in Germany, Hungary, and Rumania." *Tourism Geographies* 2, no. 2 (2000): 157–76.

Lowry, Patricia. "Flight 93 Memorial Emphasizes Contemplation." *Pittsburgh Post-Gazette*, September 13, 2005.

Meade, Teresa. "Holding the Junta Accountable: Chile's 'Sitios de Memoria' and the History of Torture, Disappearance, and Death." *Radical History Review* 79 (2001): 123–39.

Sudjic, Deyan. "Engineering Conflict." *New York Times Magazine*, May 21, 2006.

Tatlow, Didi Kirsten. "Gao Yubao on Documenting Unit 731's Brutal Human Experiments." *New York Times*, October 21, 2015.

Williams, Paul. *Memorial Museums: The Global Rush to Commemorate Atrocities*. Oxford: Berg, 2007.

Young, James E. "The Counter-Monument: Memory against Itself in Germany Today." *Critical Inquiry* 18, no. 2 (1992): 267–96.

———. "Daniel Libeskind's Jewish Museum in Berlin: The Uncanny Arts of Memorial Architecture." *Jewish Social Studies* 6, no. 2 (2000): 1–23.

Zhao, Xiaolong. "The Landscape Planning and Design of Japanese Imperial Army Unit 731 Site Park." *Electrical and Control Engineering* (ICECE), conference proceedings, August 2011.

Contributors

Michael Berenbaum is a writer, lecturer, and conceptual developer of museums and historical films. He is director of the Sigi Ziering Institute at the American Jewish University. He was president and chief executive officer of the Survivors Shoah Visual History Foundation and the director of the United Holocaust Research Institute at the United States Holocaust Memorial Museum. From 1988 to 1993 he was the project director of the United States Holocaust Memorial Museum, overseeing its creation.

Father Patrick Desbois is director of the Episcopal Committee for Relations with Judaism. He has been internationally recognized for his extraordinary work in uncovering the mass graves of Jews in Eastern Europe. His book *Holocaust by Bullets* has been recognized as one of the most important recent contributions to our understanding of the Holocaust. Father Desbois has recently been appointed as endowed professor to the Center for Jewish Civilization at Georgetown University.

Insa Eschebach is the director of the Ravensbrück Memorial Museum situated in the former Democratic Republic of Germany. She is the author of *The Ravensbrück Women's Concentration Camp*. Eschebach's recent work has focused on the postwar sovietization of the memories of the Ravensbrück women's camp.

Esther Farbstein is the director of the Holocaust Education Center at Michlala Women's College in Jerusalem. She is the foremost contemporary Hasidic Israeli historian specializing in the history of the Holocaust. Her books *Hidden in Thunder* and *The Forgotten Memoirs* are recognized exemplars of the new genre of Orthodox Jewish historiography.

Contributors

Habbo Knoch is a professor in the Department of Modern and Contemporary History at the University of Cologne, Germany. He is the former director of the Bergen–Belsen Memorial Museum. He is the coauthor of *Bergen-Belsen: Neue Forschungen Wallstein Verlag*.

Lawrence L. Langer is professor emeritus of English at Simmons College in Boston as well as the foremost scholar of the Holocaust in the field of literature and testimony. *The Holocaust and the Literary Imagination* (1975), his first work on the Holocaust, was followed by *The Age of Atrocity: Death in Modern Literature* (1978); *Versions of Survival: The Holocaust and the Human Spirit* (1982); *Holocaust Testimonies: The Ruins of Memory* (1991); *Admitting the Holocaust: Collected Essays* (1995); and *Preempting the Holocaust* (1998). He is also editor of *Art from the Ashes: A Holocaust Anthology* (1995).

Paul A. Shapiro is the director of the United States Holocaust Memorial Museum's Center for Advanced Holocaust Studies. He is the recipient of the Cross of the Order of Merit, Germany's highest civilian recognition, for his contributions to the study of the Holocaust. Shapiro was instrumental in opening the International Tracing Service archive, based in Bad Arolsen, Germany, and making its contents available to Holocaust survivors and scholars around the world.

Leo Spitzer is the Vernon Professor of History Emeritus at Dartmouth College. The recipient of numerous fellowships, including a John Simon Guggenheim Foundation and a National Humanities Center award, he writes on photography, testimony, and Jewish refugee memory and its transmission. His most recent book, coauthored with Marianne Hirsch, is *Ghosts of Home: The Afterlife of Czernowitz in Jewish Memory*. He is also the author of *Hotel Bolivia: The Culture of Memory in a Refuge from Nazism*; *Lives in Between: Assimilation and Marginality in Austria, Brazil and West Africa*; *The Creoles of Sierra Leone: Responses to Colonialism*; and coeditor, with Mieke Bal and Jonathan Crewe, of *Acts of Memory: Cultural Recall in the Present*. He is currently working on *The Americanization of Poldi*, a memoir about Jewish refugee immigration in New York in the decade of the 1950s and, with Marianne Hirsch, on a book of essays on photography and the Holocaust.

Contributors

Henri Lustiger Thaler is an author, filmmaker, and editor of seven books and scholarly articles, most recently focusing on the Orthodox Jewish experience in the Holocaust. He is the series editor of *Memory Studies: Global Constellations* for Routledge. He is the chief curator at the Amud Aish Memorial Museum in Brooklyn, a professor of cultural and historical sociology at Ramapo College of New Jersey, and an associate researcher at CADIS of the Ecole des Hautes Etudes en Science Sociales, Paris.

Annette Wieviorka is one of the best-known French historians of the Holocaust of her generation. She is the author of many scholarly books and articles. Her book *The Era of the Witness* has become a seminal source in the field of the memory and history of the Holocaust. Her other works include *Auschwitz Explained to My Child*, *The Eichmann Trial*, *The Nuremberg Trial*, *Deportation and Genocide*, and others.

Paul Williams specializes in the representation of political histories in museums. Since 2008 he has worked for Ralph Appelbaum Associates, a New York–based museum planning and design firm. Prior to that, Williams spent several years teaching in the museum studies graduate program at New York University. He is the author of *Memorial Museums: The Global Rush to Commemorate Atrocities*. Other recent publications include "Memorial Museums and the Objectification of Suffering," in *The Routledge Companion to Museum Ethics: Redefining Ethics for the Twenty-First Century Museum*, and "Hailing the Cosmopolitan Conscience: Memorial Museums in a Global Age," in *Hot Topics, Public Culture, Museums*.

Index

Italic locators reference figures/tables in the text.

"abspritzen," 16, 19–20
"adoptive and intellectual witnessing" (Hartman), 1
Adorno, Theodor, 57
"Afterdeath of the Holocaust, The" (Langer), 2–3, 15–30
Agamben, Giorgio, 56, 57, 59
Age of Suspicion, The (Sarraute), 31, 48n3
aguna, 61
Aktion Reinhard camps, 195, 209, 210
Alexianu, Gheorghe, 106, 113, 121
All Rivers Run to the Sea: Memoirs (Wiesel), 92
American Jewish Committee, 194, 204, 212
American Jewish Joint Distribution Committee, 64, 65
American Military Zone, DP camps, 4, 5, 64, 65, 78n30, 78n32
Améry, Jean, 22
Ancel, Jean, 109, 127n10
And the World Remained Silent (Wiesel), 39
Anne Frank: The Diary of a Young Girl, 35
anniversaries, 32, 35, 176–77
antifascism: museums and memorials, 175, 176, 182, 224; organizations, 147, 163n5
Antonescu, Ion, 105, 106, 109, 111, 125
Appelbaum, Ralph, 194
Arad, Michael, 227
Arafat, Yasir, 202
archaeological surveys, 199–202, 212

"archaeology of death," 24
architectural design: memorials and museums, physical contexts and memory, 205, 205–8, *207*, 218, 219, 221–22, 224–25, 227–30; memorials and museums, planning, 169, 194–95, 196, 198–202, 205–8, 209
archives. *See* historical documentation
Argentina, 223, 227
"arrogated choice," 59
art. *See* architectural design; artistic and cultural opportunities, concentration camps; sculpture and statues
artifacts: memorials and museums, collection and use, 186, 193–94, 199–200, 203, 210–11, 220, 222; memorial sites, consideration, 169; sensitivity and respect, 203, 211, 222
artistic and cultural opportunities, concentration camps, 124–25, 184
Ashkenazi Jews, 155–56
Assmann, Aleida, 180
Association of Victims of Nazi Persecution, 169
atrocity and memory, 16, 20, 22, 25
Auerbach, Rachel, 37
Auschwitz, First Testimonies (Weiss), 42
Auschwitz and After (Delbo), 16
Auschwitz-Birkenau camp: direction, 73–75; discovery and liberation, 32, 134–35; evacuation, survivor testimonies, 3, 47; film depictions, 42–43; memorialization, 7, 32; museum

Index

Auschwitz-Birkenau camp (*cont.*)
  and artifacts, 193; perpetrator experiences: memory, 2, 15–16, 19–20; survivor experiences: memory, 10–11, 16–18, 21, 27, 42–43, 44, 61, 67–76, 87, 92; survivor memoirs, 4–5, 16, 39, 54, 62, 66–76, *69,* 79n37, 178–79; victim testimonies, 35
Auschwitz Prozess (trials; 1963–1965), 2–3, 11n4, 16, 19, 20
"Auschwitz Scrolls," 35
"authored testimonies," 45
Avigdor, Yaakov, 84, 88, 90–91, 93–94, 97
Avigdor, Yitzchok, 54–55, 59
Avrech, Yishaya, 81

Babyonyshev, Alexander, 144
Bak, Sam, 56, 78n32
Baker, Andrew, 194, 204
Belhaddad, Souad, 47
Belzec extermination camp: establishment, 127n8, 197; history and events, 197–98, 208–9, 211–12; victims, 193, 195–96, 197, 198, 206–8, 209–11, 213–16n11; witness testimonies, 8–9, 211, 213–16n11. *See also* Belzec Memorial
Belzec Memorial: archaeological surveys and guides, 199–202, 212; memorial and museum described, *205,* 205–17, *206, 207;* memorial and museum planning, 8, 192–95, 198–205, 212. *See also* Belzec extermination camp
"Belzec Memorial and Museum: Personal Reflections, The" (Berenbaum), 8–9, 192–217
Benjamin, Walter, 8
Berenbaum, Michael, 8–9, 192–217
Bergen-Belsen, 60–61, 230
Berkhoff, Karel, 156–58, 164n12, 165n26
Berlin, Germany, 219–20, 229–30
Bernath, Andrei, 124
Berr, Helen, 35

Berri, Claude, 39
Bessarabia and Bessarabian Jews, 106–7, 108, 110–11, 113, 114, 161
Besser, Chaskel, 200
biblical stories and passages, 93, 96–97, 205, 206
Birkenau. *See* Auschwitz-Birkenau camp
Black, Peter, 204
"Black Book" of Soviet Jewish history, 147, 163n7
"black boxes" (recorders), 221–22
Bloodlands: Between Hitler and Stalin (Snyder), 158, 165n27
Bloomfield, Sara J., 204
Boder, David, 4
Bogdanovka camp, 108–10, 111
Borlant, Henri, 36–37, 38
Borowski, Tadeusz, 79n37
Borwicz, Michel, 34
Boulavka, Anna, 138
Brandenburg Memorials Foundation, 182
Browning, Christopher, 41, 42, 43, 209–10
Buber-Neumann, Margarete, 174, 187n15
Buchenwald camp, 63–64, 77n25; hologram "survivor" interaction, 10; memorials, 170, 171, 176, 223–24; works about, 179
Buchenwald—Mahnung und Verpflichtung (Bartel), 179
Buchmann, Erika, 178, 179, 188n18
Budapest, Hungary, 224–25
Bukowina province and Bukowinan Jews, 106–7, 108, 110–11, 113, 114, 161
Burdened Woman (Lammert), 170, *172,* 173–75
burial customs, 143, 196, 223
Bush, George W., 204
Buzek, Jerzy, 200
bystanders as witnesses, 33; concentration camp areas, 208–9;

Index

mass graves, and Desbois work, 6, 25, 27, 131, 132, 142–43; memory creation and recording, 132–33, 135–43; official interviews and documentation, 6, 135–38

capos. *See* kapos
Cariera de Piatr! camp, 108, 110–11, 127n10
Carruth, Cathy, 57
Cayrol, Jean, 40
Celan, Paul, 45, 50n34, 111
"celebratory memory," 21
cemeteries, 173, 196, 200–202, 223
censorship. *See* propaganda and censorship
Central State Archive of the Russian Federation/Uzbekistan, 151–52
chemical weapons, 220
chickling pea, and paralysis, 116–22
children: camp complexes, 168, 176; camp incarcerations and death, 7, 26, 69–70, 72, 109, 168, 214–16; ethical protection and survival, 92, 153, 195–96; as witnesses, 33, 35, 37, 38, 135
Chile, 223
China, 140, 220–22
"choiceless choices," 59, 121
Christian iconography, 173–74, 175
"Chronicle of a Single Day" (Goldin), 21–22, 29n9
civilian casualties of WWII, 149, 152, 158
class and hierarchical divisions: concentration camps, 171, 180, 184; Soviet territories, evacuation experiences, 153, 154–55, 156, 158
Clinton, Bill, 204
collaboration: accusations and trials, 45–46; Soviet, 146; villager threats and coercion, 133, 137–38
collective consciousness, 16; Jewish memory and action, 3–4; post-WWII Europe, 3; survivor population decline effects, 9

collective memory: collective forgetting and counter-memory, 174; "scaling of public memory," 218, 224, 231, 232n2; survivors' memory neglected, 7; witnessing and listening, 57
collectivization, 134
Comité Vrouwen van Ravensbrück, 176–77, 187n14
Committee for the Preservation of the Jewish Cemeteries in Europe, 200–201
"common memory," 17–18, 21, 22
communication processes: memorials and museums, 10, 186, 209; memory transmission, 2–3, 10–11, 140; primary witnesses and messages, 2, 56, 132–33, 138; theory, 10, 57; underground/camp communication networks, 120, 123, 129n34. *See also* listening
concentration and labor camps: German memorial activism, 7–8, 169; historical artifacts, *63, 64,* 186; history and testimony, 41–45; labor, 72–73, 92, 107, 109, 111, 181, 183–84; liberations, 32, 38, 55, 59, 126, 134–35, 168, 173, 176–78, 184; memoirs, 4–5, 5–6, 16, 18–19, 24, 39–40, 41, 44, 54, 62, 66–76, 69, 112–20, 178–79; population and bystander witnesses, 208–9; societal conditions and organization, 5–6, 17, 36, 45, 74–75, 107–11, 114–15, 122–24, 168, 174, 180–81, 186; survivors'/victims' lack of memorialization, 6–7, 170–71, 175, 176–78, 185; survivors'/victims' memories, 8–9, 16–19, 26, 36, 45, 46–47, 54–55, 61, 63–64, 67–76, 92–93, 112–20, 124–25, 180–86, 211, 213–16n11. *See also* memorial sites; museums; specific camps
constructed memory: concentration camps, 7; survivors/victims' lack of memorialization, 6–7, 170–71, 175
Council for Protection of Monuments in Poland, 194–95

"counter-memories," 174
cremation and crematoriums: design, labor, and use, 44, 70–71, 72, 73; memorial sites, 169, 170, *171*, 173; sabotage, 71
Cremer, Fritz, 176, *177*, 224
Crossing the Line (Rassinier), 43
Cru, Jean Norton, 43
crying, 40–41, 44–45
cultural and artistic opportunities, camps, 124–25, 184
cultural meaning interpretation, memoirs, 5, 57–58, 81–82

Dachau camp, memorial, 182
Daghani, Arnold, 111
databases, 84, 87, 159
Days and Memory (Delbo), 16, 17–18
"Death Fugue" (Celan), 45, 50n34
"deathlife": Langer discussion, 2, 16–17, 18, 22, 23, 57, 76n8; survivor descriptions and sentiments, 16–17, 39–41, 54–55, 61
de Certeau, Michel, 40
deconstruction research *(khurbn-forshung)*, 4
"deep memory": consciousness, and Langer accounts, 2–3, 16, 17–19, 20, 23–24, 25–26, 27, 76n8; descriptions, 18, 22, 23; literary treatments, 16–17, 21–22, 24; vs. celebratory memory, 21
Defonseca, Misha, 19
Delbo, Charlotte, 16, 17–18, 21, 27, 36
demography. *See* survivor populations
denial and memory: Holocaust revisionism, 141, 146–49; non-Holocaust genocides, 221, 223; SS officers and guards, 2–3, 15–16, 19
deportation and relocation: Jewish displacement and extermination, 106–7, 108–10, 112–15, 206–7, 208; memorial representations, 206–7, 208; Soviet sentencing and deportations, 146, 149, 150, 157, 162, 163–64n11, 165n17;

survivor stories and suppression, 36–37, 37–38, 45. *See also* evacuation experiences; refugee experiences
Desbois, Patrick, 131; bystander testimony, 6, 24–26, 132–38; global work, 140–42; interview, 6, 131–43; mass graves investigations, 6, 23–24, 27, 131, 132, 142–43; works, 24, 25, 138
Diary of a Young Girl, The (Frank), 35
Dinesen, Isak, 1
disease, evacuating populations, 154
disease, in camps: communicable diseases, 109, 113, 114, 121, 123; inspections, 121; toxicity and paralysis, 116–22
displaced persons: aid organizations, 64; camp descriptions, 78n32; survivor work and memoirs, 4–5, 62, 66–76, 78n30; witness testimony efforts, 60–61
divine providence, 86, 93–94, 95–96
divine revelation, 94–95
doctors' accounts, 116–21, 184
documentation. *See* historical documentation
Doubson, Vadim, 159–60, 165n28
dreams, 178
Drowned and the Saved, The (Levi), 36, 49n15
Duszenko, Franciszek, 195
Dvorzeski, Meir, 59

eastern vs. western perspectives, 134–35, 139–40
education: museums and memorials, 10, 142, 186, 196, 198, 208–9, 219–20; outreach projects, 141–42
Ehrenburg, Ilya, 147, 158
Eichmann, Adolf: pretrial interrogations, 126n6; trial, 32, 33, 37–39, 40, 46, 49n21, 49n22
Einsatzgruppen, 105, 208
Eleod, Ákos, 224–25
Emmerich, Wilhelm, 67

Index

emotions and expressions, 40–41, 44–45
Empire of Trauma, The (Fassin and Rechtman), 31
English language: memoirs, 4–5, 66, 83, 99n12; terminology, 33
Ère du soupçon, L' (Sarraute), 31, 48n3
Erlich, Berish: biography, 62–66, 79n37; historical artifacts, *63, 64, 65, 69,* 78n30; memoir, 4–5, 54, 66–76, 78n33, 78n34
Erlich, Nusyn Pinchus, 62, 77n21
Eschebach, Insa, 6–7, 168–91
evacuation experiences: Auschwitz, 3, 47; class and hierarchical divisions, 153, 154–55, 156, 158; occupied Soviet territories, 6, 144–62; official and primary documentation, 152–53, 159–61, 162; works about, 151–52, 152–56, 158, 160–61
"evasive memory": bystanders, 25, 26; Holocaust perpetrators, 2, 16, 19–20; Holocaust victims, 18; temptations, Holocaust history and witnessing, 3, 28
extermination camps: perpetrators' actions and memory, 16, 19–20; similarities and differences from concentration camps, 127n8; survivors' and process descriptions, 8–9, 70, 211, 213–16n11; victim testimonies, 35
extermination methods. *See* gas chambers and extermination; mass shootings and extermination
Extraordinary State Commission, work and reports (Soviet Union): interview testimonies and corroboration, 6, 135–37; as knowledge repository, 2, 6, 159–60
Eynikayt (newspaper), 147

faith, religious: Germans, 134, 170; rabbis' Holocaust writings and effects, 85–91, 94–97; Soviet Union, 139; strength of soul, self, and community, 92–93; survivors and victims, 60, 67, 84, 85–86
false testimonies and memory: errors and approaches, 43–44; Holocaust perpetrators, 2, 16, 19–20; Holocaust victims and survivors, 19, 42, 43–45; media influence, 42–43, 218–19
family experiences: bodies and burial, 143, 203, 223; camp solidarity, 92, 174–75, 176, 195–96; Soviet evacuations and relocations, 153, 161; survivor stories and suppression, 36–37, 38
Farbstein, Esther, 5, 55, 81–104
farmers, bystander witnessing, 6, 25, 27, 33, 140
Fassin, Didier, 31
Feferman, Kiril, 160–61
Feldman, Shoshana, 56
films: archaeological surveys, 199; documentaries, 33–34, 40–41, 210; Eichmann trial, 37–39; features, 23, 39, 42, 46; influence on memory, 42–43; interviews projects, 33–34, 37–38, 40–41, 42–44, 136, 137, 179–81, *181,* 221
"Flight and Evacuation of Civilian Populations in the USSR, The" (Shapiro), 6, 144–67
Flight 93 Memorial, 228–29
Fogiel, Esther, 38
food. *See* hunger and starvation; kosher observances
forced collectivization, 134
forced labor: Soviet citizens, 150, 164n12; Transnistria, and Romanian Jews, 106, 111
Forgotten Memoirs, The (Zachor project), 83, 99n12, 101n44
Fortunoff Video Archive, 37–38, 41, 42–43
Foundation for the Memory of the Shoah, 44
Fox, Arendt, 194
Fragments (Wilkomirski), 19, 44
France, Holocaust memory, 168

Index

Frank, Anne, 35
Frankl, Viktor, 18–19
Frauen von Ravensbrück, Die (book; 1959), 179
Freed, James Ingo, 198
French language, 33, 35
Friedenson, Josef, 63–64, 78n29
Friedländer, Saul, 35

Ganzfried, Daniel, 44
Gascar, Pierre, 24, 28
gas chambers and extermination: memoirs and testimonies, 67, 68, 70, 72, 73, 210, 215–16n11; memorial sites, 196, 200, 211; method, 20, 44, 70, 197, 215–16n11
genealogical records and databases, 84, 159
genocides: historic and modern responses, 36, 140; physical contexts, memorials, 9, 218–31; Rwanda, 46
geography of memory, 9, 218–31
German language: memoirs, 4–5, 66; terminology, 33
Germany, postwar: concentration camps and memorial activism, 7–8, 169; forced labor reparations, 164n12; memorials, creation, 6–7, 170–71, 175–78, 219–20, 223–24, 229–30; reconciliation, 7–8; reunification and effects, 181–82, 185–86, 224
germ warfare, 220
Gerstein, Kurt, 210
Gilbert, Martin, 78–79n37
Gillis, John R., 186
Glab, Jan, 210–11
Globocnik, Odilo, 210
Golbert, Rebecca L., 127n16
Goldberger, Pinchas Asher, 88, 100n20
Goldin, Leyb, 21–22, 29n9
Gran, Wiera, 46
Greenberg, Irving, 200, 204
Greenblatt, Stephen, 229
Greenwald, Yosef, 87

Grunewald, Ralph, 194
Grunwald, Yehoshua, 84, 92, 95–96
Grūtas Parkas (Lithuania), *225*, 225–26, *226*
gulag deportations, 146, 149, 150
Gutter, Pinchas (hologram "survivor"), 10

Hackenholt, Lorenz, 210
HaCohen, Avraham, 91–92
"halakhic witnessing," 57, 58, 60–61, 66–67, 86–87, 96
"Halakhic Witnessing: The Auschwitz Memoir of Berish Erlich" (Lustiger Thaler), 4–5, 54–80
Halbersztadt, Jerzy, 192, 205
Halbwachs, Maurice, 231
Hammermann, Gabriele, 182
Handelman, Don, 176
Handke, Emmy, 178
Hanukkah, 89
Harbin, China, 220–22
Harris, David, 204
Hartman, Geoffrey, 1, 174
Harvest of Despair (Berkhoff), 156, 164n12, 165n26
Haupt, Adam, 195
Hausner, Gideon, 37
Hawthorne, Christopher, 228–29
Hendler, C., 84
Hering, Gottlieb, 210
Herzfeld, Shmuel, 203
hierarchical divisions. *See* class and hierarchical divisions
Hilberg, Raul, 34
historians, 3, 39, 41–45, 142, 178–80
historical commissions: creation, Holocaust survivors, 3–4; former Soviet states, 151; interview testimonies and corroboration, 6, 135–37; as knowledge repositories, 2, 6, 159–60
historical documentation: genealogical databases, 84, 159; historical archives and education, 141–42, 219–20;

244

Index

historical commissions, collection and compilation, 3–4, 151; human witnessing, goals, 33–34, 140–43, 160, 179, 219–20; journalistic approaches and voices, 21–23, 34, 49n20, 147, 152, 158, 159–60, 179–81; rabbinic works (survivors'), 5, 55, 82–83; Soviet investigation archives, 2, 6, 135–37, 151–52, 156, 159–60; Soviet postwar society and information policy, 146–50, 150–51, 153, 156–58; survivor records and literature, 5, 41, 62, 77n23, 81–82, 83, 152–53, 160, 179–86; technological advances and tools, 10, 159; Warsaw Ghetto, 21–22, 23, 34, 37, 49n20, 62. *See also* historical writing; interviews

historical items. *See* artifacts

historical sites. *See* memorial sites

historical truth: discovery via witness testimonies, 136, 137; educational outreach, 141–42; evasion, Holocaust memorials, 170–71; weighing with survivor/witness testimonies, 3, 27, 39, 41, 43–44, 82, 85, 136–37, 159–60, 179, 183–84

historical writing: Germany in WWII, nonfiction, 158; historians' Holocaust pasts, 178–79; power of primary witnesses, 9, 41, 178–79; problems and challenges, 3, 41, 85, 192; research experiences, 4, 40, 41, 179–86; USSR in WWII, nonfiction, 145–46, 150–62

historic artifacts. *See* artifacts

hithazut, 60

Hoheisel, Horst, 229–30

holiday observance, 86, 89

Holocaust and Genocide Studies (journal), 159–60

Holocaust and Historical Methodology, The (Stone), 5

Holocaust by Bullets, The (Desbois), 24, 138

Holocaust denial and revisionism: Soviet Union, 146–49; Ukraine, 141. *See also* denial and memory

Holocaust in the Crimea and the North Caucasus, The (Feferman), 160–61

Holocaust literature: allusions, 22; concentration camp memoirs, 4–5, 5–6, 16, 18–19, 24, 36, 54, 62, 66–76, 112–20, 178–79; diaries and letters, 6, 34, 35, 41; era reporting, 21–22; genre generalizations, 4; genre scope, 81; primary witnesses' works, 2, 4, 6, 16, 24, 33–34, 35–36, 39–40, 54, 62, 66–76, 69, 81–82, 112–20, 178–79; rabbinic works/memoirs, 5, 55, 58, 61, 82–98; readership, 35–36, 44. *See also* interviews

Holocaust within Jewish history, 93–94

Holodomor museum (Ukraine), 224

Horowitz, Sara, 174–75

Höss, Rudolf, 44, 78n37

Hungary, 224–25

hunger and starvation, 21–22, 23, 55, 64; abstinence and resistance, 121; food conditions, 107, 115, 116–20, 121–22, 184; "natural" extermination, 109, 110, 224

Hurwitz, Leo, 38, 40

If This Is a Man (Levi), 35, 36

Ils étaient juifs, résistants, communistes (Wieviorka), 33

"imagined memory," 42–43, 218–19, 231

infrastructure development, German invasions, 105–6, 111

Inside a Nazi Slave-Labor Camp (Browning), 41

Inside the Drancy Camps (Laffitte), 41

intellectual memory, 18

"intellectual witnessing" (Hartman), 1

interactive learning tools, museums and memorials, 10, 186, 209

International Tracing Service of the International Red Cross, 5, 77n23, 164n12

interviews: Desbois, and bystander witnesses, 6, 27, 131–43; evacuees, 160–61; Holocaust perpetrators,

Index

interviews (*cont.*)
16, 19–20, 33; processes, 42–43, 179–81; video and film, 33–34, 37–38, 40–41, 42–44, 136, 137, 179–81, *181*, 221; Wieviorka, and witnesses, 33; witnesses and survivor testimony, 4, 8–9, 33–34, 37–38, 40–41, 42–43, 132–33, 179–81, 211, 213–16n11

Israel: survivor relocation and integration, 36, 37–38; trials, 45–46

Israeli Center for Holocaust Survivors and the Second Generation, 203

Izrael, Avraham, 96–97

Japanese occupation of China, 220–22

Jewish Anti-Fascist Committee (Soviet Union), 147, 163n5

Jewish history, 93–94, 124

Jewish life: kosher observances, 92–93; mitzvot, 86, 87–89; rabbis, post-Holocaust, 96–97; rabbis, pre-Holocaust, 83–85

Jewish martyrology, 59

Jewish resistance movement: rabbis and Jewish ethics, 90–92; Warsaw Ghetto, 33–34, 60

Jockusch, Laura, 4

Joint Distribution Committee (JDC), 64, 65

journalism. *See under* historical documentation

Judenräte, 45, 90–91

Kaddish prayer, 143, 196, 216
Kaduk, Oswald, 16
Kaganovitch, Albert, 152, 164n14
kapos: camps work and organization, 72, 73, 75, 107, 122; testimony and trials, 45–46
Kapsukas, 225, *226*
Karski, Jan, 33–34, 210
Kassow, Samuel, 23, 34, 62
Kasztner train, 93, 101n46
Keniston, Kenneth, 192

Kessler, Arthur, 112–13, 114, 115, 116–21, 126

keys, 211

khurbn-forshung (deconstruction research), 4

Kiddush Hashem and *Kiddush Hahayim*, 59–60

Kiedrzynska, Wanda, 179

Klarsfed, Beate, 44

Klarsfed, Serge, 40, 44

Klehr, Josef, 16, 19–20

Klemperer, Victor, 34

Knigge, Volkhard, 169

Kogon, Eugen, 179

Korczak, Janusz, 195–96

kosher observances, 92–93

Kumanev, G., 144

Kuwalek, Robert, 192, 205

Laffitte, Michel, 41
Lager Vapniarka, 5–6, 105, 111–26
Lammert, Willi, *172*, 173–75
Landsberg DP camp, 78n32; survivor experiences and artifacts, 63, *64*, 64–66, *65*, 78n30; survivor memoirs, 4–5, 62, 66–76
Lang, Berel, 1
Langbein, Hermann, 178
Langer, Lawrence: "The Afterdeath of the Holocaust," 2–3, 15–30; terms and influence, 56–57, 59, 76n8
languages and translation: archival materials, 142; concentration camps' language, 60, 61; LTI, 34; memorial sites' languages, 196, 206, 208, 211; survivor writings, 35, 66, 82, 83, 99n11, 99n12; "witness," 33
Lanzmann, Claude, 33–34, 40–41, 210
lathyrus sativus, 116–22
Lau, Yisroel Meir, 201, 203
Laub, Dori, 56, 57, 111
Lau-Lavie, Naftalie, 203
Lazare parmi nous (Cayrol), 40
"Lazarus" character and theme, 39–40

Index

Lemberger, Moshe Nosson Nota, 85–86, 89, 92
Lenin, Vladimir, 225, *225*, *226*
Lerman, Miles, 192–94, 203–4, 212
Leval, Gerard, 194
Levi, Primo: dreams, 178; on life with death, 16–17; turns of phrase and quotations, 4, 36, 60; voices for voiceless and "drowned," 54, 55, 56; witnessing, memory, and transmission, 10–11, 36, 54, 55, 56, 57, 178; works and writings, 25, 35, 36
Libeskind, Daniel, 227
lice, 117, 122, 123
Lichtenstein, Hillel, *65*
Lin, Maya, 227
listening: necessary attitudes, 25, 26, 42, 141; "otherness," 57; reluctance/refusal, 4, 45, 178
literary allusions, 22
Lithuania, 84, 225–26
"Locating Loss: The Physical Contexts of Genocide Memorials" (Williams), 9, 218–34
"love stories," 138–39
LTI *(lingua tertii imperii)*, 34
Lucie Aubrac (1997), 39
Luckert, Steven, 204
Lustiger Thaler, Henri: Desbois interview, 6, 131–43; "Halakhic Witnessing: The Auschwitz Memoir of Berish Erlich," 4–5, 54–80; text introduction, 1–11

Mada v-Ha-Hayim (Zaichyk), 97
Magnus, Laura Surwit, 204
Majdanek camp: Erlich at, 63; museum and artifacts, 7, 192, 193, 195, 205, 212
Maksudov, Sergei, 144, 159–60
Malinauskas, Viliumas, 225
Manley, Rebecca, 144, 151–52, 152–54
Mann, Franceska, 67, 74, 78–79n37
Man's Search for Meaning (Frankl), 18–19
marriage status, 61

Marsalek, Hans, 179
martyrology, 59, 60, 78n36
mass graves: extermination camps, 70–71, 196, 199, 200–203, 206–7, 215, 216; location and witnessing, Desbois project, 6, 23–24, 27, 131, 132, 142–43; non-Holocaust genocide, 223; in *The Season of the Dead* (Gascar), 24; site memorials and cemeteries, 170, 173, 196, 199, 200–203, *205*, 206–7, 222–23
mass shootings and extermination: public occurrences, and witnessing, 133, 135–36, 138, 142–43, 157; Soviet Jews, 157; survivor testimonies, 37–38; Transnistrian camps, 109, 111, 113
maternalism, 174–75, 176
Mauriac, François, 39
Mauthausen-Gusen, 54–55
McLuhan, Marshall, 10
medical care: camps, 116–20; hygiene, 123; Soviet Union and evacuees, 153, 155
medical experimentation, 38, 75, 220–21
Meerbaum-Eisinger, Selma, 111
Meisels, Zvi Hersch, 60–61, 67, 87, 92, 96
Mekadshei Hashem (Meisels), 92
memoirs. *See* Holocaust literature; survivors' and victims' testimonies; specific works
"Memoirs Not Forgotten: Rabbis Who Survived the Holocaust" (Farbstein), 5, 55, 81–104
memorial commemorations. *See* memorial dates; memorial sites
memorial dates, 32, 35, 176–77
memorial sites: ceremonies and events, 176–78, 212; creation and design, 8, 169–70, 173, 175–78, 192–96, 198–217, *205*, *206*, *207*, 218, 221–22; functional and educational aspects, 8, 23, 168, 182, 186, 196, 198, 208–9, 219–20; overlooking survivors and victims, 6–7, 170–71, 175, 176–78, 185, 193, 224; shortcomings, 17, 170–71, 175–78, 196, 223–24; site-memory relationships,

Index

memorial sites (*cont.*)
7–8, 9, 218–31; stereotyped characterizations, 42–43, 175; survivor memories, purposes and legacies, 8–9, 32, 142–43, 170–71, 178–86, 211; "witness sites," 32–33, 48n5, 142–43. *See also* museums

Memories of the Eichmann Trial (1979), 37–39

memory. *See* "celebratory memory"; collective consciousness; collective memory; "common memory"; constructed memory; "counter-memories"; "deep memory"; denial and memory; "evasive memory"; false testimonies and memory; "imagined memory"; intellectual memory; memorial sites; quotations; sensory memory; survivors' and victims' testimonies; time

Memory of the Shoah (Veil), 44
Mengele, Josef, 42, 73
mercy, 93
Michelet, Jules, 40
Mickenberg, David, 198
Mickevicius, Vincas, 225, *226*
"micro-histories," 140
Miller, Leszek, 202
minimalist aesthetics, 227–30
Ministry of Cultural Affairs (GDR), 169
miracles, 68, 86, 94, 95, 97
Misha: A Memoire of the Holocaust Years (Defonseca), 19
mitzvot, 86, 87–89
Moll, Otto, 72
monuments. *See* memorial sites
Moscow, Russia, 148, 152, 154
Motherland in Danger: Soviet Propaganda during World War II (Berkhoff), 156–58, 165n26
Mouchard, Claude, 45
mourning: bodies, location and burials, 143, 203, 223; memorial sites, symbols, 170–71, 176, 196

Mujawayo, Esther, 46
Muller, Filip, 67–68, 78n35
Murdoch, Paul, 228
muselmann, 59
Museum of Evidence of War Crimes, 220, *220–22*, 222
museums: archival information, 152, 164n12, 179, 180; developer experiences and witnessing, 8–9, 192–95, 198–217; education and outreach, 141–42, 182, 186, 219–20; geography and place, 9, 218–31; national symbols, 134; potential shortcomings, 17. *See also* memorial sites; specific museums
music, 124–25, 129n35

Nanjing Massacre Memorial Museum, 222
nationalism, 141, 228–29
National September 11 Memorial & Museum, 223, 227
Nazi Germany and the Jews (Friedländer), 41
Nazi propaganda, 157, 161
Nedvedova-Nejedlá, Zdena, 184
"negationism," 43–44
Neumann, Philipp, 179
New York State Supreme Court, 203
Night (Wiesel), 39
nightmares, 178
Nikiforowa, Antonia, 178
Nissenbaum, Isaac, 60
NKVD, 146–47, 154
Noah, 96
Nora, Pierre, 9, 231
Nowakowski, Jacek, 192, 194, 205
Nuremburg International Tribunal, 79n37

Oberhauser, Joseph, 210, 212
"objective choice," 59
Ohrdruf (Buchenwald), 63–64, 77n25
Oklahoma City Memorial, 9, 228
Operation Reinhard camps, 195, 210
oral testimony. *See* interviews

Index

"ordinary memory," 17–18, 21, 22
Ordinary Men: Auxiliary Police Battalion 101 and the Final Solution in Poland, 209–10
Organization for Reconstruction and Training (ORT), 78n32
Orthodox Judaism: camp populations and leadership, 65, 65–66; concept and terminology, 98n3; historiography, 5, 83, 88, 93; mitzvot, 86, 87–89; particular Holocaust perspectives, 55, 57–60, 82, 86; rabbi consultations, memorial sites, 199, 200–203; villager witnesses' testimonies, 139. *See also* rabbis and scholars
Oyneg Shabbos archives, 21–22, 23, 34, 37, 49n20, 62

Pagis, Dan, 208
Paper Tiger (Rolin), 33, 48n7
Papon, Maurice, 38, 49n23
paralysis (physical), 116–22
parks, 224–26
peasants: bystanders, mass graves, 6, 25, 27, 131, 132, 142–43; food sources, 109, 112
Pechora camp, 108, 110, 111, 127n10, 127n16, 127–28n17
Perlov, David, 37–38, 41
Pester, Yaakov, 96
Phillips, Edward, 204
photographic evidence, 184, 209, 210, 220, 221, 222. *See also* films
physical sites. *See* geography of memory; memorial sites
Pidek, Zdzislaw, 199
Pieta representations, 173–74
Pinchuk, Victor, 141
Pinochet, Augusto, 223
place, and memorial contexts, 9, 218–31
Podklebnick (survivor; *Shoah*), 40–41
poetry, 208
Polish culture and history, 193, 194, 202, 209–10

Polish Institute of National Remembrance, 193
political prisoners: Ravensbrück memorial archivists, 178; Ravensbrück memorialization focus, 7, 171, 175, 176, 180; Vapniarka, 113–14, 115, 122
population data. *See* survivor populations
presentism, 33
Pressac, Jean-Claude, 44
priests: Desbois' research and documentation, 6, 131–43; hiding Jews, 90
primary witnessing: evacuation, primary documents, 152–53, 160–61, 162; false testimony, 19, 42, 44–45; focus and importance, 2, 9, 41, 160, 179; paradox of Holocaust witnessing, 56; types and forms, 1; witnesses' words on witnessing, 10–11, 54, 56. *See also* survivors' and victims' testimonies
prisoners of war: French, 24; Soviet, 73, 118, 149, 150
propaganda and censorship: memorial events and ceremonies, 176–78; Nazi messages, 157, 161; Soviet Union, 147, 150–51, 153, 156–58, 161, 162, 224
public consciousness. *See* collective consciousness
public memory. *See* collective memory
public personae, survivors, 37–38, 174
publishing as protest, 97–98

questioning and answering: hologram "survivor" capabilities, 10; questions of survivors, 94
quotations: memory and place, 9, 231; memory and transmission, 10–11, 56, 186; prisoners, on labor, 183–84

rabbinical education, 84, 91
rabbis and scholars: concentration and DP camps, 65, 124; consultations, extermination camp memorial sites,

rabbis and scholars (cont.)
199, 200–203; European presence and history, 83–85; halakhic witnessing and guidance, 58–61, 86–87, 96; Jewish life and history, 83–85, 86–87, 96–97; rabbinic works/memoirs, 5, 55, 58, 61, 82–98; scholarly responses to Holocaust, 4, 5, 58, 78n36, 82–83, 88, 89–90, 93–94, 97–98; Warsaw Ghetto history, 62

Rabinowitz, Baruch, 91
Rabinowitz, Shlomo Chanoch, 62
radio communication, 129n34
railroads and trains: concentration camp transportation, 112, 133, 214–15; escapes, 91–92; memorial and museum elements, 193, 207, 208–9
rape, 46, 47, 155, 178, 187n15
Rassinier, Paul, 43
Ravensbrück camp, 168–69, *169*; art and iconography, *172*, 173–75, 176, *177*; memorial creation and descriptions, 169, 170–71, 173, 175–78, 182–84, 185–86; official publications, 179; size, 7, 168, 173, 185–86; survivors and memories, 176, 178, 179, 180–86, *181*, *183*; survivors' and victims' lack of memorialization, 6–7, 170–71, 175, 176–78, 185. *See also* Ravensbrück Memorial Museum
Ravensbrück Group of Mothers (Cremer), 176, *177*
Ravensbrück Memorial Museum, *171*; archives, 179, 180; creation and history, 169, 170–71, 175–86; exhibitions, 182–86, *183*, *185*; sculpture, *172*, *177*. *See also* Ravensbrück camp
"Ravensbrück Women's Concentration Camp: Memories in Situ" (Eschebach), 6–7, 168–91
Rechtman, Richard, 31
reconciliation efforts, national, 7–8
Red Army: concentration camp liberations, 110, 168, 176, 177, 178, 194; concentration camp memorials focus, 176–78; Jewish soldiers, 146, 156, 158, 161, 163n6; POWs, 150; retreats, 113, 116
Red Cross. *See* International Tracing Service of the International Red Cross; Russian Red Cross; Swedish Red Cross
Reder, Rudolf, 8–9, 211, 213–16n11
refugee experiences: occupied Soviet territories, 6, 144–62; rescues by Jewish communities, 91
regional archives, 151–52
Reich, Walter, 202
relics. *See* artifacts
religious belief. *See* faith, religious
relocation. *See* deportation and relocation; evacuation experiences
Rème, Christiane, *181*
reparations, 164n12
representation, Holocaust stories and topics, 9–10, 55–56
"representation-as" (Lang), 1
requisitioning of labor, 133, 135, 137–38
rescue attempts: hiding and saving Jews, 90, 138, 139; Kasztner train, 93, 101n46; rabbis', 91, 94; refugees, within Jewish communities, 91
resistance efforts: concentration camp inmates, 5–6, 111, 121, 122–25; Jewish ethics and resistance, 90, 91–92; Warsaw Ghetto, 33–34, 60
reunification, Germany, 181–82, 185–86, 224
Ribbentrop-Molotov Pact (1939), 149
Ringelblum, Emanuel, 21, 22, 23, 34, 49n20, 62
Rolin, Olivier, 33, 48n7
Romania and Romanian Holocaust: ghettoes and camps, 107–22; memoirs and descriptions, 5–6, 105–30; WWII and politics, 113, 116, 125–26
Roma peoples, 142
Rosen, Ilana, 98n2
Rosenberg, Alexander J., 64

Index

Rossif, Frédéric, 46
Roszczyk, Marcin, 199
Rothenberg, Moshe, 84
Russia. *See* Soviet Union history
Russia at War: 1941–1945 (Werth), 145–46, 165n23
Russian Red Cross, 159
Rustow, Margrit, *183*
Rwandan genocide, 46

Sachsenhausen camp, 63, *64,* 170, 176
Salsitz, Norman, 203, 210
Sarraute, Nathalie, 31
Schepansky, Israel Shabbtai, 93
Schillinger, Josef, 67, 74, 78–79n37
Schindler, Pesach, 59
Schindler's List (1993), 23, 39, 42–44, 49n26
Schlager, Yechiel Michel, 85–86
Schlesinger, Elyakim, 200–201, 203
Schudrich, Michael, 200–202
sculpture and statues, 170, *172,* 173–75, 176, *177,* 224–26, *225, 226*
Season of the Dead, The (Gascar), 24, 28
Segal, Raz, 82
Seidman, Hillel, 65
self-defense questions, and victim-blaming, 20, 94
self-fragmentation: life and death, 16–17, 39–40, 54–55; literature examples, 21, 22, 39–40; survivor experiences, 16–17, 17–18, 21, 39, 40–41, 54–55
"self-representation," 3, 36
Sen-Sandberg, Steve, 15
sensory memory, 18, 231
September 11, 2001 attacks, and memorials, 223, 228–29
Shabbat observance, 88–89
shailos, 58
Shapira, Kalonymus Kalman, 60
Shapiro, Paul, 6, 144–67
Shoah (1985), 33–34, 40–41, 210
Shoah Foundation, 141, 142
Shternshis, Anna, 160

Simon, Nathan, 112, 114, 115
Smith, Martin, 194
Snam, Liesbeth, 176–78
Snyder, Timothy, 158, 165n27
Sobibór extermination camp: archaeological remnants, 199; camp remains, 195, 213; establishment, 127n8
social and cultural opportunities, camps, 124–25, 184
"'Solidarity and Suffering': Lager Vapniarka among the Camps of Transnistria" (Spitzer), 5–6, 105–30
Solyga, Andrzej, 199, 212
Sonderkommandos: descriptions, 71; testimonies, 8–9, 67–68, 211, 213–16n11
songs, 124–25, 129n35
soup kitchens, 21, 23
Soviet Commission and reports. *See* Extraordinary State Commission, work and reports (Soviet Union)
Soviet Union history: collapse, 150–51, 164n12, 180; ethnic minorities, 149, 153, 155–56, 158, 163–64n11, 165n23, 165n27; German-Romanian invasion, 106, 110, 113, 116, 125, 148, 156–57, 160–61; Holocaust witnessing and memory, 134–35, 139–40, 146–49, 150–51; industry and economy, 145, 147–48, 152, 157, 158; media policy, 147, 150–51, 153, 156–58, 161; refugee and evacuation experiences, 6, 144–62; regions and republics, 144–45, 147–48, 149, 151, 155, 158, 161; Soviet Jews, WWII, 146–50, 152, 153, 155–56, 157–61, 162; studies and works, 145–46, 147, 150–52, 152–54; Ukraine disinformation, 224. *See also* Red Army
Spielberg, Steven, 23, 39
Spitzer, Leo, 5–6, 105–30
split selves. *See* self-fragmentation
Srebnik, Simon, 34
Srebrenica massacre (1995), 223
SS officers and guards: attacks and resistance efforts, 67, 71, 74, 78–79n37;

Index

SS officers and guards (*cont.*)
camp activities, survivor memories/memoirs, 47, 67, 69–70, 71–75, 107, 213–15n11; Eastern European operations, 105–6, 208; memory accounts and camp activities, 2–3, 15–16, 19, 197–98; trials, interviews, and witness accounts, 2–3, 15–30, 19, 32, 33, 37–38
Stalin, Josef, 146–47, 149, 157, 158, 225
Starachowice labor camp, 41
starvation. *See* hunger and starvation; thirst
statues. *See* sculpture and statues
Stone, Dan, 5
Stronski, Paul, 154–56
Suchomel, Franz, 33, 210
Sudjic, Deyan, 230
suicide, 67, 78n35
survivor activism: historical commissions creation, 3–4; historical documentation, 21–22, 23, 34, 37
survivor populations: decline, and effects to witnessing and memory, 1, 9, 32, 39; names databases, 84, 159
survivors' and victims' testimonies: camp memoirs, 4–5, 5–6, 16, 18–19, 24, 36, 54, 62, 66–76, 112–20, 178–79; camp worker testimony, 8–9, 211, 213–16n11; celebratory stories and memory, 21; complicity and guilt, 26–27; evacuees, 152–53, 160–61, 162; faith expressions, 60, 67, 84, 85–86; false, and errors, 19, 42, 43–45; focus and importance of primary witnessing, 2, 9, 32, 35, 41, 56, 160, 162, 179; memory and memorials, 8–9, 32, 170, 178–86, 211; multiplicity within, 3, 82, 180–81, 182–84; oral, characteristics and content, 22; postwar communication and authenticity, 7, 8, 41–42, 178; rabbinic works/memoirs, 5, 55, 58, 61, 82–98; and survivor silence, 4, 45–47; testimony functions, 31, 34, 35–36, 37–39, 40–45, 55–56, 81–82, 178. *See also* Holocaust literature; interviews; primary witnessing
survivors' guilt, 94
Swedish Red Cross, 177
Szajna, Jozef, 198
Szoborpark (Budapest, Hungary), 224–25
Szpilman, Wladyslaw, 46

Tabau, Jerzy, 79n37
Tashkent, 147, 151, 155–56
Tashkent: Forging a Soviet City (Stronski), 154–56
technological advances and tools, 10, 159
temps du ghetto, Le (Rossif; 1961), 46
terrorism and memorials, 9, 223, 227–29
teshuvas, 58
testimonies, function and treatment, 31, 34, 35–36; empathy, 138; errors and approaches, 43–44; historians' opinions and usage, 41–47, 81–82, 152–53, 160–61; outside influences, 42–43, 45; trauma relief, 37–38, 135; as traumatic, 57; trials, and understanding, 37–39, 40–41, 45–46. *See also* survivors' and victims' testimonies
Thanks for Surviving (Borlant), 38
thirst: camp conditions, 115; as memory, 18
Tighina Agreement (1941), 105–7, 108, 126n1
Tigre en papier (Rolin), 33, 48n7
Tillion, Germaine, 179
time: effects on memory and testimony, 135–37; literary treatments, 21; survivor experiences, 40
"Todesfuge" (Celan), 45, 50n34
Todt Construction Company, 106, 111
To the Tashkent Station: Evacuation and Survival in the Soviet Union at War (Manley), 151–52, 152–54

Index

trains. *See* railroads and trains
translations. *See* languages and translation
Transnistria (Romania and Moldova), 5–6, 105–30, 127n10
trauma: Holocaust events, 135; testimony as trauma relief, 37–38, 135, 138; testimony as traumatic, 57
Treblinka extermination camp: archaeological remnants, 199; establishment, 127n8; memorial, 195–96, 198, 205, 212–13; Warsaw Ghetto populations, 23, 34, 62, 195–96
Trezise, Thomas, 57
trials: Belzec SS forces, 212; Eichmann trial, 32, 33, 37–39, 40, 46, 49n21, 49n22; kapos, 45–46; Nuremburg International Tribunal, 79n37
Trksak, Irma, 184
truth. *See* historical truth
Tuszynska, Agata, 46
typhus, 109, 113, 114, 121, 123
Tyulenev, Ivan, 145–46

Ukraine: Holocaust revisionism and education, 141; Holodomor museum, 224; Jewish displacement and extermination, 106–7, 108–9, 112–13, 133; mass graves, 6, 23–24, 131, 132, 142–43; population evacuations, Soviet Union, 157
Ullman, Micha, 229
Ulysses Betrayed by His Own (Rassinier), 43
Und di Velt hot geschwingn (Wiesel), 39
Under Two Dictators: Prisoner of Stalin and Hitler (Buber-Neumann), 187n15
uniforms, 107
United States Holocaust Memorial Museum: Belzec memorial aid and development, 193–94, 198, 199–200, 202, 203–5, 210, 212; education outreach, 142; history and leadership, 192–94, 202

Unit 731 Memorial Museum (Harbin, China), 220, 220–22, 222

Vapniarka camp, 5–6, 105, 111–26
Veil, Simone, 3, 44, 46–47
Vera Gran. The Accused (Tuszynska), 46, 50n36
Verner, Paul, 176–77
victim blaming, 20, 94
Vidal-Naquet, Pierre, 44
Vietnam Veterans Memorial, 205, 227
Voices under the Ashes: Manuscripts from Auschwitz's Sonderkommandos, 35

Walker, Peter, 227
"wall" style memorials, 205–6, *206,* 207, 227
Walz, Loretta, 180, *181*
Warsaw Ghetto: Erlich biography, 62–63; figures and stories, 15–16, 46, 195–96; Großaktion (1942), 23, 34, 48n12, 62; journalistic and historical documentation, 21–22, 23, 34, 37, 49n20, 62; religious leadership, 60; resistance, 33–34, 60
water, in memorials, 227, 228
"ways of walking" (Halakhah), 58–59
Weinberg, Jeshajahu, 194
Weinberg, Yechiel Yaakov, 84
Weinberger, Alter, 88–89, 91, 92–93
Weiss, Avi, 202–3
Weiss, Eric, 42
Weiss, Yitzchak Yaakov, 96
Weissmandel, Michael Dov, 91–92
Werth, Alexander, 145–46, 165n23
western vs. eastern perspectives, 134–35, 139–40
Who Will Write Our History? (Kassow), 34
Wiera Gran, l'accusée (Tuszynska), 46, 50n36
Wiesel, Elie: essays, 21; memoir passages, 92; novels, 39, 40
Wieviorka, Annette, 3, 31–53

Wilkomirski, Benjamin, 19, 44
Williams, Paul, 9, 218–34
Wirth, Christian, 210
Witnesses (Cru), 43
"Witnesses and Witnessing: Some Reflections" (Wieviorka), 3, 31–53
witnessing: defining, 33, 34, 132–33; emotional motivations, 67, 138–39; eras considered, 31–32; "halakhic," 57, 58, 60–61, 66–67, 86–87, 96; Holocaust as "witnessless," 56, 57; information transmission, 2–3, 11, 33–34, 132–33, 138; modern, 32–33, 39; public killings, 133, 135–36, 138, 142–43; survivor populations and, 1, 9, 32, 39. *See also* bystanders as witnesses; primary witnessing; survivors' and victims' testimonies; testimonies, function and treatment
Witnessing Witnessing (Trezise), 57
Wolff, Karl, 2, 15
women's concentration camps, *169;* memoir coverage, 73, 179; rape, 178, 187n15; solidarity, 174, 176; survivors' and victims' lack of memorialization, 6–7, 170–71, 175, 176–78, 185
World War I, 43, 48n4

Yiddishe Vort, Dos (newspaper), 64, 78n29
Yiddish language, works and use, 5, 39, 66, 196, 207, 211
Yosselevka, Rivka, 37–38, 41, 49n22

Zachor, the Center for Holocaust Research and Education, 83, 99n12
Zaichyk, Chaim Ephraim, 84, 91, 95, 97
Zeidman, Fred, 204
Zhukov, Georgi, 148, 162
Ziemba, Menachem, 60
Zionism, 86
Zuckerman, Antek, 33

CPSIA information can be obtained
at www.ICGtesting.com
Printed in the USA
BVOW10s1223230817
492800BV00022B/359/P